THE IVY LEAF

The Ivy Leaf

The Parnells Remembered

Commemorative Essays
by
DONAL MCCARTNEY
and
PAURIC TRAVERS

UNIVERSITY COLLEGE DUBLIN PRESS
PREAS CHOLÁISTE OLLSCOILE
BHAILE ÁTHA CLIATH

First published 2006
by University College Dublin Press
Newman House
86 St Stephen's Green
Dublin 2
Ireland
www.ucdpress.ie

ISBN 978-1-904558-60-6 hb
978-1-904558-59-0 pb

Cataloguing in Publication data
available from the British Library

Typeset in Ireland in Plantin and Fournier
by Elaine Burberry, Bantry, Co. Cork
Text design by Lyn Davies
Index by Jane Rogers
Printed on acid-free paper in England
by MPG Books, Bodmin, Cornwall

To the cherished memory of Máire Tobin

*

Contents

Preface

In writing these essays and preparing them for publication, we have incurred debts to many people which are only partially repaid by public acknowledgement. Our greatest debt is to the current and former members of the Parnell Society: Leslie Armstrong, Bernie Bianchi, Joe Buckley, Bernadette Crombie, Anne Goff, Patricia Gordon, Nuala Jordan, Carla King, Deirdre Larkin, Mairin Lindsay, Patricia Molloy, Eunan McKinney, P. J. Mathews, Joe McCullagh, Frank Murray, Edmond O'Donnell, Joyce Padbury, Bernadette O'Reilly, Pat Power, Noel Shiels, Noel Tierney, the late Máire Tobin, Frank Turvey, Fionnuala Waldron and Alex White. We are grateful to each and every one of them, individually and collectively, for their assistance, support and friendship.

Many of the essays in this collection are directly or indirectly related to particular locations. We would like to express our thanks to Jean Costello of Avondale House, Coillte Teo., Kilmainham Jail and the House of Commons in London; the cemetery authorities at Glasnevin, Ilfracombe, Littlehampton and Mount Auburn, Boston; and the local communities in Bordentown, New Jersey and Valley, Alabama.

The production of the book has benefited greatly from the expertise of Barbara Mennell and the staff of UCD Press. The Research Committee at St Patrick's College facilitated the use of a little research assistance at a critical moment. We would also like to thank Theresa O'Farrell for her invaluable assistance. Finally we wish to acknowledge the support of Peig McCartney and Mary Moore.

DONAL MCCARTNEY
PAURIC TRAVERS
Dublin, February 2006

Illustrations

Abbreviations

DMP	Dublin Metropolitan Police
GAA	Gaelic Athletic Association
GOM	Grand Old Man
HC Debs	House of Commons Debates
IHS	*Irish Historical Studies*
IRB	Irish Republican Brotherhood
LDF	Local Defence Force
MP	Member of Parliament
NAI	National Archives of Ireland
NLI	National Library of Ireland
PRHA	President of the Royal Hibernian Academy
RHA	Royal Hibernian Academy
UCD	University College Dublin
TCD	Trinity College, Dublin
TD	Teachta Dála
VC	Victoria Cross

Commemoration History

Donal McCartney
Pauric Travers

The essays collected in this volume commemorate the Parnells of Avondale. They were written by the joint authors mainly for public events organised by the Parnell Society, established in 1986, as part of its mission to promote an interest in the life and times of the Parnell family and their relevance for contemporary Ireland. These aims have been pursued through the organisation of an annual Spring Day, Summer School and Autumn Weekend, all at Avondale, and other commemorative events elsewhere in Ireland and abroad.

'Commemoration History' has become a popular and sometimes contentious form of history in Ireland in recent years. The marking of significant anniversaries, especially centenaries is not new or recent – as commemorations as diverse as the 1798 centenary, the centenary of Catholic Emancipation in 1929 and the fiftieth anniversary celebrations of the Easter Rising demonstrate. However, the 25 years after 1966 saw a more muted approach to such public commemorations, for reasons not unrelated to political developments north and south, and the emergence of the revisionist school of thought which was critical of nationalist orthodoxies and questioned the tendency towards hero-worship in much popular history.[1] Internationally, in the same period, the growth of a broader definition of history and the rise of social, economic and women's history undermined the preoccupation with great men and high politics.

More recently, and particularly since the mid-1990s, Ireland has experienced a strong wave of commemoration and commemoration history. In 1991, the centenary of the death of Charles Stewart Parnell was marked by ceremonies at Avondale and Glasnevin – the former presided over by the then Taoiseach, Charles Haughey. Commemoration of the 150th anniversary of the famine was co-ordinated by a national committee which subsequently evolved into the '98 commemoration committee.[2] The Act of Union and the Emmet rebellion have since been the subject of commemorations, the former understandably confined largely to academic circles. This emergence or re-emergence of 'national' commemorations has coincided with the advent of post-revisionism and the Northern Ireland peace process. It has also attracted widespread popular interest and both reflected and contributed to a new public mood which, for good or ill, is more self-confident, matter-of-fact and unapologetic in relation to historical issues. There is, it would appear, a greater consensus about the 'national past' warts and all, a greater willingness to commemorate it and a deeper appreciation of the importance of doing so. The post-revisionist 'national story' is more inclusive and less simplistic than its predecessor but it undoubtedly serves similar civic and social purposes. Therein lies its compelling attraction for its exponents and its inherent dangers for its critics.

Commemoration, like any form of remembering, is an instinctive human and social activity but it can be shaped and manipulated. For some, the decision of the Irish government in October 2001 to re-inter the bodies of the 'forgotten ten' executed in Mountjoy in 1920–1 was a wholly appropriate act of commemoration and, in the words of An Taoiseach, Bertie Ahern, discharged a debt of honour stretching back eighty years; for others, it was a self-conscious assertion of the succession rights of the Irish state to a particular tradition and a challenge to the expropriation of that tradition by Sinn Féin.[3] Similarly, Tom Dunne and others have seen in the '98 commemorations a self-conscious political agenda which distorts the nature of events in the 1790s to provide a wholesome model for post-peace-process Ireland. Incipient republicanism, egalitarianism and democracy are highlighted and naked sectarianism elided, or so it is alleged.[4] According to Roy Foster, 'commemorationist history', as he terms it, is 'always present centred'. In the 1798 commemoration, historical memory was 'bewilderingly recycled into spectator sport and tourist attraction'.[5]

The history of the response to and commemoration of the 1916 Rising and its leaders, especially Pearse and Connolly, is another instructive example of the insights to be gained from the examination of how we remember the past. Widespread condemnation by Dubliners, politicians, churchmen and the press had marked the initial response to the Rising. Within a matter of weeks, however, the rebels had been transformed into heroes and martyrs. And this venerated image – the official and orthodox view of our history – became entrenched over the next fifty years.

Commemoration of the Rising began almost immediately.[6] No public commemoration took place in 1917 because of a proclamation forbidding public displays in Dublin during Easter week, but ceremonies were organised in all subsequent years. The Treaty Split and civil war had a significant impact with the commemorations dominated by anti-Treaty republicans. In 1925, Eamon de Valera called for the setting aside of a national day of commemoration for those who had laid down their lives for the Republic in and since

1916. The following year, on the tenth anniversary, the Free State government showed little interest in staking a claim to the legacy of the Rising. Ten years later in 1936, with Fianna Fáil in power, the official commemoration was more active but generated hostile comment from republican critics. The 25th anniversary in 1941 was marked by large celebrations throughout the country, culminating in a huge military parade in Dublin. The occasion was used as a rallying point for the nation and was a direct response to the threats to Irish neutrality during the Second World War.

Glorification of the Rising reached its peak in the Golden Jubilee year of 1966. The triumphalist mood was dominant. Official state celebrations in Dublin resonated in the numerous commemorative events held in provincial cities and towns throughout Ireland. All national newspapers carried extensive supplements. Telefís Éireann, then only four years old, surpassed anything it had yet attempted. A crowded week of commemorative programmes included a dramatised reconstruction of the Rising, entitled 'Insurrection', which was shown over eight consecutive nights (from Sunday to Sunday), each episode lasting one-and-a-half hours, and followed on seven nights with sensitive profiles of the seven signatories of the Proclamation. And throughout the same week, Radio Éireann broadcast a great variety of programmes relating to 1916. The official commemorative ceremonies concluded on the evening of Saturday 16 April: in his address President de Valera reminded his audience of the ideals of 1916 yet to be accomplished – the restoration of the Irish language and the reunification of the country.[7]

The high-water mark of the 1916 brand of nationalism was registered in the 1966 commemorations. With the commencement in 1969 of the Northern 'Troubles', however, Yeat's terrible beauty was to become more terrible than beautiful. The argument that the so-called 'cult of 1916' during the fiftieth anniversary celebrations led directly only a few years later to thirty years of violence in Northern Ireland is simplistic. However, the glory and pride formerly associated with the Rising became major casualties of the car-bombs, assassinations and other atrocities perpetrated in many cases, ironically by those who claimed to be acting in the name of that same 1916 Republican tradition. The power of Pearse and Connolly to govern from the grave was brought more and more into question or even rejected outright.

Because of the violence and sectarianism in the North, the official commemoration of the 1916 Rising was abandoned in 1970. Throughout the next 35 years, the government's decision not to hold the annual Easter military parade was reinforced by 'revisionist' historians and commentators who condemned the glorification of physical force in our history and the emphasis on heroes and martyrs, and the perpetuation of the nationalist myth that in every generation the Irish people had asserted in arms their right to freedom and sovereignty. The commemorations in 1976, 1981 and 1991 were muted and occasionally controversial. At a commemoration ceremony in Belfast, Ruairí Ó Brádaigh laid claim to the 1916 inheritance: 'It has been said that the men involved [in the Provisional IRA] were not the same as those involved in 1916. However it has been said of the men of 1916, that they were not the same as those of 1798.'. The truth, Ó Brádaigh declared, was that the Irish struggle would be won by those currently engaged in the fight.[8]

The announcement by the Taoiseach, Bertie Ahern, at the Fianna Fáil Ardfheis in October 2005, that the military parade would be restored at Easter 2006 and preparations made for the centenary of the Rising in 2016 reflects another swing of the pendulum. The decommissioning of its arms by the IRA and the return to less violent politics in the north facilitated the decision to reinstate the military parade but, inevitably, critics have interpreted the change of heart as an attempt by Fianna Fáil, to reclaim 1916 from Sinn Féin. Addressing a conference entitled 'The Long Revolution: the 1916 Rising in Context', President Mary McAleese expressed the hope that the commemoration of the shared anniversaries of the Rising and the Somme would contribute to peace and reconciliation and 'a shared pride for the divided grandchildren of those who died, whether at Messines or in Kilmainham'.[9] It remains to be seen whether the reinstated commemoration of 1916 will rise above faction, as in the case of Parnell, and meet the challenge to become instead an occasion of genuine national self-examination.

It is not the intention here to adjudicate on these arguments about commemoration history but merely to place them in a context. Such conflicts are commonplace and reflect enduring differences about the nature of history and its uses. An awareness of such differences and the deeper significance of commemoration are essential tools of the historian seeking to understand the Irish or indeed any past. In recent years, it has become commonplace for historians to look at symbols, ceremonies and commemorations in much the same way as anthropologists look at the rituals of so-called primitive societies.[10] Such rituals are 'a kind of language' which, when we learn to decode and understand it, can reveal much about the society which produces them. Commemorations present a dual perspective – on the time, events and individuals being commemorated and on those doing the commemorating.

In Ireland, as in many other societies, commemoration of the dead has been used as a potent element in the endorsement of a particular political culture or the challenging of the *status quo* and the creation of an alternative. Monuments to fallen heroes, political funerals at Glasnevin, Wolfe Tone commemorations at Bodenstown, Collins commemorations at Béal na mBláth, commemorations of the siege of Derry and the Battle of the Boyne, St Patrick's Day parades, even street names, have been sites of contest and conflict and the raw material for historians seeking to unravel the complex interaction of history, memory and identity. Such conflicts are all laden with deeper meanings for those equipped to interpret their significance. Who and what we remember, how we remember and who shapes the act of remembering are vital dimensions of the relationship between past, present and, indeed, future.

The commemoration of the dead and the 'dead generations' played a significant role in the development of romantic nationalism in Ireland. Parnell's relationship with romantic nationalism is examined in the opening essay in this collection. It is argued that despite his significance in the evolution of the nationalist movement, he could not be categorised as a 'romantic nationalist'.

In some respects, Parnell had more in common with O'Connell who bestrode the Irish stage in the first half of the nineteenth century in the same way as Parnell bestrode it in the second half. In between came the famine and the phenomenon of mass emigration. As a result, Parnell's Ireland was orientated towards America as surely as O'Connell's was orientated towards Europe. Parnell grasped this and was well placed to turn it to advantage. While the influence of his American roots has been reassessed by Jane Côté, it remains true that the closeness of the Parnell American ties has not been fully appreciated. In April 2001, the Parnell Society undertook an extensive journey exploring these links in Boston, home of the Tudors and resting place of Fanny Parnell; Bordentown, New Jersey where the Parnells had a residence; and Valley, Alabama where John Howard Parnell embarked on an experiment in peach farming, assisted by tenants from the Parnell estate in Avondale. While the latter enterprise ultimately failed, it did have some impact on the development of the peach industry in the South and the descendants of these 'planters' still live in Alabama. The fruits of this exploration are recounted in 'In the Footsteps of John Howard Parnell: Memories of an American Journey' (chapter 8), while 'Parnell and the American Connection' (chapter 3) assesses Parnell's relationship with the United States from both a personal and political perspective. The effect of both of these essays is to demonstrate that the Parnell links with the United States were more active and dynamic than previously supposed.

The main purpose of the 2001 journey was to mark the grave of Fanny Parnell with a fitting monument. Since its foundation, the Parnell Society has been committed to exploring the contribution to Irish history of all the members of the Parnell family. As well as having a significant influence on the political development of their better-known brother, Anna and Fanny, in particular, are significant figures in their own right. Fanny who was born in 1848 was close to Charles and contributed to his early political awakening. As a patriotic poet and writer, she attracted favourable notice from advanced nationalists, especially in America. Her poem 'Hold the Harvest' was described by Michael Davitt as the Marseillaise of the Irish peasant. The Ladies' Land League was her brainchild. She died at Bordentown in 1882 and was buried in the Tudor family vault at Mount Auburn cemetery in Boston. In 2001, the Irish Ambassador to the United States, Mr Sean Ó hUiginn, unveiled a stone of granite carved by a Wicklow stonecutter and transported to Boston by the Parnell Society. The stone carries the inscription 'Fanny Parnell (1848–82) Irish Poet and Patriot'. The moving oration delivered on that occasion by Donal McCartney, President of the Parnell Society, belatedly acknowledges her contribution.

Anna Parnell was born in 1852 and drowned tragically in Devon in 1911. In 2002, the Parnell Society placed a marble stone on her grave at Holy Trinity Church in Ilfracombe. It bears an inscription with her own words 'The best part of independence . . . the independence of mind.' How apposite these words are is well illustrated in the tribute from Donal McCartney and the accompanying essay which approaches Anna Parnell's outlook and identity through her political activism and her poetry (chapter 9). The under-estimation of her importance by contemporaries and later historians is all the more poignant given the estrangement from her brother which followed his suppression of the Ladies' Land League and his abandonment, as she saw it, of the radical agrarian platform.

This essay also places Anna in a wider context and addresses the Englishness of the Parnells. If they were an Irish family with a strong American orientation, the Parnells had English roots and retained pronounced English characteristics. Davitt described Charles Stewart Parnell as an 'Englishman of the strongest type, moulded for an Irish purpose'.[11] Parnell moved easily between at least two worlds without being fully at home in either. He certainly mastered and manipulated the subtle inter-cultural nuances necessary to mobilise completely different constituencies. That much is clear from 'Reading Between the Lines: the Political Speeches of Charles Stewart Parnell' (chapter 4), an essay which marks the visit of the Parnell Society to Committee Room 15 in the House of Commons in 2003, and which challenges the received wisdom about Parnell as an orator.

The balancing of disparate and often competing forces in Ireland, Britain and the United States lies at the heart of the political genius of Charles Stewart Parnell. He also had to balance social and personal relationships, a task which proved enormously difficult. 'The Blackbird of Avondale: Parnell at Kilmainham' (chapter 2) considers a pivotal movement in his political and personal life and in the development of the national movement and highlights the tangled relationship between public and private spheres. Parnell's reorientation of his priorities away from land agitation and towards the political movement for Home Rule was politically and personally pragmatic.

It is reasonable to surmise that the instability of his early home life – his father died in 1859 when Charles was 13 and his mother was frequently absent on her travels – combined with a wider insecurity in relation to his cultural identity had an impact on Parnell's relationship with women. 'Parnell's Women' (chapter 5) explores his relationship with a number of women, but particularly Katharine O'Shea. Katharine offered him what he never enjoyed – domestic stability. 'At the Graveside' (chapter 7) acknowledges this debt and the huge injustice done to the reputation of Katharine in her lifetime and subsequently by the political opponents of Parnell.

The essays in this collection are evocative of time and especially of place – Avondale, Alabama, Boston, Bordentown, Brighton, Glasnevin, Ilfracombe, Littlehampton and London. Six of these were locations where one or another member of the Parnell family resided – seven if one includes Kilmainham. Four are locations of graveyards in which Parnell family members are buried. Of the graveyards, Glasnevin has pride of place. The funerals of O'Connell in 1847 and Parnell in 1891 were the two great political demonstrations of nineteenth-century Ireland. Parnell's funeral and its deeper meaning are examined in 'Under the Great Comedian's Tomb: The Funeral of Charles Stewart Parnell' (chapter 6). It is placed in the context of other political funerals before and since.

After Parnell's interment, Glasnevin became a place of pilgrimage. 'The Thurible as a Weapon of War: Ivy Day at Glasnevin' (chapter 10) examines the rise and decline of the Ivy Day commemoration as the great social and political event in the Dublin and national calendar in the century after 1891. As time passed, Parnell passed from politics to history, a transition which is discussed in 'From Politics to History: The Changing Image of Parnell' (chapter 11). The Ivy Day commemoration continues annually with a short ceremony and an oration – two of these recent orations are included here – those of 1982 and 1988.

These essays deal with history and historiography: they are both an exercise in commemoration and an attempt to use commemoration to provide an insight into shifting relations between history and memory in the case of Charles Stewart Parnell and his family. While they cannot escape completely the allegation of being present centred, they treat the past as sacred; they avoid putting words into the mouths of the dead for a modern audience but allow them speak for themselves. The Parnell legacy has moved beyond the claims of faction; it is not the 'plaything of political faction'. This collection explicitly examines the past in the context of the past for the sake of understanding it.

CHAPTER I

Parnell

Nationalism and Romance

Donal McCartney

What we call Romantic Nationalism was the product of two forces – one political, and one cultural. The political element emerged mainly out of developments associated with the French Revolution. The cultural current came from the contemporary Romantic Movement in literature, antiquarianism and the arts generally. It was the co-mingling and interaction between the cultural and political developments that produced the Romantic Nationalism which so many peoples came to experience during the last two centuries.

In Ireland the Romantic Movement owed much to poets like Moore, Ferguson and Mangan; and to scholars like Petrie, O'Donovan, O'Curry and the many learned antiquarian societies that were such a feature of early nineteenth-century Ireland. All of these streams fed into the popular advancement of Romantic Nationalism through the channel of Thomas Davis, the Young Irelanders, the *Nation* newspaper and similar publications.

A political aspiration – whether of the Wolfe Tone/Robert Emmet republican variety, or the more moderate constitutional type of Grattan and O'Connell – already claimed that Ireland had the right to be an independent state. This political claim now fused with the cultural idea which held that the Irish people constituted a nationality quite distinct from the English. The result of the fusion of these two ideas – one political and one cultural – was the concept of the nation state and the diffusion throughout Ireland of the force we came to know as Romantic Nationalism.

A nostalgia for what was deemed to be Ireland's glorious past was a prime characteristic of Romantic Nationalism. In its more extravagant manifestations it was claimed that our ancestors had polished the Greeks, and that Gaelic was the language of the Garden of Eden.[1] The rediscovery, preservation and eventual restoration of the national language grew out of that nostalgia. The glorification of arms as the means for re-establishing an independent nation state became another leading characteristic of Romantic Nationalism. As the

German historian, Treitschke, said: 'It is war which turns a people into a nation'. Cuchulain, the Fianna, Brian Boru, Red Hugh O'Donnell, Owen Roe O'Neill, Sarsfield, the Irish Brigade, Clare's Dragoons, Tone and Emmet – all had to be praised in song and story, and when the call came again, had to be emulated.

Following on the French Revolution's democratic ideal, and Herder's insistence that each people had its own unique character, the people themselves, as well as their culture, came to be idolised. This adulation of the folk added a further powerful element to Romantic Nationalism. O'Connell told his mass audiences that they were the finest peasantry in the world. And Davis wrote of his 'rich and rare land':

> No men than hers are braver –
> Her women's hearts ne'er waver;
> I'd freely die to save her,
> And think my lot divine.[2]

Romantic Nationalism, therefore, romanticised about a glorious past; about the splendours and antiquity of the Irish language and culture; about the heroic chivalry of military force; and about the unsurpassed virtues of the Irish people. From Emmet in 1803 down to Pearse in 1916 Irish political figures breathed this atmosphere of Romantic Nationalism.

Where does Parnell fit into all of this? The short answer is that personally he doesn't fit in at all. He is unique among nineteenth- and early twentieth-century Irish political leaders in that all of the major characteristics of Romantic Nationalism are absent from his ideology. Far from being nostalgic about Ireland's past, it was said of him that he knew nothing of Irish history. His ignorance of the subject was, indeed, proverbial. 'I never saw a sign of his knowing Irish history', wrote Gladstone.[3] His lack of knowledge in the area was confirmed by allies like John Devoy and his biographer, Barry O'Brien. On one occasion when O'Brien made reference to O'Connell's alliance with the Whigs, Parnell confessed: 'I am very ignorant of these things . . . I have read very little.'[4]

Some commentators, while admitting that O'Connell was a reformer, would deny that he was ever a nationalist. The same commentators have no hesitation in accepting Parnell as a nationalist. Yet O'Connell was touched by the Romantic movement to the extent that he purposely held his great monster meetings at the most famous sites in Irish history – Tara, Cashel, Kells, Mullaghmast, Clontibret; Drogheda and Wexford (with their memories of Cromwell), Limerick, Kilkenny, Enniscorthy, and the series was planned to end at Clontarf – symbolically with the expulsion of the invader. At all of these historic locations O'Connell was, in the words of John Blake Dillon, 'searching the depths of the nation's memory'. Or, if we prefer, tugging at the heartstrings of Romantic Nationalism. In stark contrast, this historical litany of Ireland's memorable sites meant little to Parnell.

Nor did Parnell show any awareness or interest in the Irish language as a driving force in the growth of nationalism. The stirrings that eventually led to the foundation of the Gaelic League were already long in existence. Several societies throughout the nineteenth century had given their attention to the language. The latest of these – the Society for the Preservation of the Language – had been established in 1877, two years after Parnell entered parliament. When the Intermediate Education Bill was introduced in 1878, the Society petitioned, successfully, to have Irish included as an examination subject. In parliament it was not Parnell but his Home Rule colleagues O'Connor Power, the O'Connor Don and Isaac Butt who spoke in favour of the language.

In a widely publicised letter accepting the position of patron of the GAA in 1884, Parnell's close ally, Archbishop Croke, issued what amounted to a clarion call for the de-Anglicisation of Irish society.[5] Before the Gaelic League was founded, Tim Healy in parliament denounced the policy of teaching Irish-speaking children through English as absurd and as English philistinism.[6] And William O'Brien, one of Parnell's closest lieutenants, described Irish as the distinguishing characteristic of nationality, one of the oldest and dearest of our national possessions; and he urged young nationalists to learn the living tongue.[7]

Although surrounded by colleagues and allies who were responding to the quickening of cultural nationalism and the Irish-Ireland ideal, the proclaimed leader of the Irish race at home and abroad remained untouched by the subject. There was little indication that he ever concerned himself with the plight of the language, or with its preservation – much less with the advocacy of its revival as the spoken tongue. Thomas Davis's famous proposition that 'a nation without a language is a nation without a soul' simply meant nothing to Parnell.

The key to Parnell's non-Romantic nationalism lay in the acute practicality of his mind. The extremely pragmatic streak in his nature was evidenced in his lifelong absorbing interest in applied science and engineering, and in mining. On his first visit to America his interest was in seeing the workings of mills and cotton factories. And he was in grave danger of being killed in Alabama while sketching the roof of a newly designed railway bridge hundreds of feet above the Warrior river, because he wanted to adapt the design of the roof for the new sawmills he proposed constructing in Avondale. At the centenary of Independence exhibition in Philadelphia in 1876, during his second visit to America, his chief interest was in the Machinery Hall.

In Kilmainham Jail in 1881–2, a well-wisher had sent him an expensive musical-box which played the tune, 'The Wearing of the Green'. Parnell's only interest was in dismantling it to show his fellow prisoners how it worked mechanically. At Eltham in 1885 when cohabiting with Mrs O'Shea, she had an extra room built on to her house to serve as Parnell's own workroom where he pursued his scientific tests. In Brighton he spent hours measuring the span of the roof of the rebuilt railway station, drawing up architectural plans and reducing to scale for his new cattle shed in Avondale. At Brighton, too, he spent months trying to invent a ship which would cut through the sea without the sensation of the motion of the waves. Models of this ship were made and tested at the Chain Pier in Brighton. But time ran out before his invention was completed.

It may well be that the practical side of Parnell came from the fact that his mother was American which made him half-American by blood and, as William O'Brien claimed, five-sixths in sympathy.[8] He had perhaps inherited, and certainly admired, those qualities of youthful energy, strength and practicality with which he believed Americans approached issues. A practical man in his hobbies, the same virtue of practicality – not romanticism– was the essential ingredient of his politics.

His career in parliament began as an obstructionist because he was convinced that disruption of the normal business of the House of Commons was the one pragmatic way of drawing Parliament's attention to the wrongs of Ireland. These vigorous tactics, disapproved of by his party leader, Isaac Butt, had also the effect of drawing attention to himself. And two years after he had entered Parliament, he was elected president of the largely Fenian-controlled Home Rule Confederation of Great Britain in place of the much more moderate Butt.

Then, when the agricultural crisis of the late 1870s, threatened a re-visitation of the horrors of the Great Famine of the 1840s, Parnell's response was typically practical. It also showed, however, another of his enduring characteristics: a readiness to take serious calculated risks.

'Do you think, Mr Kickham', he asked the old Fenian leader 'that the people feel very keenly on the land question?' 'I am only sorry to say', answered the Fenian purist, 'that they would go to hell for it'. [9] For it was orthodox Fenian doctrine that the people should concentrate their energies on establishing first the Irish Republic to which all other reforms could be added later.

Despite the priorities of the President of the Supreme Council of the IRB, and the public condemnation of the meeting by John MacHale, Archbishop of Tuam, Parnell went to Westport on 8 June 1879 and memorably exhorted the people to 'hold a firm grip on your homesteads and lands. You must not allow yourselves to be dispossessed as you were dispossessed in 1847'.[10] He realised that the protection of the tenants required a nationwide organisation and agitation. As president of the Land League, Parnell was the first Irish political leader to appreciate and exploit the American connection, and win critical financial and political support for the cause. His two and a half months fund-raising tour of over 60 North American cities earned for him the title of Uncrowned King of Ireland.

Despite success and adulation, he remained his cool pragmatic self. Anything that threatened what he regarded as achievable had to be firmly rejected. That is why he suppressed the Ladies' Land League, and opposed Davitt's dreams of land nationalisation as utopian. And although his declared objective was peasant proprietorship, yet he was prepared to accept the 1881 Land Act because it conceded the famous 3FS – fair rent, free sale and fixity of tenure – introduced the principle of dual ownership, and established a Land Court which protected the tenants from rack-rents. In this, as in so many other incidents, he displayed the art of the practical statesman: keeping his principles intact, while acting according to circumstances.

The Land War increased and intensified support for Home Rule. And during the course of the agrarian agitation, Parnell, long the *de facto* leader of nationalist Ireland, was formally elected chairman of the parliamentary party. He could now concentrate his own remarkable skills and all the force of his much strengthened party on the business of winning an independent parliament for Ireland. Romantic Nationalism entered no more into Parnell's political or Home Rule objectives than it had into his social or Land League agitation. But when it comes to the question of Home Rule, the problem for his contemporaries, as well as for his biographers and historians since, is in trying to determine what precisely were Parnell's objectives.

There were occasions when he sounded as extreme as any Fenian. At Cincinnati in 1880 it was reported that he had said: 'None of us . . . will be satisfied until we have destroyed the last link which keeps Ireland bound to England.' It was precisely this kind of statement that kept the Fenians and their American allies, Clan na Gael, on his side. Famously, in Cork in 1885, he declaimed:

> No man has the right to fix the boundary to the march of a nation; no man has the right to to say to his country: 'Thus far shalt thou go and no further', and we have never attempted to fix the *ne plus ultra* to the progress of Ireland's nationhood, and we never shall.[11]

It was this speech that made Pearse proclaim that Parnell had the separatist's instinct. And while Pearse denied that Grattan, O'Connell or Redmond were separatists, he assigned Parnell to the same separatist Pantheon as Tone, Davis, Lalor and Mitchel. In 1891, addressing an audience in Navan as 'the men of royal Meath', he added the comment that someone in the future might have the privilege of addressing them as 'the men of republican Meath'. One is reminded of Cromwell's dictum: 'He goeth furthest who knows not whither he is going'.

Depending on his audience and the occasion, he was as likely to be heard declaring a position at the other end of the nationalist spectrum. If not exactly in the same breath with which he declared in Cork that Home Rule might not go far enough for Irishmen in the future, at least in the same month in 1885 he was in negotiations with Joseph Chamberlain about a proposal to give Ireland a central board of local government – something akin to a glorified county council. (It is only fair to say, however, that Parnell made it clear that the Central Board could never be accepted as a substitute for Home Rule). But, then, in 1886 he said he would accept Gladstone's limited Home Rule Bill as a 'final solution' to the Irish question.

It is not that Parnell was a mere opportunist or purposely ambivalent. But each power group – the Fenians, the Land League, the parliamentary party, the Church and the government – took from his words the interpretation that best suited its own agenda. And he, while aiming at the principle of an independent parliament, deliberately avoided all doctrinairism about the details of the ideal constitutional status for Ireland. With no interest in abstract theories of government, he concentrated on political action to achieve what was feasible. This gave him a certain flexibility which saved him from being tied down to any one specific constitutional structure. So while the *strategy* aimed at an independent parliament, the *tactics* took such steps and used such weapons as were available, nearest at hand and realistic.

On the question of the use of force to achieve political ends, again Parnell will be found to have been quite bellicose on occasion depending on the circumstances. He certainly cannot be described as a pacifist; and he did not go along with O'Connell's dictum that political freedom was not worth the shedding of a single drop of human blood. He was not a revisionist ready to condemn all appeal to arms in Irish history. But neither, on the other hand, did he romanticise about the rebellions of Wolfe Tone, Emmet, Young Ireland or the Fenians.

His comments on Robert Emmet were quite characteristic. Once someone was talking slightingly of Emmet's rebellion. Parnell interjected: 'Emmet was not such a fool as many foolish people think. There was Napoleon with his Army of England cooling his heels at Boulogne. Any success in Ireland might have decided him to cross. Emmet's idea of striking at the Castle to begin with was a good one. He might have done better without bothering about uniforms.'[12] In Parnell's book, to hit at Dublin Castle was practical. To bother about uniforms was romantic.

His attitude to the use of force was determined by the same litmus test he applied to any political device. Did it work? Was it practical? His argument against rebellion in his time was that Ireland did not have the arms nor the numbers to take on the Empire. And geographically, Ireland was too small a country for a rebellion – there was not room enough to run away.

Washington, he said, had won against the English by running away, that is by being able to retreat. In Ireland he would have had to surrender in six weeks.[13] His offer to resign after the shock of the Phoenix Park murders is the more reliable indicator of his attitude to the use of force. Not only did he regard the recourse to arms and insurrection as impractical, but he also saw it as politically detrimental.

I have argued that Parnell was not the Romantic Nationalist, but the eminently pragmatic politician. Although he himself was not the Romantic Nationalist, his followers transformed him into the Romantic Hero. And therein lay his power to mesmerise; and therein lay his continuous appeal long after his death. The peasantry of the Land War; the party members who gladly submitted to his control; the clergy who chaired the constituency meetings; and the poets and writers of the literary revival,– all were captivated in the spell he cast over them.

Even his political opponents and the hostile British press, while bitterly denouncing him, admitted that he 'stood head and shoulders' above his fellow parliamentarians.[14] Gladstone, who had been 60 years in the House of Commons and Prime Minister on four separate occasions, said:

> Parnell was the most remarkable man I ever met . . . He did things and he said things unlike other men. His ascendancy over his Party was extraordinary. There has never been anything like it in my experience of the House of Commons. He succeeded in surrounding himself with very clever men, with men exactly suited for his purpose . . . he had a most efficient Party . . . The absolute obedience . . . the military discipline in which he held them was unlike anything I have ever seen . . . and Parnell was supreme all the time.[15]

The mystique he possessed is widely attested to, even by those who afterwards led the ranks of the anti-Parnellites. His charisma was based on a happy combination of many elements. It had something to do with his charm and good looks and his honoured name; it had something to do with the paradox that he was a Protestant landlord leading a Catholic peasantry in revolt against landlordism. And unlike the stereotyped, flamboyant Irish orator, he was unusually silent and composed; and when he spoke he used words only sparingly, but effectively. Politically, he was an outsider, alienated from his own landlord class. As a non-romantic he was different from the Romantic Nationalists in his own party. And socially, he was ever the loner. Somewhat of a mystery man to his colleagues, nevertheless they acknowledged his indomitable will and courage, his sheer political instinct and sense of timing.

Parnell may not have read much of the romanticised history of his country, but he lived and worked among men and women who had. In him the various strands of the Irish historical experience came together – the constitutionalism of Grattan and O'Connell, the republicanism of Tone and Emmet, the romanticism of Young Ireland and the Fenians, and the agrarianism of Fintan Lalor and Michael Davitt. Irish history, so it seemed, culminated in and lived through Parnell. He was identified – and identified himself – with the wrongs, the needs and the aspirations of the Irish people.

Possessing marked historical as well as political imagination, he grasped not only what was politically feasible in his time, but also what was appropriate, deeply felt and desired. Parnell had come to be idolised as the agent and incarnation of the national will. He moved as if by instinct into what was ripe for development, and then forward to the next step in the progress of Irish nationalism – from obstruction to the New Departure, to the Land League, to the machine-like efficiency of the Parliamentary Party, to the Home Rule Bill. His words and deeds seemed to be the surest and best of his time.

By any reckoning his achievements in the 16 years of his political career had been considerable. He succeeded, as no other Irish politician, before or since, succeeded in bringing together all shades of nationalist opinion at home and abroad. Physical force Fenians, radical agrarian agitators, moderate parliamentarians, and conservative bishops united in a grand alliance behind his leadership. And they applauded as he performed the breathtaking tight-rope act between revolutionary agitation and constitutionalism. 'Parnell's policy', said a colleague, 'was neither "constitutional" nor "unconstitutional", but a judicious combination of the two'. [16]

Through the Land League he began the dismantling of landlordism – thus changing the face of the countryside, for the transfer of the ownership of the land amounted to a social revolution. It heralded also a political and democratic revolution. For the landlords had been the main support of the Union; and with the destruction of landlordism and the Protestant Ascendancy the whole structure of the Union with Britain began to totter.

Another of his achievements was the creation and skilled leadership of the first modern, disciplined party machine. Every nationalist candidate for parliamentary elections was required to sign a pledge stating that in the event of his election he would 'sit, act and vote with the Irish Parliamentary Party', and if, in the opinion of the majority of the Party he failed to do so, that he would resign his seat forthwith.

Parnell was not so autocratic as to insist on filling seats with his own creatures. But because of his status among the people, he was sometimes requested to provide a nominee, as in a revealing telegram he once received from Kerry: 'We'll elect a broomstick if you'll give it a name'.[17] Following unprecedented success in the 1885 general election, Parnell's party held the balance between the Liberals and the Conservatives in the House of Commons. The result was that Gladstone announced the conversion of the Liberals to the principle of Home Rule. And the Conservatives, as a substitute for Home Rule, declared for the conciliation of Ireland in what came to be called the policy of 'killing Home Rule with kindness'.

Energies and aspirations and the latent nationalist sentiment of the people had found an outlet in the Land League and Home Rule agitations. And it was Parnell who provided the messianic leadership for all that mighty upsurge. His triumphs as well as his tragic fall released powerful forces, and no doubt contributed, if in mysterious ways, to the emergence of the Gaelic League and the Anglo-Irish literary revival, the rise of Sinn Féin, the reinvigoration of the IRB, and gave rise to a literary Parnellism exemplified at its best in Yeats and Joyce. It can be argued that his fall made 1916 possible – perhaps even necessary. But the ambiguity of his methods make it possible also to argue that his legacy was rather to constitutional nationalism and the parliamentary tradition of Dáil Éireann.

Parnell's fall was due to his love affair with Mrs O'Shea. Ironically, the non-Romantic Nationalist of public life had turned out to be deeply romantic in his private life. His background had prepared him for just such an affair. He was only seven when his parents virtually separated. His mother took herself and her daughters off to Paris and London for their education and to launch the older ones as debutantes. Parnell was brought to a boarding-school for girls near Yeovil, in Somerset, by his father who was anxious that the child should spend some time with a surrogate mother and away from his brother John, whose stammer he was beginning to imitate.[18] At thirteen Charles was the only member of the family at home in Avondale for the sudden death of his father.

In his mid-twenties he had a serious love affair with an American heiress whom he met in Paris. When she moved to Rome with her parents, Parnell followed her. When she returned to Newport, Rhode Island, he followed her there, only to be told that she no longer wished to marry him. Charles was depressed for weeks; and his brother was convinced that as a result of this jilting Charles later sublimated his energies in politics. His first six years in politics – the years of obstruction in Parliament, of the land agitation, of the American tour and the campaign for the control and direction of the flagging Home Rule Party – had been remarkably intense. During this time he had travelled frequently between Avondale and London and to public meetings throughout Britain, the USA and Ireland, living in lonely hotel rooms and to a great extent in social isolation. Then, in 1880, when he had been no more than two months as chairman of the party, he met Mrs O'Shea. He was then 34, and she a year and a half older. Lonely and tense from overwork, he was ripe for romance.

She, too, was ready for something more exciting in her life. Katharine Wood had married Captain O'Shea when she was 22. His travels for long periods abroad on failed business enterprises had made him very much a part-time husband. Because of the prolonged absences in the Captain's lifestyle, Katharine said that: 'A formal separation of a friendly sort' had been 'tacitly accepted'; and that years of neglect, varied with quarrels, had killed her love for her husband long before she met Parnell.[19] With an absent, financially embarrassed husband, she became companion to her rich old Aunt Ben, who purchased a nearby house for her niece in Eltham, and paid for the Captain's chambers in London. After her husband was elected as a Home Rule MP for County Clare in 1880, Katharine invited some of his fellow MPs, including Parnell, the now famous new leader of the party, to dinner in a London hotel.

The Parnell–Mrs O'Shea love affair, which began instantly, was destined to be one of the consuming passions of modern history. Its intensity sprang from a hunger felt by two who had been deprived of a loving relationship for so long. An attractive and warm-hearted woman, she provided him with all of the comforts of a home life that he had never known. And he acknowledged that he felt 'home-sick' whenever he was not staying with her.[20] Before the rest of the world Parnell was, as she said, 'an iron mask of reserve'. Publicly, the man of ice; privately, deeply passionate. Gladstone once remarked on Parnell's 'coldness and reserve'. She replied that he was a volcano capped with snow.[21]

After the revelations of the divorce court, when Gladstone, like everyone else, knew more about their relationship, he changed his verdict and said that 'the man who was a rock to all the world was like a bit of wax in the hands of a woman'.[22] The difference between the non-Romantic Nationalist of public life and the romantic lover in private, is fully revealed in Parnell's letters to Mrs O'Shea. These letters, simple in style, from a man who put so little else on paper, testify to how smitten he was.

His infatuation was evident in letters which told her that even a note or a telegram from her seemed to have become a necessary part of his daily existence; or how much she had occupied his thoughts all day. And from Avondale he enclosed a sprig of heather with his best love. Later letters show him caring and worried about her health; anxious when she is troubled; and constantly reassuring her of his love.

In the earliest letters (July 1880), he wrote to her as 'Dear Mrs O'Shea'. Three months later he is addressing her as 'My Own Love'. Six months after their first meeting (Jan. 1881), it was 'My Dearest Wifie'. Then from Kilmainham Jail, it had become 'My Own Darling Queenie'. As in public life he had fascinated the Irish people, so in private, a romantic such as Katharine was charmed by his devotion. She described herself as having been 'swept into the avalanche of Parnell's love',[23] which she said was always 'tender and considerate'.[24] Twenty years after his death she wrote: 'Parnell loved me as never woman has been loved before'.[25]

Then, came Captain O'Shea's divorce action against his wife and Parnell. In his public career Parnell had been regarded, even by British ministers, as an honourable man, true to his word, one you could do business with. Dignified and proud, he was the idol of his people. The contrast between the hero of public life and the wife-stealing, home-breaking, deceitful cad that was portrayed in the divorce court could hardly have been more shocking or more devastating in its effect. Because the action was undefended, the Captain's evidence and the lurid stories of his witnesses could not be tested in cross-examination. And Parnell was presented as having recklessly engaged in a furtive and squalid affair with a colleague's wife. In that dangerous intersection where public career and secret affair meet, Parnell fell victim. He was deserted by a majority of his Parliamentary Party, by most of the electors in the constituencies and by all of the bishops.

At the outer crust of the relationship were all the apparently shabby details of deception, duplicity and infidelity – the secret messages and meetings, the lies, the aliases, the rented love-nests, and from time to time the melodrama. Yet at its core was a love story of great and enduring intensity, tenderness and harmony – Katharine content with her role as the mistress-in-the-background; Charles content with his domestic hobbies; and the couple keeping themselves very much to themselves socially, and happy with their horses and dogs and walks on the Sussex Downs.

But they were unfortunate in the era in which they lived and loved. A century later Katharine could have accompanied her Irish political leader wherever, and have been received the world over as his devoted partner. One might well ask why the affair of eleven years could not have become open. And one might well ask why the O'Shea marriage could not have been formally ended long before it scandalised the public. The Captain had kept up the pretence partly, no doubt, because of the expectation of sharing Aunt Ben's considerable fortune. And Katharine had stayed officially married to him, partly because she feared the effect divorce might have on her lover's political career. And Parnell had accepted the situation, not only because of consideration for Katharine's wishes, but partly also because he was no stranger to taking risks and courting mystery.

And if all this was not enough, the then current, restrictive divorce laws in England, especially as they applied to women, and the illegitimacy laws as they applied to children, militated against ending the charade of the O'Shea marriage – that is until it appeared that Aunt Ben's will had made Katharine the sole beneficiary. The divorce proceedings enabled the will to be challenged in court, and the settlement arrived at meant that Katharine had to share the money left to her by Aunt Ben with her own avaricious siblings and with Captain O'Shea.

My argument has been that Parnell was not a Romantic Nationalist. But he lived in an era of Romantic Nationalism and was surrounded by colleagues who were greatly influenced by its spirit. It was this spirit of Romantic

Nationalism that had helped make him into the Romantic hero, and had raised him to the peak of political power as the Uncrowned King. In his liaison with Mrs O'Shea, however, he was very much the romantic. That secretive life of romance collided head on with the public career of the Romantic Hero. Neither element in Parnell's nature – the romantic and the heroic – would or could give way to the other. The force of the collision, it might be said, not only toppled him from power, but was, indeed, responsible for his death only three months after his marriage.

In his mid-twenties the rejection of his love by one woman had helped direct this non-Romantic Nationalist into politics; and in the process gave us one of Ireland's greatest ever leaders. In his mid-thirties and forties the fulsome reciprocation of his love by Katharine O'Shea eventually destroyed that remarkable career; and in the process gave us the most tragic story of romance in Ireland's history.

'The Blackbird of Avondale'

Parnell at Kilmainham

Pauric Travers

The ghosts of Kilmainham have a thousand stories. These stories are moving, tragic and diverse. They tell of crime and punishment, poverty and hardship, oppression and sometimes even death. Charles Stewart Parnell was one of those ghosts. Arrested on 13 October 1881 and imprisoned without trial, Parnell was held at Kilmainham until 2 May 1882, when he was released under the terms of the so-called Kilmainham Treaty.

In the scale of things, Parnell's interlude at Kilmainham was untypical. If one discounts the impact of imprisonment without trial on a country gentleman, the experience in the main was not particularly traumatic and he was generally well treated. A popular ballad of the time lamented that the 'cold prison dungeon' was no fit habitation for the 'blackbird of Avondale' but, in truth, Parnell's lodgings were relatively comfortable.[1] Parnell was not an 'ordinary ghost of Kilmainham'. Even in the narrower category of political prisoners, his story lacks the drama of impending transportation or, worse still, execution. Yet his term at Kilmainham was of considerable significance for Parnell personally and politically, for the Ladies' Land League, for the land agitation and for the nationalist movement generally.

The decision to arrest Parnell had one unexpected outcome. There is no period of Parnell's life about which so much is known. The letters, interviews, official reports, diaries and memoirs allow an unusually detailed insight into his political thinking and personal outlook. Gladstone may have blundered in deciding to arrest Parnell, but for that particular blunder we should be eternally grateful.

For many of the most notable political prisoners who passed through its gates, Kilmainham marked a culmination or climax, followed by exile or even worse. In Parnell's case, the Kilmainham experience came relatively early in his political career and it marked not so much a climax as a transition from one phase to another. While Parnell entered politics in 1875 and gained some

notoriety for his defence of the Manchester Martyrs in the House of Commons and the policy of obstructionism, his political career did not take off until 1879 through his leadership of the land agitation. His famous Westport speech in June 1879,[2] when he outlined the principles of fair rent and fixity of tenure, provided the embryo movement with its programme and inaugurated an intense period of parliamentary and extra-parliamentary activity focused on the land question which lasted until the Kilmainham Treaty. In October 1879, the National Land League was established with Parnell as President and Michael Davitt, A. J. Kettle and Thomas Brennan as joint secretaries. The League which grew rapidly countrywide operated on two levels, public and covert, with Parnell maintaining a skilful if sometimes precarious balance.

The response of the Liberal government to the land agitation was coercion and concession. In 1881 two Coercion Acts were passed: the Protection of Person and Property Act and the Peace Preservation Act. Following the arrest of Davitt, who spent more than a year in jail, Parnell resisted pressure from some of his Land League colleagues to withdraw from the House of Commons and lead a no-rent campaign in Ireland. His caution seemed to be rewarded when Gladstone introduced a new land bill. Gladstone's Second Land Act, the Land Law (Ireland) Act, 1881, was a radical measure which was inconceivable without the land agitation. It conceded the three F's, at least in theory, and established the principle of dual ownership, a revolutionary step but one already dismissed by Parnell as unworkable.[3] A Land Commission was established to make loans to tenants for the purchase of their holdings and to fix fair rents. While the concession fell short of what the leaders of the Land League and their supporters might have wished, in retrospect the 1881 Act can be seen to have marked the beginning of the end of landlordism. Inevitably there was disappointment, not least among small tenant farmers whose hopes had been raised only to be dashed.

The leadership of the Land League was divided on how to respond to the Act with moderates arguing that it was a reasonable measure of reform, while the radicals, including the Fenian element, argued that it should be rejected out of hand as it did not meet their demands and its implementation was in untrustworthy hands. The uneasy coalition which the League represented seemed likely to split but a compromise was reached. A Land League convention in Dublin rallied behind Parnell's recommended course of 'testing the act' by referring selected cases to the rent tribunal. While John Dillon accurately derided this as a 'milch cow for the lawyers', it was essentially a holding position designed to buy time while keeping contending forces united.[4] It is at this vital moment and with the unrest in the countryside continuing that Parnell was arrested and imprisoned in Kilmainham.

While Parnell's arrest caused a sensation in Dublin and throughout the country, it did not come as a complete surprise. The Government had made clear its intention to act firmly against what it saw as sedition, and many of the leaders of the Land League were already in prison. W. E. Forster, the Chief Secretary, had been urging Parnell's arrest for some time. On 8 October, in a speech at Leeds, Gladstone had launched a strong personal attack on Parnell, contrasting his leadership unfavourably with that of O'Connell and Butt and warning him not to impede the operation of the Land Act:

> He [Parnell] desires to arrest the operation of the Land Act; to stand as Moses stood between the living and the dead; to stand there not as Moses stood, to arrest, but to spread the plague . . . If it shall appear that there is to be fought a final conflict in Ireland between law on the one side and sheer lawlessness upon the other, if the law purged from defect and from any taint of injustice is still to be repelled and refused, and the first conditions of political society to remain unfulfilled, then I say, gentlemen, without hesitation, the resources of civilisation against its enemies are still not yet exhausted.[5]

Parnell responded at Wexford on 9 October in a tone of calculated defiance:

> The Irishman who thinks that he can now throw away his arms, just as Grattan disbanded the Volunteers in 1782, will find to his sorrow and destruction when too late that he has placed himself in the power of a perfidious and cruel and unrelenting English enemy.[6]

The widely expected response from the Government was not long delayed. The *Irish Times* hinted that something was afoot, noting that although the Lord Lieutenant was absent from Dublin, Forster had left Dublin for a cabinet meeting the previous day and that everyone knew it was about serious matters. The *Irish Times* speculated that Cabinet had decided on 'firm action'.[7] Indeed it had. On 12 October, after five hours of discussion, the Cabinet decided that Parnell should be imprisoned under the Coercion Act. Forster immediately contacted Dublin Castle to make the necessary arrangements, suggesting that it would be best if the arrests were made early the following morning.[8]

Announcing Parnell's arrest, Gladstone echoed his Leeds speech and justified the Government's decision on the basis of the need to vindicate law and order, the rights of property, the freedom of the land and the first elements of political life and civilisation. Gladstone argued that Parnell, for whatever motives, was engaged in an anarchical oppression of the people of Ireland.[9] The *Irish Times* immediately linked the arrest with the Wexford speech:

> The Government yesterday took the decisive step of arresting Mr Parnell. The action is sudden, bold and authorised by the Cabinet . . . Mr Parnell will be the last man himself we should say to complain of the latest move if an unexpected

and stern one in the game which he has been playing so closely with the government. He declared against them mortal war in Wexford and they reply by putting him in prison.[10]

It is clear that Parnell was aware that the Government was likely to act and that he framed his Wexford speech to provoke such a response. That evening when two members of his party discreetly inquired about instructions in the event of his arrest, Parnell reputedly responded with the famous retort, 'Ah, if I am arrested Captain Moonlight will take my place'.[11]

Parnell had returned to Dublin via Avondale, and stayed at Morrison's Hotel on Dawson Street.[12] He was arrested there on the morning of 13 October by two detectives. When Superintendent Mallon and his colleague arrived, Parnell kept them waiting for half an hour while he dressed. He dismissed prompting from a porter that he should make his escape. A cab was then called to take him to Kilmainham, but not before he had written a note to Katharine O'Shea which he insisted on posting himself. This letter contained a remarkable sentence:

> Politically, it is a fortunate thing for me that I have been arrested, as the movement is breaking fast, and all will be quiet in a few months when I shall be released.[13]

This would suggest that by October 1881 Parnell had concluded that the land agitation had reached the end of its useful life and was beginning to disintegrate. If this interpretation is accurate, then it demonstrates a high level of astuteness and tactical awareness. However, notwithstanding Parnell's undoubted prescience, it was not inevitable that the imprisonment of the leaders of the Land League would lead to the end of the Land War. On the contrary, imprisonment without trial was as likely to produce a surge in popular support and might have led to even greater militancy. It is instructive to look at a roughly similar moment in the spring of 1918 when the nationalist movement was at a crossroads. Warned that they were going to be arrested, the leaders of Sinn Féin decided that there would be political advantage in not evading arrest. De Valera and the other Sinn Féin leaders were duly arrested on foot of an imaginary German plot. Significantly, however, Michael Collins and Harry Boland evaded arrest. In this case, far from the arrest of the political leadership leading to a calming of the situation, it facilitated the passing of the initiative to the most militant wing of the movement.[14] That outcome was as likely in 1881, bearing in mind that Parnell's arrest did produce a huge increase in agrarian crime. Thus Parnell's strategy was high risk.

If Parnell viewed Kilmainham as an interlude during which calm might be restored and a new course set, that view was not shared by many of his colleagues who saw an opportunity to galvanise support and add new impetus to the agitation. Parnell's arrest generated a wave of public sympathy. Even the *Irish Times* acknowledged this but thought it was more a feature in the country than in the city. From all over the country there were reports of public meetings and motions of protest condemning, as one resolution put, 'in the strongest terms that the English language will allow the arbitrary seizure of Charles Stewart Parnell' and pledging to carry on the struggle against land-lordism. In Cork, it was reported that the arrest had caused a 'great sensation'. From Boyle, in County Roscommon, a correspondent reported that

> the arrest of Mr Parnell and his consignment to Kilmainham prison was received with positive bewilderment, although nobody seemed surprised. In fact, his seizure was daily expected. More uncontrollable excitement and, indeed passion, than prevails here would be hard to imagine.[15]

Parnell and the Kilmainham prisoners quickly became national heroes. Ballads were written and sung on street corners about their predicament:

> The fowler way-laid him in hopes to ensnare him,
> While I here in sorrow his absence bewail,
> It grieves me to hear that the walls of Kilmainham
> Surround the dear Blackbird of sweet Avondale.[16]

'The Blackbird of Avondale or the Arrest of Parnell' is among the finest in the Irish ballad tradition; other efforts display less artistic merit or, as in the case of 'Could Kilmainham Jail', show evidence of the mock-heroic lampoon:

> Come all ye gallant Irishmen, and listen to my song
> Whilst I a story do relate, of England's cruel wrong.
> Before this wrong all other wrongs of Ireland do grow pale
> For they clapped the pride of Erin's Isle into 'could' Kilmainham Jail.[17]

This verse which has been taken as a genuine street ballad by historians, including St John Ervine and Robert Kee, was in fact written by Sir John Ross, last Lord Chancellor of Ireland, and his former school friend Percy French. Among the gifts which poured into Kilmainham for Parnell were food, flowers, verse and a music box that played the 'Wearing of the Green' and other rebel ballads. Not all of the verse was sympathetic:

> O Mr Parnell, O Mr Parnell,
> Cease to do evil, and learn to do well.[18]

Six weeks after his arrest, one of Parnell's fellow prisoners received a letter from a colleague testifying to their new-found hero status:

But cheer up. You were very dear to us before your imprisonment but your arrest immortalized you. Your name is a household word and mothers teach their little children to learn the names of Ireland's imprisoned heroes and what more noble than to suffer for dear motherland. In this, I envy you, but I suppose I am not worthy of so high an honour. I was daily expecting to be arrested for weeks after you were taken and here I am still at liberty.[19]

Notwithstanding the levity of tone, the observation was perceptive. Among the numerous messages of sympathy sent to Anna Parnell on the imprison-ment of her brother was an address from the newly formed Boys' Branch of the Land League pledging to love their country, hate their oppressors and remain ever more loyal to the imprisoned leaders.[20] It is clear that, as St John Ervine suggested, 'Parnell in prison was as powerful as Parnell out of it – in some respects more powerful'.[21] His imprisonment strengthened his leader-ship, particularly among the radicals inside and outside Kilmainham who criticised him for being too moderate. His unexpected support for a radical 'No rent manifesto' issued from Kilmainham confirmed that position. Even John Dillon who had clashed repeatedly with Parnell was drawn back into a nationalist fold which now appeared more united than ever.

Whatever Parnell's intentions, it is hardly surprising that a self-conscious attempt was made to turn the wave of sympathy to good use. The Ladies' Land League established in January 1881 was the immediate beneficiary. The story of the Ladies' League lies beyond the scope of this essay except insofar as it impinges on the Kilmainham prisoners. Under the leadership of Anna Parnell, the League led a countrywide campaign in support of the prisoners while at the same time attempting to maintain and extend the land agitation and provide for the needs of evicted tenants. *Pace* suggestions of mismanage-ment and financial naivety, the extent to which the Ladies' League succeeded on all three fronts remains a remarkable achievement and makes all the more extraordinary the disdain with which the women's organisation was subse-quently treated by the prisoners on their release, and not least by Parnell himself. In fairness to Parnell, his insistence that the Ladies' Land League should wind up was consistent with his broader policy for the land agitation, but his approach opened a serious breach with his sister Anna who viewed it as a betrayal.

It is evident from the papers of the Ladies' Land League in the National Library of Ireland that, at the time, many of the prisoners were extremely grateful to the Ladies' League for their attentiveness and practical support.[22] Jennie O'Toole (later Jennie Wyse Power) was indefatigable in her role as librarian and general welfare officer, even to the extent of providing curtains for Parnell's cell. She quickly learned to cater for the varied tastes of the prisoners – one prisoner explained that for the most part his colleagues were of peasant stock and did not care much for English magazines and English novels. In Galway jail, however, the prisoners must have been made of sterner stuff, or so we might conclude from Tim Harrington's urgent appeals to Jennie O'Toole regarding the disappearance of two French grammars which had been sent to them. J. P. Quinn wrote on behalf of Parnell seeking a scrap-book, gum and brush.[23]

The actions of the government gave the Ladies' League a propaganda weapon. Nowhere is this more evident than on the question of the diet of the prisoners which was self-consciously manipulated to generate public support. The prospect of the prisoners having to rely on prison fare was viewed with understandable distaste and quickly gave rise to a public campaign. A 'Prisoner's Sustenation Fund' was launched on 3 November. In response, a Meath branch of the Ladies' League passed a unanimous resolution that 'they would not allow Mr Parnell and his colleagues to subsist on prison fare as they wished if possible to have them come out strong and healthy'. A Dublin artisan sent 2s 6d, half of his earnings, with a note saying that he was sorry for the sake of 'our noble countrymen in prison' that it was not £100.[24] This campaign was seen by some of those involved in the movement as being opportunistic. The resultant debate exposed significant internal divisions and occasional outright hostility particularly among the prisoners themselves and between the rank and file and the leadership.

In the 1880s, it continued to be the case in Irish prisons that well-to-do prisoners could make arrangements for their dietary needs at their own expense. Even before Parnell's arrest, some Land League prisoners had been provided with food from voluntary subscriptions or at the expense of the League. In the case of paid officials of the League, they continued to receive their salaries and were able to use part of this money for food. With the arrival of large numbers of prisoners, a more formal arrangement was necessary. This gave rise to considerable comment from conservative critics about the favourable treatment of these prisoners which had transformed a normally harsh prison environment into something more resembling a 'high class hotel'. Parnell's Kilmainham was described as being 'like something from a comic opera by Mr Gilbert':

> The great central hall, where scarcely a sound is heard but the measured voice of the warder, was noisy – and very cheerfully so – from morning to night. A long table down the centre of the hall was littered with newspapers, magazines and books of the day, draught boards, chess boards, backgammon boards, and packs of cards. The same table at the dinner-hour bore a cloth of snowy linen, was decorated with fruit, flowers and cut glass, and upheld a weight of excellent hot dishes and wines of many kinds. It might have been a succession of Horse-show weeks in Dublin, and her Majesty's gaol at Kilmainham turned over to some

enterprising caterer who had converted it for the nonce into an elegant hotel. It might have been, but it was not; Kilmainham prison was Kilmainham prison still, but with a rather considerable difference. The prisoners for whom games and the newspapers of the day were provided, and who fared thus sumptuously every day, were the political suspects whom the hostile press (in England as in Ireland) respresented as pining in British dungeons.[25]

A succession of caterers were used to provide food. On 2 November Anna Parnell received a detailed tender from Martin Reddy of Reddy Brothers undertaking to provide what was by any standards a varied attractive fare for the prisoners at a cost of 27s 6d per man per week.[26] After some discussion, this was agreed even though it was clear that it would be significant drain on resources – hence the need for the 'Prisoner's Sustenation Fund'.

> Reddy Brothers
> 70 Great Britain St
> 2 November 1881

Miss Anna Parnell,
Hon Sec
Ladies Irish National Land League
39 Upper Sackville St

Madam,
We propose to supply the prisoners in Kilmainham with three meals per day, namely

Breakfast
Tea or Coffee with Cold Meat or two fresh eggs – any person delicate can have a chop

Dinner
Three Joints say Roast Beef, Corned Beef, Roast Chicken and Ham. A steak or chop can be had if preferred, soup three times per week say oxtail, gravy, kidney and mutton broth; A change in the meats each day;
Fish as in season

Evening
Tea or Coffee with bread and fresh butter.
We guarantee to convey the prisoners meals in a heating apparatus which will have the food as hot as if served up at their own table at home.

The Hon. Sec. or any other lady connected with 'the League' can visit the house where the food is stored and cooked and see that all are of the best quality and properly served.

We now propose to serve all before mentioned in a proper and comfortable manner for the sum of 25/6 per man per week: all drinks or extras to be charged separately.

Should the estimate meet your approval we would feel grateful for your reply as we would require a few days notice to get the heating machine ready.

And believe me to remain,
Yours Sincerely,
Martin Reddy

Note: All drinks supplied shall be of the very best brands.

Some of the leaders of the Land League suspected that Forster, the Chief Secretary, was engaged in a devious strategy of destroying the League by imposing on it the burden of providing food for the prisoners.[27] In an interview published in the *Freeman's Journal* on 8 November, Parnell stated that the sum required already amounted to £400 per week. 'We are considering', he said, 'whether we ought not to go on prison fare.' This far from casual remark which was designed to counter Forster's tactic and evoke public sympathy was met with cynicism in unexpected quarters. T. J. O'Dempsey a fellow inmate in Kilmainham noted in his prison diary:

> I do not know to whom Mr Parnell alluded by the term 'we'; but I am aware that no such subject had at all been considered or suggested for consideration by the general body of suspects in the Hall, or in the exercise ground, or in the Infirmary of the prison in which I then was and am still. Probably the statement refers to deliberations amongst the gentlemen occupying a special infirmary presided over by Dr Kenny in the vicinity of some unknown backyard of the prison and inaccessible to the ordinary suspects. (These gentlemen consist of Mr Parnell MP, Mr Dillon, Mr Kettle, Mr Thomas Brennan, Mr Boyton.)[28]

O'Dempsey was a thirty-year old Land League solicitor from Enniscorthy who was imprisoned for intimidation.[29] During his incarceration, he became increasingly frustrated that his legal practice was stagnating in his absence, particularly when his clerk informed him that his rival solicitors were busily rushing round like commercial travellers hawking for lucrative fair rent cases. To his credit, however, O'Dempsey instructed his clerk to continue to refuse to take such cases given the official position of the League.

In O'Dempsey's view which, he claimed, was shared by many of the rank and file, the Land League had money flowing in from the United States and thus had adequate funds to support the prisoners if it chose to do so. He rejected the argument that as the money was collected for evicted tenants, it could not be diverted: it had been collected for general relief and, in any case, it was now being spent on neither evicted tenants nor prisoners.[30] Suspicion of and cynicism about the paid officials of the League and the coterie who surrounded Parnell is explicit in O'Dempsey's diary, although Parnell himself was usually exempted from such criticism. If retrenchment was necessary, it should 'begin with lopping off the luxuries and salaries of the pampered few who inhabited the regions "upstairs" inaccessible to the common lot of the ordinary Hall.'[31] Rumours about this group abounded – it was said that the previous April League prisoners had been persuaded to go on prison diet but rebelled when they saw one of the leading advocates of that course 'dining sumptuously out of a silver dinner service'.

O'Dempsey insisted that he had no objection to going on the prison diet but he strongly opposed doing so to 'see what the country would do' and manipulating the issue to launch a national collection to support the prisoners. That, he said, would be to make 'begging machines' of the prisoners – something which offended the susceptibilities of many prisoners who like O'Dempsey had a strong sense of their own respectability and what was proper. As O'Dempsey saw it, there were three main groups among the prisoners: men like himself whose livelihood required them to be free; salary and luxury men – 'drinkers of champagne and eaters of wild fowl' who surrounded Parnell and probably kept him in the dark; and poor men, many of whom were dependent on grants for their families and who would therefore do what they were told.

In the weeks that followed, rumour was rife among the prisoners that they would be asked to go on prison diet and that Parnell himself would be coming to address them on the subject. This did not happen. Instead Parnell was again interviewed by Edmund Dwyer Gray from the *Freeman's Journal*. On 21 November the prisoners were startled to read in the *Freeman* that they had one and all resolved to go on prison diet immediately.[32] The *Freeman* appealed to the country for subscriptions for a fund established by Dr Joseph Kenny. O'Dempsey claimed that this was regarded by a large section of the prisoners as 'undeserved by the country and degrading and humiliating to the suspects themselves'. An attempt by the leadership to get prisoners to sign a pledge to go on prison diet generated hostility and almost led to blows. In the end, all but 16 signed.

Despite opposition, the prisoners went on prison diet on 1 December. Because of the noteworthiness of the day, an unusually detailed picture of the routine for at least some of the prisoners that day survives. O'Dempsey recorded in his diary:

> The long threatening has come at last and here we are in the presence of the hard conditions of prison diet. Eight oz of stirabout on a dinner plate – in a circular even

plateau – meal good – but only half cooked, very thin and almost cold. Barely half a pint of skimmed milk, already tinged with sourness. My companion (Heffernan) and I ate one third of our supply of meal with the entire quantity of the milk, such as it was.

What a fool Forster and his British Government were, ever to allow any supplies from outside to reach his prisoners. This is what, if honestly administered without any surreptitious mitigations, will try the sincerity of some of our upper ten who have sentenced the honest men, who did the work of the country, to starvation. I have determined so far as I can to see that they are rigidly held to their bond, and I venture to think that, if carefully watched, they will be starved out in less than a week.

Before the day was out, it was reported by 'vigilant malcontents' that five baskets of food were seen in the Hall at dinner time. For the less fortunate, dinner, served at half past one, consisted of a pint of thin soup 'tolerably palatable and hot. Heffernan got a maggot in his. Eight oz of boiled fresh beef cut up in tough slices. Half a dozen potatoes. Both were cold.' O'Dempsey and Heffernan tried to crisp the potatoes on the fire in the infirmary – a smoky task. There was a slightly improved diet for those in the infirmary – a pint of skimmed milk and a lump of white bread for breakfast; two ounces of rice boiled in milk and meat every day for lunch.

After dinner, O'Dempsey went as usual to the exercise yard. At four o'clock he returned to the Hall where an unusual incident occurred which illustrates Parnell's leadership style. He appeared among the ordinary prisoners, made his way over to O'Dempsey's group and spent almost an hour conversing with them. Parnell began by asking how the prison diet was doing. He suggested that it might be improved by getting bread and milk or tea in the morning instead of stirabout and milk. He also thought the soup could be made more appetising and suggested a number of other improvements. He adverted to the great saving being achieved by the men taking prison food. The conversation then moved on to the propriety of seeking rent reductions and the treatment of prisoners in previous periods of history including 1867. Duffy, one of the group, who had been a prisoner in Kilmainham for two years during the Fenian period, recalled that if you looked crooked at a warder you would be manacled.[33]

Throughout this conversation, O'Dempsey was uneasy. He suspected that Parnell was not being fully informed by the coterie around him so he had sent him a remonstrance signed by 18 prisoners outlining their grievances. He was unsure if this had reached Parnell but had the distinct impression that the advocates of what he termed 'the starvation policy' were highly uneasy when this conversation was going on. The sudden appearance of Parnell and his engagement with O'Dempsey suggests that he had indeed received the letter or at least was well aware of the discontent in relation to diet. But neither made any direct reference to it. At the end of an eventful day the prisoners were given a bowl of bad tea and a piece of brown bread without butter.

Not long after Parnell's encounter with the ordinary prisoners, a new initiative was introduced which won the approval of all sides – all prisoners were given two bottles of stout per day at the expense of the League. As the money began to pour in from the country, there was also a compromise on the whole food issue. A sum of £9,000 was raised, about sufficient to provide one meal per prisoner per day. Each prisoner was given an allowance of £1 per week for food to be used as he saw fit – Anna Parnell felt that to be sufficient an allowance of £1 5s 0d would have been required. She had favoured an allowance system from the start but the Land League leaders had preferred to bring in caterers. The new arrangement commenced on Christmas Day, 1881. Parnell admitted to Katharine that, in practice, those who could afford to, could get all their food from outside.[34]

How long Parnell himself subsisted on prison diet is not clear. As we have seen, he made a point of emphasising his solidarity with the rank and file on the issue. On 8 December, he told Frank Hugh O'Donnell that the porridge was uneatable and it was impossible to tell the tea from the coffee. However, the next day he wrote to Katharine O'Shea telling her that all his food was coming from the governor's kitchen; he had earlier assured her that he was not on or only nominally on the prison diet and, that they were living on 'all the good things of the world, game etc'. This would seem to confirm O'Demspey's suspicions of a double standard, a view shared by F. S. L. Lyons who concludes that on the whole Parnell in Kilmainham suffered more from indigestion that malnutrition. He confessed that the purpose of the row was to persuade the government to improve the quality of the food for the ordinary prisoners and thus save the League from having to deplete its own resources.[35]

If the prison diet issue was politicised in a way which makes it difficult to disentangle fact from propaganda, the same was true of the general health of the prisoners. Nowhere is that more true than in the case of Parnell himself. On the one hand, prolonged confinement in Kilmainham, no matter how benign the regime, was hardly conducive to general health and well being, not least for those more used to comfortable surroundings. Despite official denials, there is ample evidence of this. On the other hand, it was in the best interest of a movement intent on maximising public sympathy to highlight or even over-state the plight of the prisoners and the conditions in which they were confined.

The prison journal of O'Dempsey contains several references to minor ailments suffered by himself and other prisoners, some of them he thought brought on by the change in prison diet.[36] On the day before Parnell's arrest, a meeting of North Dublin Union heard a report from Dr Kenny on the precarious state of health of Andrew Kettle who was held at Kilmainham.[37]

Commenting on the loss of his health at Kilmainham, Kettle later remarked that it was curious that 'all the sedentary and town fellows felt Kilmainham as a holiday, but the robust, open-air, country people generally went physically wrong'.[38] Dr Kenny himself was arrested shortly afterwards, on 24 October, and was given an opportunity to observe and treat many of the Kilmainham prisoners. A year older than Parnell, Kenny was a well-respected medical practitioner who had studied at the Catholic University Medical School and at the College of Physicians and Surgeons in Edinburgh. He lived in Gardiner Street and was medical officer to the North Dublin Union, of which Kettle was a member. He was a member of the Executive of the Land League and had treated several prisoners in different prisons, including Michael Davitt. At the instigation of Forster, the Chief Secretary, he was dismissed from this position at least partly because of his role in embarrassing the government on the issue of the medical condition of the prisoners. When his dismissal was raised in Parliament, it became a source of embarrassment, not least to the Prime Minister who had not been consulted. Gladstone considered the dismissal 'monstrous', 'unwarrantable' and a misuse of the Coercion Act.[39]

From his Kilmainham journal, it is evident that Kenny had concerns about a number of prisoners, including Parnell but particularly John Dillon and Michael Boyton.[40] Dillon had only recently been released from an earlier term of imprisonment and was dyspeptic and possibly consumptive. An English visitor who saw Dillon on 12 November reported to Joseph Chamberlain that he was 'in consumption and to keep him in Kilmainham for a winter means to sacrifice his life'. Dillon's health did indeed deteriorate rapidly and he was in and out of the infirmary. The dietary change on 1 December resulted in vomiting and stomach cramps. Eventually Parnell himself wrote to the *Freeman's Journal* in relation to his condition. Although the authorities publicly insisted that his health while poor gave no ground for immediate concern, the possibility that Dillon might die resulted in an bizarre initiative from Chief Secretary Forster under which an offer was made to release Dillon on condition that he immediately went to the continent for health reasons. Dillon's refusal and the publication of the offer resulted in further embarrassment of the government.[41]

The irony of Parnell's intervention on Dillon's behalf is that his own health was also giving grounds for concern. His sister, Emily, visited him the week after he was arrested. She found him paler and thinner: 'his eyes were heavy, and it was evident that confinement, deprivation of his liberty, and want of fresh air, were even at this early date beginning to tell on his health and strength'. On later visits, she recalled, she 'could not fail to perceive the change for the worse in his appearance, which each time was more and more apparent'. Emily was convinced and this view was shared by his brother, John Howard, that Parnell's six months in Kilmainham 'shook his constitution and undermined his health to such an extent that he never recovered but was ever after extremely delicate and subject to divers ailments and illnesses.'[42]

Parnell's health was never robust and it cannot have been improved by prolonged confinement in Kilmainham. While the evidence for the family's retrospective conclusion is inconclusive, Dr Kenny's journal, transmitted routinely to the prison authorities, does chart a growing concern about Parnell's health. He reported that on 30 October Parnell had suffered from violent spasms and severe abdominal pain. Kenny told the authorities that Parnell suffered from an 'affection of the heart' and warned that prolonged confinement might have serious consequences. On 15 November, Dr Kenny reported that Parnell was suffering from loss of appetite, insomnia and sciatica. He requested permission to visit him in his cell nightly as it might be necessary to faradise him or give him morphia injections. On 17 November, he reported that Parnell was sleeping better after sulphur baths and electrical stimulation. Frank Hugh O'Donnell visited Parnell on 8 December and reported that he had had a seizure the previous night, brought on by insufficient fresh air and exercise.[43]

The prison medical officer, Dr William Carte, took an altogether different view of Parnell's health, repeatedly insisting that Kenny was exaggerating. Born in Limerick in 1830, Carte grew up in Tasmania. He trained in the College of Surgeons and served in the Crimea. He was Surgeon to the Royal Hospital Kilmainham from 1859 until his death in 1899.[44] Carte reported that on the day of his reported seizure, he had seen Parnell playing handball. Later when he was summoned to visit him in his cell, Parnell told him he had been unwell but had now recovered.

Perhaps the most reliable insight into Parnell's medical condition is to be gained from his letters to Katharine O'Shea, although even here the reliability is mitigated by a consistent attempt by Parnell to reassure rather than to alarm his lover. On 1 November, Parnell told Katharine that he had been temporarily indisposed but assured her that this was quite normal for prisoners early in their sentences and that she should ignore exaggerated newspaper reports. Parnell frankly admitted that he and Kenny were constantly having to 'invent little maladies' to facilitate visits by Kenny or to have him kept in the infirmary where the prisoners had greater freedom.[45] One of these inventions was 'heart affection' but he reassured her that he never felt better in his life. On 5 November, Parnell wrote to Katharine:

> You will be anxious to know what my short illness was about. It was of a very unromantic kind – not the heart but the stomach. I had not much appetite for some days and was tempted by a turkey to eat too much, thence very severe indigestion and considerable pain for an hour.[46]

Later he warned her not to be alarmed if the *Freeman's Journal* reported that his condition had worsened explaining that it was a means of exerting pressure on the authorities not to move him from his room.[47] On 3 December, he reported that he was 'exceedingly well', all his aches and pains had disappeared and he had acclimatised well. It is clear from these letters that Parnell did suffer some ailments, including feverish colds and stomach upsets, both normally associated with prisons. As to whether Kenny or Carte should be relied on, doctors may differ and patients die, but not in this case: Parnell who was 175 pounds when he entered Kilmainham had put on five pounds before his release and complained of getting fat.

To keep himself fit, Parnell played handball in the prison yard. He boasted that although he had not played for twenty years, he had beaten 'one of the most practised players in the place'.[48] Prisoners were allowed into the yard for up to six hours per day. By one account, Parnell's activities in the yard also included target practice with an air gun.[49] His sister Emily claims he played football and that he was at liberty to engage in as much recreation as he chose in 'an enormous, well-ventilated hall, which had a balcony all round and resembled an opera house, minus the seats'.[50] We know that Parnell played chess regularly but, if we are to believe one playing partner, not to any great standard.[51] He talked regularly with his colleagues John Dillon, J. J. O'Kelly, Dr Kenny, Thomas Brennan and William O'Brien. O'Brien recalled it as a 'pleasant little company': Parnell was 'no professor of table talk. At table, as everywhere else, he was simple, genial and unpretentious'. Lights out was at 9.00 p.m. but Parnell often read late into the night. By his own account, the newspapers and journals he had sent to him in Kilmainham included *The Times, Pall Mall Gazette, Universe, Engineer, Engineering*, and the *Mining Journal*.[52]

Given the constant meetings of the leaders, and the regular stream of visitors, Parnell did well to have time for such pursuits. Lyons has calculated that Parnell saw his solicitor 42 times during his imprisonment. He also gave numerous interviews to journalists and kept up a stream of correspondence, some posted through official channels and some smuggled in and out. Emily claims that when one secret letter was discovered he spent a week in solitary confinement but there is no independent corroboration of this.[53]

One contemporary critic complained that the political prisoners received so much correspondence that the prisoners were hard pressed to keep up.[54] As letters referring to prison conditions or the political situation were routinely intercepted by the prison authorities, Parnell used various means to ensure confidentiality in his communications. Not all his fellow prisoners were so fortunate. In a humorous and moving letter, Dennie Hannigan from Limerick wrote to his children apologising that a long letter he had written had never reached them. However, this latest message also fell foul of the authorities. A positive aspect of such censorship of mail is that fragments of the stories of anonymous prisoners have been preserved, prisoners including the unnamed Munster land leaguer who spoke only Irish. One night he claimed he could hear his wife talking in the hall. His fellow prisoners laughed at the thought that she could be heard all the way from home but he explained that she had 'come by telegraph'.[55]

Enforced separation from loved ones was one of the most difficult parts of imprisonment and Parnell was no exception in this regard. If his imprisonment was not in other ways traumatic, his enforced separation from Katharine O'Shea who was carrying his child was a source of increasing strain. It is difficult to avoid the conclusion that his confinement in Kilmainham was important in Parnell's developing relationship with Katharine. It is significant that she was the person he chose to write to on the morning of his arrest. Bearing in mind the risks involved and Parnell's much vaunted reserve, the letter is startling in its intimacy:

> My Own Queenie, – I have just been arrested by two fine-looking detectives and write these words to Wifie to tell her that she must be a brave little woman and not fret after her husband.
>
> The only thing that makes me worried and unhappy is that it may hurt you and our child.
>
> You know, darling, that on this account it will be wicked of you to grieve, as I can never have any other wife but you, and if anything happens to you I must die childless. Be good and brave, dear little wifie. Your own husband.[56]

Parnell had a photograph of Katharine with him throughout his imprisonment and he wrote to her regularly. Given the delicacy of his position, both the frankness and the frequency of the correspondence are remarkable. The letters reflect a growing frustration with prison on Parnell's part and an impatience at their separation. On 14 December, he threatened to resign his seat and quit politics so that they could be together. In February, he wrote regretting that he had not gone directly back to England from Wexford after his infamous speech, thus avoiding arrest. Two days later, their daughter Claude Sophie was born. Within weeks, Parnell unsuccessfully sought permission from the authorities to be released temporarily, ostensibly to vote in a parliamentary division.[57] When he learned that his daughter had not long to live, Parnell's desperation increased. Early in April, he applied and was granted temporary release to attend the funeral of his sister Delia's son, who had died suddenly in Paris. Parnell was released on parole from 10 to 24 April. Emily Monroe Dickinson writes that Parnell spent a fortnight in Paris endeavouring to console their grief-stricken sister.[58] That is true but what she does not mention is that Parnell detoured on the way to Paris, overnighting at Eltham and calling again on his return journey to see his dying child.

This is not the place to rehearse in detail the negotiations which led to the Kilmainham Treaty and the release of the prisoners in which Captain O'Shea played an important role. On his way to and from Paris, Parnell had discussions with O'Shea about the political situation and also had meetings with Justin McCarthy and Frank Hugh O'Donnell, which generated a flurry of behind-the-scenes activity involving O'Donnell, Joseph Chamberlain, Forster, the Chief Secretary, Gladstone and his son, Herbert. O'Shea later visited Parnell in Kilmainham on 29 April and, crucially, Parnell wrote to McCarthy indicating in broad outline the conditions which ultimately were incorporated into what the Tories immediately described in derogatory terms as 'the Treaty of Kilmainham' or the 'discreditable Kilmainham compact'.[59] The 'Treaty' was an informal agreement that Parnell would accept the Land Act and end the campaign in return for an amendment to extend the fair rent clauses to leaseholders, measures to protect tenants with heavy arrears of rent and, of course, the release of the prisoners. Suffice it to say that it marked a watershed in Parnell's career and in the land agitation. Parnell's flirtation with semi-revolutionary agitation was ended, although that did not become clear for some time. Likewise the Land League itself, the leaders of which had not been consulted in advance about the agreement, rapidly disintegrated. While the agitation continued in new guises, it never regained the drive and cohesion of its early years.

At the time, Tim Healy described the Kilmainham Treaty as 'one of the most sagacious arrangements that ever enabled a hard-pressed general secure terms for his forces'. Later he dismissed it as a device to enable Parnell to get back to Mrs O'Shea as quickly as possible.[60] Conor Cruise O'Brien has described the Treaty as 'essentially a business like recognition' by Parnell that the land agitation had achieved all it could and that a change of direction was necessary.[61] Parnell had arrived at this conclusion before his arrest, and his sojourn in Kilmainham allowed him to formalise this shift. However, in analysing his actions and disentangling cause and consequence, it is impossible to separate fully personal and political motivation.

Gladstone for his part was happy to avail himself of a way out of the impasse which had developed. Imprisonment without trial of up to 1,000 prisoners including a number of MPs was never likely to be anything other than a temporary expedient, unsustainable in the long term. By April 1882, he had become convinced that, as well as land reform, Ireland needed political reform, including the establishment of some form of local representative institutions.[62] Once Parnell had indicated his willingness 'to cooperate cordially for the future with the Liberal Party in forwarding Liberal principles and measures of general reform' which he did in a letter on 28 April,[63] such reform became a real possibility. While Gladstone dismissed talk of a 'Treaty' or even 'reciprocal assurances' or 'tacit understandings' as 'ridiculous' and insisted 'there was no treaty', John Morley, his biographer, conceded that 'the nature of the proceedings was plain enough'.[64] Gladstone was convinced that political progress was dependent on moderate leadership in Ireland; as is evident from his refusal to countenance Parnell's offer to resign in the wake of the Phoenix Park murders, he acknowledged that Parnell was a moderating force.

The significance of the Kilmainham Treaty was obscured by the Phoenix Park murders. They made a conciliatory initiative on the part of the Government less likely in the short term, not least because the late Chief Secretary, Lord Frederick Cavendish, had been appointed because of Forster's resignation in protest against such a policy of appeasement. Cavendish was both a friend of Gladstone and his wife's nephew-in-law. However, the murders did have some positive results for Parnell: they made a public attack on his policy from critics such as Davitt much less likely and they confirmed his reluctance to continue his close involvement in semi-revolutionary politics.

Parnell was released from Kilmainham on 2 May 1882, thus ending an interlude of enormous personal and political significance in his career. He emerged with his leadership of the party and country significantly enhanced and the future direction of the movement fixed on a course of his choosing. It also seems plausible to suggest that imprisonment had an important impact on his relationship with Katharine O'Shea. In explaining the background to the release of Parnell to the Queen, Gladstone declared that two forces had been locked in combat in Ireland – the Land Act and the Land League. The Cabinet was satisfied that those who governed the League now accepted that they had been defeated. A more accurate gloss might have been that the League had been defeated, but that Parnell's leadership had been strengthened.[65] In the words of Barry O'Brien, 'Parnell, in his cell at Kilmainham proved a greater power in Ireland than the British Minister, surrounded by all the paraphernalia of office and authority.' [66]

CHAPTER THREE

Parnell and the American Connection

Donal McCartney

Parnell was the first and arguably the most successful Irish political leader to exploit Irish-America. That he was half-American by birth was to prove of immense advantage in his effort to win American and Irish-American support for his policies.

The following is an abridged version of his mother's family tree – the Tudors of Boston.[1]

JOHN TUDOR (1709–98) emigrated from England with his mother when he was six. He began his adult career with a bakery business; then became a general merchant and trader; made a fortune in real estate; and became a respected and influential citizen of Boston.

HIS SON, WILLIAM (1750–1819), educated at Harvard; joined the law firm of John Adams (later second President of the United States) whom he could count among his personal friends; appointed Judge Advocate of the continental army. Among William's children were William jr, Frederick, Emma and Delia.

WILLIAM JR (1779–1830) was founder of the *North American Review*, 1815; US Consul in Peru; Chargé d'Affaires in Rio.

FREDERICK (1783–1864), known as the Ice King, made a fortune shipping ice to the tropics; he married Euphemia (Effie) Fenno (1815–84) later active in the women's suffrage movement and founder of a hospital for women and children. She gave a reception in her home in honour of her great-nephew, Charles, during his visit to Boston in January 1880; and when Fanny died in July 1882 her remains lay in her great-aunt's home before burial in Mount Auburn cemetery.

EMMA (1785–1866) married the wealthy Robert Hallowell Gardiner.

DELIA (1787–1860) married Charles Stewart who was born in Philadelphia, the son of eighteenth century Ulster emigrants; became a captain, later commodore and rear-admiral in the US navy. They had two children, Charles Tudor (1818-1874) who died unmarried; and Delia Tudor (1816–98) who married John Henry Parnell whom she had met while the young master of Avondale was on a tour of North America. They became the parents of eleven surviving children including Charles, John Howard, Fanny and Anna. Charles Stewart Parnell's mother, sisters and brother sojourned for long periods in America.

PARNELL'S FIRST VISIT TO AMERICA, 1872

While staying with his American uncle, Charles Tudor Stewart, in Paris in the early 1870s, Charles Stewart Parnell, at the age of 24, met an American beauty, Miss Woods, the daughter of wealthy parents from Newport, Rhode Island. It was a case of love at first sight. While in Paris, they were almost inseparable and were apparently engaged. The Woods family moved to Rome and Parnell decided to follow her there. A letter which he received from his uncle warning him against Roman fever brought him ungallantly back to Ireland. He wrote to Miss Woods telling her that he would come to her in Paris on her return. His hypochondria had proved stronger than his passion. He kept his word and visited her again that winter in Paris. Parnell then returned to Avondale to prepare it for his American bride (following the pattern of his father's betrothal).

Back in Ireland, he received a letter from Miss Woods announcing her departure for Newport, Rhode Island, and nothing at all about their engagement. He hastened back to Paris only to find the bird had flown. He set out at once in the Spring of 1872 for the USA.[2] He had three objectives in mind: the first of these was the pursuit of his fair one; the second – ever the practical man that he was – to look into his coal-mining investments; and thirdly, to visit his brother John, who earlier had gone to Alabama where he had a farm devoted to cotton growing and peaches. (He was never the man for one option only.) In Newport, he was graciously but heartlessly received. Sullen, dejected and jilted he spent three weeks recovering in Alabama talking farming and partridge shooting. He detested the cooking, was not at ease with the blacks but very interested in the coal mines. Near Birmingham, while travelling with his brother, they had an almost fatal train accident, and spent a month in a scruffy hotel in lieu of any available nursing home and where Charles nursed brother John whose injuries had been the more severe. He travelled to Virginia, where he already had some investments in the mines. There he narrowly missed being decapitated in a cage going down the mine. Taking to heart what a fortune-teller had forecast for him in America, he and John returned to Ireland on New Year's Day 1873. One impression he formed during his first visit was that the Irish were despised in America. What impact the American federal system may have had on his political thinking was not recorded; but the visit to this southern American state was only two years before his involvement in the Home Rule movement in Ireland.[3]

SECOND VISIT, 1876

After Parnell's defence of the Manchester Martyrs in Parliament in June 1876, the Fenians never lost sight of him again and Parnell never lost sight of them. Fenians and advanced nationalists organised a public meeting at Harold's Cross on 4 July 1876 in connection with the centenary of American Independence. Parnell proposed the main resolution of the meeting which was an address of congratulations to the United States. O'Connor Power and Parnell were chosen to present this address from 'the Irish people' to President Grant. Parnell left two weeks ahead of O'Connor Power in order to spend time with his mother, sister Fanny and brother John, who were then staying in a New York hotel. The delegates obtained an interview with President Grant, who refused to accept the address until proper formalities had been observed. Back in Washington, the Secretary of State insisted that diplomatic protocol should be adhered to and that the address should be presented through the British Ambassador. The Ambassador was unlikely to have approved of such phrases in the address which alleged that while America had enjoyed a hundred years of freedom, Ireland had 'borne seven centuries of oppression'. The Ambassador claimed that he could not act without instructions from London. The two delegates took the line that it was none of the Ambassador's business and that they were acting on behalf of the Irish, not the British, people. President Grant, according to a remark which Parnell made to his brother, John, was 'a vulgar old dog'. Politically rejected this time, on his second visit to the USA, Parnell took the opportunity of visiting Philadelphia, where his interest lay chiefly in new stone-cutting machinery, which might be useful for his own quarries, and the new roofs for suspension bridges, which might be adapted for sawmills and cattle-sheds in Avondale. He again visited the Virginia coal mines. Following the Presidential rebuff, Parnell then paid for an address to the American people and sailed home leaving O'Connor Power to arrange for its presentation to Congress.

The rebuff had done Parnell no harm at all in nationalist circles. Landing at Liverpool he said 'America, I love, reverence and respect and look for a great future for that country'. He asserted that it was not the American people who had rejected the address, but the President who had so far forgotten his position as the leader of a great nation as to take orders from a British Ambassador. He also spoke of having seen a revue of five or six thousand militia in New York and wondered whether we would ever see in Ireland such a national militia to protect the interests of Ireland as a nation. The English government, he said, knew Ireland was determined to be an armed nation and feared to see her so, remembering how in 1782 with arms in their hands, a section of the Irish people had wrung legislative independence from England. Without a full measure of Home Rule, he continued, Ireland would never be content.[4]

The impact which Parnell was having on the Fenians and on their Clan na Gael allies in America is dramatically revealed in a letter written by J. J. O'Kelly to John Devoy on 5 August 1877. O'Kelly, a Fenian and agent for Clan na Gael, and who had worked with Devoy on the *New York Herald*, and was its London correspondent, met Parnell and Biggar in the Paris hotel of John O'Leary. He wrote:

> I had a long chat with Parnell and Biggar, the former is a man of promise, I think he ought *to be supported*. He has the idea I held at the starting of the Home Rule organisation – that is the creation of a political link between the conservative and radical nationalists. I suppose the lunatics will be content with nothing less than the moon – and *they* will never get it. The effect of Parnell's attitude has been simply tremendous and if he were supported by twenty or thirty instead of seven he could render really important services. He has many of the qualities of leadership – and time will give him more. He is cool – extremely so and resolute. With the right kind of support behind him and a band of *real* nationalists in the House of Commons he would so remould Irish public opinion as to clear away many of the stumbling-blocks in the way of progressive action.[5]

Part of Parnell's strength lay in leaving those he charmed guessing. A fortnight later, O'Kelly wrote again to Devoy:

> The day parliament broke up I had a long chat with Parnell. He is a good fellow, but I am not sure he knows exactly where he is going. However, he is the best of the parliamentary lot. He is going to America in November and I would advise you to see him and have a long talk with him over affairs . . . Butt is a little frightened by Parnell's popularity. . . . I have always tried to convince you of the great moral effect of having Ireland represented by men like Parnell, O'Donnell and Biggar even if they were not prepared to advance one step further and I hope recent events have convinced you of the correctness of my views.[6]

O'Kelly's espousal of Parnell in August 1877 was an accurate foreshadowing of what in fact did materialise as a result of what Devoy called a 'new departure' in Irish national politics when making his public overture to

Parnell more than a year later (October 1878). O'Kelly – Fenian colleague and close friend of Devoy since boyhood – must be credited with having had some influence in directing Devoy's and Clan na Gael's formidable support behind Parnell. As a consequence of those meetings with Parnell in Paris and London in August 1877, O'Kelly had found himself on his own road to Damascus, and was to become Parnell's zealous disciple, a Parnellite MP, fellow prisoner with his leader in Kilmainham, and faithful adherent after the Parnell split. As for Parnell, Irish-American goodwill and patronage was to play a significant role in the progress of his political career.

IRISH-AMERICAN NATIONALISM

In the four decades following the Great Famine, over 3 million people born in Ireland settled in the USA. By 1890, there were already more people of Irish birth or origin in the USA then in Ireland itself, and there were more people of Irish birth or origin in New York than in Dublin. These immigrants included the famine-stricken refugees, the 'Poor Irish' whom Parnell, during his first visit to the USA in 1872, found to be everywhere despised. In the days before the American Civil War of the early 1860s, they competed with the blacks for the lowest paid jobs in the great cities of America. These Irish immigrants also included a hard-core of politically conscious refugees who, in 1858, established in America the Fenian organisation, and were later joined by a further group who had been deeply involved in IRB activity in Ireland in the 1860s. The Fenians in America were faction-ridden and from the late 1860s were supplanted by a new organisation, Clan na Gael, in which John Devoy, former IRB activist exerted a powerful influence. Although Clan na Gael was also to have its share of splits and factions, it proved in the long run to be more effective than the American Fenians and maintained a more effi-cient connection with nationalist Ireland. These were the social and political refugees of whom Yeats was to write:

> Out of Ireland have we come.
> Great hatred, little room,
> Maimed us at the start.
> I carry from my mother's womb
> A fanatic heart.[7]

It would be a great mistake, however, to see all those millions of Irish-Americans as being of the one political mind and having the same fanatic heart.

As in the home country itself, there were great diversities: Irish-American nationalism had its committed, conservative constitutionalists, as well as its extremist physical force element, as well as its social reformers whose priority was the reform of the Irish land system. Hostility to England, ranging from intense hated to milder feelings of opposition, certainly constituted part of the psychological make-up of Irish-American nationalism.

Immigrants had carried with them bitter memories of famine, poverty, eviction and oppression. They had been fed, too, on the traditions of Wolfe Tone's republicanism, Robert Emmet's speech from the dock, O'Connell's emancipation and repeal mass movements, and Young Ireland's idealism. And as they flocked into the great industrial cities of America – New York, Boston, Chicago, Philadelphia, San Francisco, St Louis – they had brought with them also the powerful consolations of Catholicism and the community-binding agency of a popular and public religion.

Nor should we overlook the negatives which were part of their baggage – the sense of shame of having had to flee from a land and a society and a system that had failed them; the perception of having been humiliated and a fury with themselves for allowing the famine to happen; the feelings of inferiority and a desperate desire for acceptance and respectability. It is hardly surprising if some, as they stepped on the first rung of the social ladder, wanted no more to do with 'the most distressful country' and its politics; or that they should model themselves on the White Anglo-Saxon Protestants whose political status and financial success they envied. Sturdier and prouder spirits among the immigrants, in order to dissolve the sense of shame and inferiority, faced up to the challenge and wanted to transform Ireland into an independent state modelled on their adopted 'land of the free'.

Irish-American nationalism, therefore, was not simply something that had been imported from Ireland: it also owed much to the immigrants' experience of America. It was a response to their own needs in a land, where, for the most part, they were among the lowest social and economic strata.

In what was supposed to be the land of opportunity, the immigrant was faced with a great deal of prejudice against his race and his religion. What was officially named the American Party, but is better known to history as the Know Nothing nativist movement, was bitterly anti-immigrant and anti-Catholic. Its bigotry was directed especially at the poorer Irish in the cities of the eastern seaboard. The encounter with the Know Nothing movement increased the Irish immigrants' feelings of alienation and oppression; and was easily taken by them as an extension of English, or at least Anglo-American Protestant prejudices against them.

Patrick Ford, afterwards the very influential founder and editor of the *Irish World* in New York, articulated the agony felt by the despised Irish. Ford emigrated from Galway at the age of four. He said that he brought nothing with him from Ireland – nothing tangible to make him into the Irish-American nationalist and agitator that he became. It was Boston of the 1850s, he said, that shaped his life when he first went searching for a job and everywhere encountered notices which read: 'No Irish need apply'. He then realised that what was against him was the fact that he was Irish and Catholic. It was this experience that made him aware of Ireland; and he began to read everything he could lay his hands on about his native country. He came to the conclusion that he was the victim 'of the conditions of poverty and enslavement' that engulfed the land of his birth. He decided that 'it was necessary for everyone of Irish blood to do all in his power to change that state of things'.

The immigrants' consciousness of being victimised because of the degraded state of their native land was recognised, too, by Michael Davitt. In a speech to the Irish-Americans, Davitt said: 'You want to be regarded with the respect due to you; that you may be thus looked on, aid us in Ireland to remove the stain of degradation from your birth. . . . And [you] will get the respect you deserve'.[8]

The response of the Irish Americans to the circumstances in which they found themselves came in a variety of ways. They played an active role in the Knights of Labour; they formed associations for mutual aid such as the Irish Catholic Benevolent Union; they formed secret societies like the Molly Maguires on models such as they had known in the agrarian secret societies back home. On the political front, they could enthusiastically endorse the American Republican antipathy to monarchy and the traditional hostility of America to England, its old colonial master. These attitudes found ready echoes among the Irish-Americans. In their adopted land, they imbibed American principles of freedom, equality and democracy; and these ideals the exiles were anxious to communicate to their own native land. American missionary fever entered their blood. They called for the independence of small nations. They organised to help their native country achieve its independence. Their objective was to make of Ireland an America back home so that their country might 'take its place among the nations of the earth'. By achieving Irish independence, they would also be countering the sense of inferiority and raising the level of respect for the Irish in America. The most powerful of the Irish-American nationalist organisations with these objectives in mind was Clan na Gael.[9]

Yet, the factions and the divisions among the Irish-Americans remained – partly because of the personality clashes, but also because the priorities among Irish-Americans varied. For some their first allegiance was to Ireland; for others it was to Irish-America; and there were also those whose first allegiance was to America, as Daniel Cohalan would later remind de Valera. What was lacking was a movement that could bring all together. More specifically, what they were instinctively crying out for was a leader – one who could restore to them their pride; a hero in the glory of whose achievements they could bask. They dreamt of a messianic figure who could reform the land system; smash landlordism; and win an independent Ireland. By 1879, no such leader had arisen among the immigrants. Nor, indeed, had such a leader appeared in Ireland since the famine.

In its early years, the Home Rule movement, when it was promoting Fenian amnesty and agitating for the better treatment of Fenian prisoners, had enrolled amongst its supporters a number of leading IRB figures. The understanding in some Clan na Gael and IRB circles had been that if Home Rule methods had not succeeded after a three years' trial, there would be a reversion to Fenian methods. It now seemed, however, that Home Rule had reneged on its early promise. Yet, it also appeared to the more pragmatic within Clan na Gael that the sea-green incorruptibles among the IRB in Ireland, those republican purists under Kickham and O'Leary who would have no compromise with the parliamentary nationalists, lacked any imaginative approach to the Irish political situation, every bit as much as the Home Rulers lacked purpose and strength. From Clan na Gael's point of view, the Home Rule movement with its own divisions, its lack of strong leadership, and without direction and purpose was on the point of disintegration. It was tottering to its grave along with the ailing Butt. It came to be generally agreed among the Irish-Americans that the young and more aggressive Parnell offered the best and perhaps only prospect.

In these circumstances, Clan na Gael sought to grasp the initiative. Inspired by Devoy's dynamism, Clan na Gael moved on two fronts: first, it established a revolutionary directory which would control and co-ordinate both Clan na Gael and IRB activities; and second, it proffered an open alliance on specific terms with the more extreme party among the Home Rulers. This is known as Devoy's New Departure. On 25 October 1878, Devoy sent a cablegram to Kickham, head of the IRB, which, if Kickham approved, was to be shown to Parnell. It proposed that the American nationalists would support Parnell and his friends if he would agree to certain conditions. These included:

1   that Butt's demand for federal Home Rule should be replaced by a general declaration in favour of Irish self-government;
2   that there should be vigorous agitation to achieve peasant proprietorship as the solution of the land question with immediate concern to abolish evictions;
3   that Irish MPs should all vote together in parliament and adopt an aggressive policy;
4   that they would promote the freedom of all struggling nationalities.

Parnell gave no formal reply; but acted as if these had always been part of his policy.

Meanwhile, back in Ireland the economic depression of the late 1870s had deteriorated to such an extent that the spectre of famine was once again hanging over the land. In these worsening conditions – food shortage, rising food prices, unpaid high rents, increase in evictions and a corresponding increase in agrarian crime – the Land League was founded to protect the tenantry from a repetition of the Great Famine. It was as president of the National Land League, founded in October 1879, that Parnell, accompanied by John Dillon, set out on what was Parnell's third visit to the USA. The objective was to raise a fighting fund for the Land League; but since conditions had worsened in Ireland even while the delegates were crossing the Atlantic, Parnell announced on landing that they were also seeking a separate fund for famine relief.

DIFFICULTIES HE ENCOUNTERED

Parnell was to face many difficulties, and even downright hostility in America. He faced two enemies, wrote the proprietor of the *Chicago Daily News*: the friends of England, and the hare-brained Irish who had no faith in constitutional methods but wanted to use guns and powder. He was a young man at the very outset of his political career. He had stepped into a veritable minefield. He had to make sure that he did not become the tool of his hosts, Clan na Gael, and that the Land League was kept independent. On the other hand, he had to be careful not to offend Clan na Gael so as to lose their support. If they controlled him, his political future was doomed. If they refused all assistance to him, he was also doomed. Only a man as adept as he showed himself to be could avoid becoming embroiled in the intricacies of Irish-American politics. He also wanted the support of the Irish-Americans outside the revolutionaries; and he wanted to be able to appeal to responsible non-Irish Americans. A number of Catholic churchmen and papers were suspicious of what the *New York Herald* called his 'rank communism'. His natural enemies were the Anglo-Americans or WASPS and the Know Nothing elements. He was to experience strong newspaper criticism. He was criticised for his opposition to the two Dublin relief funds – the Duchess of Marlborough's and the Lord Mayor's. Elements in Clan na Gael were strongly opposed to Parnell's own famine relief fund, on the grounds that he should be concentrating on the political objectives of the tour. On the other hand, he was criticised in the American press for mixing politics with charity.

THE ORATOR

In general, the American press were to be disappointed with Parnell as a speaker. He was clearly not in the same mould as their own American orators. He engaged in no theatricals and no oratorical flourishes. They had expected a more dramatic performance especially from an Irish agitator. Instead, he was described as being as cold as an iceberg; without style or animation; with an awkward manner and a thin voice that failed to get to the heart of his audience. For someone who was always nervous before meetings, having to perform before so many critical audiences must have been a real ordeal.

On the other hand, one young American reporter said that before Parnell had spoken six words, he recognised Parnell's superiority to any other person present, either on the platform or in the audience. He said that the dress, the action and the face of the man were regal.[10] The rhetorical display, therefore, may not have lived up to the expectations of the hostile critic; but, as far as Irish-America was concerned, the message was what mattered. And it was Parnell's message, and his own sincere belief in it, that always impressed audiences as diverse as peasants in the West of Ireland, politicians in the House of Commons and the Irish in America. His talent was not that of the captivating orator, but rather that of the expert communicator.[11]

An interesting insight into Parnell as an orator very much alive to the importance of the role of the press in getting his speeches accurately reported to the public beyond his immediate audience is to be found in an article entitled 'An Irish Reporter's Tribute'. This anonymous reporter wrote:

> He adopted the system of never speaking more than would make about the ordinary column of a newspaper, and over and over again when the enthusiastic plaudits . . . might well have tempted him to prolong a speech he would just give that column and no more. One result of this was it developed that method of epigrammatic condensation which made his utterance so strikingly effective and another that he was sure to get a perfectly satisfactory report, for that column was invariably good 'copy', acceptable to every paper, and expressed in such a way as to make it a pleasure to report or read it.[12]

THE TOUR

The tour was mainly organised by Clan na Gael. But societies of a non-revolutionary character as well as Americans of repute, irrespective of party politics, were invited to participate. It lasted two and a half months during which Parnell spoke in 62 cities. This involved travelling many long hours in Pullman cars; addressing public meetings on the East Coast and in the mid-West, in the Southern states and in Canada. It was a gruelling task: shaking hands, attending receptions, listening to addresses of welcome, marching in processions, making speeches, holding press conferences and briefing sessions. It was something akin to the whistle-stop campaign of an American presidential election. It meant that he hardly spent two consecutive nights in the same hotel. In all he had covered 16,000 miles. On the night of 8 March 1880, when he returned to his hotel in Montreal, a telegram awaited him. It read: 'Parliament dissolved. Return at once.'

HOW HE WAS RECEIVED

Everywhere he had been met with great honour, beyond all his expectations, and certainly well beyond what would be usual for someone of his comparatively junior political status. He was given the singular honour of addressing the American House of Representatives in Washington. Only a few very distinguished strangers had been accorded this privilege previously. He also accepted invitations to address joint meetings of the State Senate and the House of Representatives in Virginia, in Iowa and in Kentucky; and he was formally received by the legislatures of New York and Wisconsin. He was received also by President Rutherford Hayes.

State governors, city mayors, leading citizens and clergymen, vied with each other to greet him and spoke in support of his cause. He received the freedom of several cities including Buffalo, Louisville (Kentucky), Springfield (Illinois), and Chicago (where he addressed the largest individual meeting of his tour, when 10,000 were gathered into the Exposition Building). In several of the cities, he was escorted by Irish-American military regiments, police squads and benevolent societies. He was given a 21 gun salute at Toledo and a 32 gun salute at Des Moines and welcomed by a salvo of cannon elsewhere.[13]

'The Battle Song of the Republic' was sung to new words:

> Says every true American, Parnell thy cause is ours,
> We pray for Heaven's blessing to strew your course with flowers
> The land-sharks dare not harm thee with our united powers,
> To set Ireland free
>
> Welcome, welcome,
> Onward, onward, etc.
> To set Ireland free. [14]

WHAT HE SAID (A) TO THE AMERICANS

Certain points were emphasised over and over again in all his speeches. He laid great stress on the idea that American public opinion could determine Ireland's future. The day after his arrival, before an estimated 8,000 people at Madison Square Garden, he declared that 'the American people are virtually the arbiters of the Irish Question'. And he opened his address to the House of Representatives in Washington by announcing that:

> The public opinion of the people of America will be of the utmost importance in enabling us to obtain a just and suitable settlement of the Irish Question.

He claimed that the public opinion and sentiment of a free country like America was entitled to find expression wherever it was seen that the laws of freedom were not observed. It would be a proud boast for America, he added, if, having obtained, secured and ratified her own freedom, she were now to obtain for Ireland the solution of this great question beginning with the land. He apologised that the dire consequences of the Irish land system had compelled the representatives of a proud nation to appear as mendicants before the world. And he vowed to the House of Representatives that, with American help, 'This shall be the last Irish Famine'. This kind of observation by Parnell recognising America's world role, was bound to appeal to the American missionary spirit.

He appealed, too, to the anti-English, anti-imperialist feeling that was still prevalent in America. In Boston, he asserted that the British government did not hesitate to spend 10 to 20 million a year on childish and cruel wars in all parts of the world. Surely, he said, it would be better to devote their attention to securing the happiness and prosperity of their own people, instead of destroying that of other people abroad. Here were echoes of that stirring phrase in the American Declaration of Independence about the right to Life, Liberty and the Pursuit of Happiness.

In appealing to American sentiment Parnell was ever ready to draw attention to his own American blood. 'I who boast American blood', he assured Congress, 'feel proud of the importance which has been universally attached to American opinion.' He was the grandson of a great American war hero, Commodore Charles Stewart, whose name he bore; and his publicity managers made the most of it when marketing their Irish visitor. The *Boston Pilot* carried a serial feature on Parnell's American ancestors, the climax of which dealt with his grandfather's heroic services to the nation. On Commodore Stewart's retirement from active service, Lincoln had conferred on him the title of rear-admiral. He had died in 1869, only 10 years before his grandson was taking Irish-America by storm.

Even Parnell's enemies on the *New York Herald*, when accusing him of fleeing from Ireland while his comrades in the Land League were being indicted, contrasted his alleged cowardice with the bravery of Commodore Stewart. As it happened, the *New York Herald* only played into Parnell's hands. He was able to show convincingly that far from deserting his comrades he had postponed his American tour, and had purposely repeated the speech for which Davitt had been indicted for sedition, in order to give the government every opportunity of arresting him too. And he reminded the *Herald* that he had gone down to the Balla eviction a few months earlier although he had been warned by the officer in charge of the constabulary that the police had received secret orders to shoot him if there were any disturbance. Here, surely, was the grandson of brave Commodore Stewart.

As if to underscore his American connections, Parnell's American mother, Delia Tudor Stewart, and three of his American-Irish sisters were prominent at a number of his public appearances. That Parnell's mission stirred something in the American political consciousness was testified to by the notabilities who showed their eagerness to join him on the public platforms.

Speaking at Boston, Wendell Phillips, one of the leading American orators of his day, said that he had come to the meeting like the rest of the audience to see 'the man that has forced John Bull to listen'.

(B) TO THE IRISH-AMERICANS

If Parnell touched sensitive chords in the liberal, humanitarian and missionary psyche of the Americans, he also knew how to play on the deepest feelings of the Irish-American immigrants. He instinctively recognised their sense of having been despised and humiliated; their longing for acceptance; their pride in the progress they were beginning to make; their memories of famine; their hatred of the landlord system; their hostility to English rule and their great psychological need to have pride in the country of their origin.

On the morning his ship docked in New York he said:

> We must hope and believe that the time is approaching when we may be able to speak of Ireland as other men speak of their own country, and that we may be able to speak of her as really and truly among the nations of the earth.[15]

This phrase, 'Among the nations of the Earth' from Robert Emmet's speech from the dock, was not lost on all those whose deepest desire was to see Ireland honoured in the world. This phrase, and others like it from Irish history, would be repeated throughout the tour as Parnell stirred the wellsprings of Irish-American nationalism. And no one doubted his determination as he constantly expressed his confidence in the inevitable emergence of Irish independence. Victory, he asserted in New York, was bound to come. 'We shall have the dreams of every patriot in all ages realised, and the orange and green will be united.'

The ostensible reason for his mission to America was not the independence of Ireland, but the promotion of the Land League's objectives. His speeches, as might be expected, therefore castigated the landlord system, described in detail the current oppression and suffering of the peasants of the West of Ireland to their relations in America, and aroused their own memories and deep resentment of the condemned system.

With consummate dexterity, he succeeded in linking the fight against the landlords with the struggle for political independence. It was already clear from his words in America that Parnell had not taken off his coat just to reform the land system. He had taken up the land question because he saw it as the engine which would most effectively contribute to the attainment of the ulterior political objective – the independence of Ireland. In New York, he had proclaimed that the solution of the land question would be the first great step to freedom. The inextricable connection in his mind between land and liberty was most succinctly epitomised in his address at Cincinnati. Here he announced: 'I feel confident that we shall kill the Irish landlord system; and when we have given Ireland to the people of Ireland we shall have laid the foundation upon which to build up our Irish nation.' Then, in that sparse, logical way of his, he said:

> Pull out that cornerstone [Landlordism], break it up, destroy it, and you undermine English misgovernment.
>
> When we have undermined English misgovernment, we have paved the way for Ireland to *take her place among the nations of the earth*. [My italics. Note that phrase again.]
>
> And let us not forget that this is the ultimate goal at which all we Irishmen aim.
>
> None of us, whether we be in America or in Ireland, or wherever we may be, will be satisfied until we have destroyed the last link which keeps Ireland bound to England.

The phrase 'the last link which keeps Ireland bound to England' was to be thrown in his face during the Special Commission which investigated *The Times*'s charges against him of conspiracy with the physical force revolutionaries.[16]

There could be no doubting the truth in the criticism that was made of him in a hostile newspaper: that he mingled humanitarian appeals for famine relief with extremist politics and sedition. There were times when he seemed to get carried away with the many military displays that greeted him. At Cleveland where 50,000 people lined the streets, and Irish-American regiments provided him with an escort, he said:

> When I saw some of these gallant men today. . . . I thought that each one of them must wish, with Sarsfield of old, when dying upon a foreign battlefield, 'Oh that I could carry these arms for Ireland'. Well, it may come to that some day or other.[17]

Parnell, for his own purposes, was not above taking a little poetic licence with the well-known quotations of Irish history.

In Philadelphia when insisting that the land system must be changed, an enthusiastic voice shouted back at him: 'By Revolution!' Significantly, Parnell did not say 'No!' as O'Connell would have done. Instead he reminded his audience somewhat mysteriously that he had American blood in his veins too. For those who delighted in the American citizen's right to carry arms, Parnell's reference to his American blood could only have meant the endorsement of revolution.

Parnell was unusually very careful to add prudent qualifications which may not have always been heard by those who cheered the more militaristic phrases. For Parnell was a past master in ambiguity, as witnessed by this declaration at Boston:

> I am not in favour of revolutionary methods, yet still, as a sensible man, I cannot help saying that if things are allowed to continue as they are in Ireland much longer, our people will not be able to content themselves or to withstand the influences which drive them towards violent and revolutionary methods.[18]

That the greatest political revolution was not worth the shedding of a single drop of human blood, was the well-known dictum of Daniel O'Connell. It was often repeated by Irish nationalists only to be as often scornfully rejected by them. The dictum was publicly spurned by Parnell too, but with an interesting conditional clause and an additional qualifying clause. Speaking at Rochester he said:

> I am bound to admit that it is the duty of every Irishman to shed the last drop of his blood in order to obtain his rights, if there were a probable chance of success, yet at the same time we all recognise the great responsibility of hurling our unarmed people on the points of British bayonets. We must act with prudence when the contest would be hopeless, and not rush upon destruction.[19]

I guess it would be a fair summary of his position to say that in Boston what he said was: I am *not* in favour of revolutionary methods, *provided* other means work. [My italics] In Rochester what he said was: I *am* in favour of revolutionary methods, *provided* other means *don't* work. [My italics]

He himself as good as admitted to walking the acrobatic tightrope between constitutionalism and revolution when replying to the accusation of the *New York Herald* that he would not dare make in Ireland the incendiary speeches he gave in America. He assured his St Louis audience that the contrary was the case. He said:

It is far more necessary to speak strongly to the Irish people in Ireland than it is to speak strongly to them in America. In Ireland they require to be encouraged and lifted up, because they are oppressed and beaten down; in America they require to have cold water thrown upon them.[20]

We can only conclude that his allusions to physical force had the desired effects on his Clan na Gael supporters, while his prudent qualifications reassured the more moderate among his audiences. Nor was his ambivalence so much the result of any clever analysis, but was part, rather, of the sheer political instinct of the man. That very characteristic ambivalence which would enable Parnell during the following decade back in Ireland to assure simultaneously the two extremes of Irish nationalism – the constitutionalists and the bishops on the one hand, as well as the Land League radicals and physical force republicans on the other – was practised to perfection during his American tour.

HOW EFFECTIVE WAS THE TOUR? WHAT DID HE ACHIEVE?

First of all, let me indulge for a moment in a little innocent fantasy: in the might-have-beens of Parnell's American connection. After Parnell's death Michael Davitt wrote:

America had on two occasions almost rescued Parnell from the fate [the liaison with Mrs O'Shea] which ultimately wrecked his brilliant career and inflicted a ten years' national agony on Ireland and lost us Home Rule.[21]

The first of these occasions referred to by Davitt was Parnell's serious romantic affair with Miss Woods whom he had met when both were visiting Paris. The young Irishman followed Miss Woods to Rome and then to her home in Newport. 'I proposed, but she refused', he later told Davitt. He felt badly jilted. Davitt ruefully reflected:

Little did this young lady, whoever she was, imagine the wrong she was thus unthinkingly committing against Ireland and its people.[22]

The second occasion occurred shortly after the American tour. Davitt wrote:

Early in 1880 after his return from the transatlantic mission a young, accomplished and very wealthy Irish-American lady came to London and Ireland attracted by the handsome Irish leader and the romance of his public life. There could be no doubt about the trend of her wishes in regard to him. She and her father put up in Morrison's hotel, where Parnell always had his quarters when in Dublin.

Unfortunately there was no response on his part to this delicate but obvious attention. Soon after other eyes [Katharine O'Shea's] only too easily conquered and led
him captive into the snares of a fatal affection.[23]

Davitt's historical might-have-beens were based on the notion that a Parnell
married to one or other of these American beauties would never have become
involved with what Davitt, in highly moralistic tones, called, 'a double life of
wretched deception, unredeemed by a single romantic feature'.[24]

So much for the might-have-beens. And back now to the historical realities.
By any standards, and from several standpoints, Parnell's tour was a great
success. He collected what in today's money would amount to approximately
€3 m. for famine relief. He collected another half-million for separate Land
League purposes. With these latter funds he financed, for example, in the
general election of 1880, six candidates who would have been unable to pay
their own election expenses. This half-dozen were added to the camp of his
own immediate followers in the Party. Again, when Parnell purchased from
Richard Pigott his newspaper interest and established *United Ireland*, the
money came largely from this American fund. (Ironically the routine business
correspondence which Parnell then had with Pigott was later to be used by
Pigott to forge the notorious Parnell letters in which he allegedly approved of
the Phoenix Park murders.)

When departing from America Parnell founded the American Land League
which continued to contribute to the success of the parent body in Ireland.
But it was the political, rather than the financial results that mattered most.
Parnell had effectively countered the violent opposition of a powerful section
of the American press; and had attracted the attention of American public
opinion to himself. At 33½ years old, while still not leader of the party, he had
become the best-known Irish politician in America. His tour, and the publicity
derived from it, had earned a great deal of sympathy and support for Ireland's
cause from the un-hyphenated Americans. He had been singly honoured as
the first Irish politician to address the US Congress.

And if such was the effect on the non-Irish Americans, it would be difficult to exaggerate the psychological success which the tour had on the Irish-
Americans. He was the fulfilment of all their yearnings for the messianic
figure that would restore to them pride in their homeland, the leader they
could place their trust in to lead Ireland on to independence.

He was the first Irish politician to unite all of Irish-America behind
him. And he was the first to unite the Irish-American nationalists, and the
nationalists at home in a common cause. Unity gave strength. And for the first
time in history the millions of Irish immigrants had become a powerful force
in Anglo-Irish relations.

This was recognised by Sir William Harcourt (Chancellor of the Exchequer in Gladstone's government) when he wrote in 1885:

> In former Irish rebellions the Irish were in Ireland. We could reach their forces, cut off their resources in men and money, and then to subjugate was comparatively easy. Now there is an Irish nation in the United States, equally hostile, with plenty of money, absolutely beyond our reach, and yet within ten days sail of our shores . . .[25]

Parnell's American tour had great significance not only for the success of the Land League, for Irish-American morale, and eventually for the struggle for Irish independence. It was also most important for Parnell himself, and the furthering of his political career.

His successful exploitation of the American connection set the pattern for Irish nationalist leaders after him. It is arguable, however, that not even de Valera in his 18 months' mission to the USA in 1919–20 had as much success as Parnell in a far shorter period. After all, Dev quarrelled with Devoy, where Devoy had been Parnell's strongest support.

The 'Uncrowned King of Ireland' was the title not undeservedly conferred on Parnell by Tim Healy in Montreal. The momentum from the American tour carried the Uncrowned King to victory in the General Election of April 1880 less than a month after his return to Ireland. He himself was elected for three constituencies – Cork City, Meath and Mayo – and some 25 of the Home Rulers elected were reckoned to be Parnell's own men. In May, the month following the General Election, Parnell was elected chairman of the Parliamentary Party. From the point of view of Parnell's own career, therefore, the American mission had raised him unquestionably to the leadership not only of nationalist Ireland, but he had also earned the title of the 'leader of the Irish race at home and abroad'. This was the ultimate significance of Parnell's American connection.

He has had many would-be imitators of his unique success. But no other politician has ever harnessed to the extent that he did the massive political potential of the Irish diaspora.

CHAPTER 4

Reading Between the Lines

The Political Speeches of Charles Stewart Parnell

Pauric Travers

In his pamphlet *Ghosts*, written just months before the 1916 Rising, Patrick Pearse summoned the pale and angry ghost of Parnell to stand beside those of Tone, Davis, Lalor and Mitchel as the five begetters of Irish separatism. Pearse concluded that Parnell's focus was constitutional and parliamentary, but argued that he had to work with the tools at hand: his instinct was separatist, and he embodied a separatist conviction. That view of Parnell was widely accepted among Irish nationalists in the half century which followed the 1916 Rising. The predominant view among historians in more recent decades stresses Parnell's moderation, constitutionalism and his social conservatism. The historian or biographer who seeks to clarify that position is forced of necessity back to the evidence of Parnell's political speeches in an exercise which raises underlying questions of text and context, transmission and interpretation.[1] In illustrating the problems through reference to a number of the key speeches made by Parnell, I intend to question some of the long-standing assumptions about Parnell's deficiencies as a public speaker. While the questions raised relate to the career of a particular politician and can only be resolved by reference to his life and personality, they do have a much wider application: similar questions must inevitably be confronted by anyone writing political biography. Perhaps the central issue is how far we can rely on what politicians say publicly as a guide to what they believe.

Parnell left tantalisingly little in the way of carefully considered written statements of his views. There are few surviving letters or drafts of speeches and, of course, no autobiography. F. S. L. Lyons concluded wryly that the literary form he most favoured was the telegram.[2] Moreover, his regal style of leadership and the fact that he had few if any close political confidants within or outside his party, means that the evidence of his associates is often of little value. As every elector knows, the acid test of politicians is what they do rather than what they say: thus the reputations of the great nineteenth-century leaders rest mainly on their records in government. Where, as in the case of Parnell, the subject never forms or participates in a government but remains to a greater or lesser extent an outsider, the assessment is more complicated. Of course, Parnell did exercise power within his own party and in Ireland, he did succeed in influencing government through the liberal alliance, and his actions at key periods – at the time of the Kilmainham Treaty in 1882, for example – do provide an invaluable yardstick. Nevertheless, we are dependent to an unusual degree on Parnell's political speeches as a source for his political philosophy.

The *Penguin Book of Historic Speeches* brings together the words of over a hundred men and women from Moses to Mandela – who helped to change the world through the sheer power of their oratory. Ireland, as befits a country renowned for its love of language rates a special section. 'The cry of Ireland' contains three speeches each by Henry Grattan and Daniel O'Connell, and one by John Philpot Curran, Wolfe Tone, Robert Emmet, Richard Lalor Sheil, Patrick Pearse and Roger Casement. It contains no speech by Charles Stewart Parnell. At first glance, the omission may seem understandable. Parnell, we are told, was no orator: the near consensus of historians merely replicates the verdict of many of his contemporaries. In his generally sympathetic assessment of Parnell as a political speaker, Alan O'Day concludes that it is unlikely that any revisionism could transform Parnell into a moving orator.[3] And yet, if one discounts completely Parnell's powers of communication and persuasion, how does one explain his impact? If a random selection of Irish adults were invited to identify a speech by any of the people named, many could probably rise to one speech by Emmet and one by Pearse; most could probably recognise two speeches by Parnell – 'Keep a firm grip on your homesteads' (Westport, 1879) and 'No man has the right to set the boundary to the march of the nation' (Cork, January 1885).[4] Of course, the continued currency of those speeches owes much to factors which have little to do with the manner or circumstances of their delivery, but their durability does give one reason for pause before too easily writing off the powers of communication of the statesman who originally penned and delivered them.

Parnell was not a natural public speaker; he could be nervous and uncomfortable, but he could also be extremely effective, as for instance in his speech in Galway in February 1886, which to all intents and purposes broke the so-called Galway mutiny when his supporters objected to the imposition of Captain O'Shea as a Home Rule candidate. His posture was unconventional – he stood stiffly with his arms folded loosely in front of him or sometimes behind his back. He spoke in a low voice, slowly and distinctly; he rarely raised his voice or gestured or gesticulated. He had an aversion to shouting.[5] He often gave the impression of indifference to an audience which one critic suggested made him 'meagre' in his style.[6] One senior member of the IRB commented that what struck him most about Parnell was his silence: 'It was extraordinary. One was not accustomed to it. All Irish agitators talked. He didn't'.[7]

He was never comfortable with impromptu speaking and avoided the task if he could. On one occasion when he arrived late for a debate in the House of Commons, he confessed that he had not had time to prepare what he wished to say and asked a colleague to prolong the debate to allow him time to prepare himself. While he appears rarely to have spoken from a prepared script or even detailed notes – one major exception being his speech to the House of Representatives in the United States in February 1880[8] – almost all his key speeches show evidence of subtlety, forethought and care. The *Irish Times* caught much of his essential style in describing his contribution in the Commons debate on the Queen's Speech in 1881:

> Mr Parnell assumed his usual freezing tone when he got up, speaking very low and very slow but with the iciness of attitude, deliberation and distinctiveness which betokens a provoking self-possession under the gravest circumstances, and at once chills and startles the hearers.[9]

One contemporary journalist who observed Parnell's rapid ascent to the forefront of Irish politics commented:

> He had hardly one of the attributes of a popular leader. He was a landlord, and an aristocrat, and was not considered to be at all in sympathy with the Irish national cause, until he became a politician. Moreover he was educated at Oxford College, and there contracted an English accent – a serious disqualification for an Irish patriot. Then he was singularly *unimpassioned as an orator*. But his speeches were clear and always to the point. He was, besides, eminently practical, and entirely unscrupulous as to the means, so that his ends were achieved – two indispensable requisites nowadays for success in politics. He had the disadvantage of being by nature quite unsympathetic, so that his followers had not that great personal attachment for him which O'Connell, Butt and other leaders of opinion in Ireland, so readily excited in their adherents.[10] [emphasis added]

The negative comments on Parnell's oratory date from his earliest appearance on public platforms. They recur with such regularity that it would be pointless to attempt to refute them completely but they do require clarification. Sometimes the comments came from critics of Parnell, often from those within his own party who resented his dominance. Sometimes they reflect a conventional public taste which harked back to a florid, literary eighteenth-century style of public speaking which seemed to survive in Ireland longer than elsewhere. Parnell did not fit that mould: one searches in vain for literary reference or metaphor; nowhere can one find even a hint of playfulness of language. But he could speak with devastating directness. When he was asked whether he considered Parnell a good speaker, Gladstone replied 'Indeed I do, for he has got the very rarest of all qualities in a speaker – *measure*. He always says exactly as much as, and not any more nor less than, he means to say.'[11] John Morley, Chief Secretary for Ireland and Gladstone's biographer, considered that even when his speeches were least exciting or rhetorical they were studded with incisive remarks, singularly well compressed.[12] Morley observed Parnell's performance in the debate on the repressive Tory Crimes Bill in 1887. This was the occasion on which the first use was made of closure by guillotine 'the most remarkable innovation upon parliamentary rule and procedure since Cromwell'. Parnell was in poor health at the time and took only a small part in the debate but, Morley recorded, he made 'more than one pulverising attack in that measured and frigid style which, in a man who knows his case, may be so much more awkward for a Minister than more florid onslaughts'.[13] According to Morley, Parnell was severe and lofty, had a 'slow dry way' and a 'characteristic frigidity, precision and confidence'. He was 'a consummate swordsman' with 'a supple and trenchant blade'.[14]

Parnell's debut on the Irish stage was less than auspicious. A. M. Sullivan, a member of the council of the Home Rule league which interviewed the prospective candidate for County Dublin in 1874, was so impressed that he agreed to move his selection at a public meeting in the Rotunda. Selected by acclamation, the young Parnell rose to speak:

> To our dismay [remembered Sullivan] he broke down utterly. He faltered, he paused, went on, got confused, and, pale with intense but subdued nervous anxiety, caused everyone to feel deep sympathy for him. The audience saw it all, and cheered him kindly and heartily; but many on the platform shook their heads, sagely prophesying that if he ever got to Westminster, no matter how long he stayed there, he would either be a 'silent member' or be known as 'single-speech Parnell'.[15]

J. G. Swift MacNeill recalled that Parnell could 'only say a few disjointed words, then pause, then repeat himself, then try to make a fresh start, and finally abandon the effort and resume his seat'.[16] T. W. Russell who first met him during the Dublin campaign was struck by what he thought was 'his extraordinary political ignorance and incapacity. He knew nothing and I thought he would never do anything.' Another prominent nationalist remembered that his impression was that he was a 'nice gentlemanly fellow who would be an ornament but no use'. O'Connor Power also found him gentlemanly but 'hopelessly ignorant' with 'no political capacity at all. He could not speak at all. He was hardly able to get up and say 'Gentlemen, I am the candidate for the representation of the county of Dublin.' We all listened to him with pain while he was on his legs, and felt immensely relieved when he sat down. No one ever thought he would cut a figure in politics. We thought he would be a respectable mediocrity.'[17]

Not surprisingly, Parnell made little impact with the electors of County Dublin. However the following year, he was returned for Meath, a constituency one must assume where respectable mediocrity was less of a liability. Notwithstanding his unimpressive debut, there is some evidence that he adjusted to the demands of the hustings. On 16 November 1878, William O'Brien was sent to report a meeting addressed by Parnell in Tralee. 'Parnell', he recorded in his diary, 'addressed a rough-and-tumble meeting, half farmers, half Fenians, with several tipsy interrupters, and a preliminary alarm that the floor was giving way. He spoke under cruel difficulties, but fired them all before he sat down.' [18]

Parnell's political speeches fall into three main categories: election or campaign speeches in Ireland and England, speeches in the United States, and the speeches in the House of Commons – which are strangely the least well known. On 22 April 1875, Parnell took his seat in the House of Commons. He remained a member for 16 years and made a significant if intermittent contribution to debate. There were five periods of intense activity – the first associated with obstruction, the second coinciding with the Land League campaign 1879–81, the third coinciding with Home Rule in 1886, the fourth at the time of the Times Special Commission and the fifth at the time of the split in 1890–1.[19]

Parnell made his maiden speech in a debate on the Coercion Act. If, as Barry O'Brien concluded, it was short, modest and spoken in 'a thin voice and with manifest nervousness', his message was clear and unambiguous. 'I trust', he said, 'that England will give to Irishmen the right which they claim – the right of self-government . . . Ireland is not a geographical fragment. She is a nation.'[20]

In October 1875, Parnell expressed his own view of the role of House of Commons debates when he told an audience at Navan that 'we do not want speeches in the House of Commons but men who will vote right'.[21] R. Barry O'Brien generalised from this early phase of Parnell's career:

> From beginning to end, Parnell disliked speechifying. The process was absolutely painful to him. Talking was sometimes necessary to get things done (or to prevent their being done) and he was forced to put up with it. But he took no pleasure in oratory, and had not the least ambition to become a great public speaker. The only occasion on which he made or listened to speeches with any degree of satisfaction was when talking obstructed the business of the House. Biggar was, perhaps, his ideal of a useful public speaker – a man who was silent when business had to be done, but who could hold the floor for four hours at a stretch when business had to be prevented.[22]

O'Brien cites a distinguished Irish advocate who said that 'a speech was all very good in its own way, but the verdict was the thing'. In the House of Commons, the speech was 'the thing' and, Parnell, O'Brien argues, despised the speech. He wanted the verdict.[23] O'Brien's interpretation is persuasive and has proved influential – however it tends to underrate Parnell's conventional parliamentary career and to ignore the extent to which he developed a distinctive and powerful style as a public speaker, a style which was all the more effective for being different. T. P. O'Connor considered that, despite his early shortcomings as a public speaker, Parnell developed into 'one of the most potent of parliamentary debaters in the House of Commons'. [24] Swift MacNeill conceded that he possessed a gift for directness of expression and saying plainly what he desired to say. This view was shared by Gladstone who conceded in the chamber that 'no man is more successful than the honorary member in doing that which it is commonly supposed that all speakers do, but which in my opinion few really do – and I do not include myself among those few – namely, in saying what he means to say.'[25]

Parnell came to public prominence through his association with the campaign of obstruction in the House of Commons from 1877 onwards. This campaign involved delaying of government business through filibustering. Debates were endlessly prolonged and individual speeches routinely lasted for hours. It is instructive to analyse the role of the nervous, faltering Parnell in this campaign. He quickly grasped the rules of procedure of the House and took particular care to act and argue from within the conventions of the constitution as understood. Most of Parnell's interventions were short points of order, which questioned procedure. He regularly cited precedents and earlier debates. Even in his longest speeches, he retained a tight focus and did not lapse into irrelevance. In an important article, George Boyce has examined Parnell's parliamentary career in the context of Walter Bagehot's classic exposition of the English constitution published in 1866.[26] At the heart of Bagehot's interpretation was the notion that the more strident the opposition was in parliament, the better the constitution worked. In defending his obstructionist tactics, Parnell invariably posed as the defender of the system rather than its opponent.[27] *Pace* his reputation for being ignorant and never reading, it is clear that Parnell had either read and understood Bagehot or he had intuited his message. [28]

Public speeches are notoriously fraught with pitfalls for the would be analyst: the location, the audience, the circumstances of the time all sway the tone and lay false trails for the historians. For example, how much weight should we attach to Parnell's message to small farmers in Mayo? Or what he said to an Irish-American audience in Cincinnati in 1880 (even if we can establish what precisely he did say) as opposed to his more measured tones elsewhere? His apparent irredentist message to Ulster Unionists 1886 as opposed to his soothing message at the Ulster Hall in Belfast in 1890? his public endorsement of the 1886 Home Rule Bill as a final settlement of the Irish question as opposed to his rabble-rousing speeches after the split in 1890?[29]

Speeches sometimes owe more to the occasion and circumstances in which they were delivered than to a carefully considered, long-term position. In Parnell's case, however, he was not prone to being carried away. Notwithstanding his reputation for directness and plain speaking, he understood the creative value of ambiguity and the necessity to convey different messages to different constituencies even in the same speech. But almost all commentators agree that he was rarely less than clear. When Parnell declared in an interview in New York in 1880 that a true revolutionary movement should have both a constitutional and an illegal character, his pitch for Fenian support was likely to convey – was probably meant to convey – that he was part of such a movement and approved of all its aspects. However, in 1889 before the Special Commission investigating the links between Parnellism and crime, he was able to argue plausibly that he was referring to Fenianism, not to his own movement, and that he was seeking to promote constitutionalism not the opposite.[30]

Perhaps the most common objection to Home Rule was that it would lead to separation. In rallying popular support in Ireland, Parnell was inclined to stress how much Ireland was demanding while in reassuring the opposition the emphasis was on how little. Hence, for example, the careful balance of the apparent *carte blanche* in his rousing '*ne plus ultra*' speech, with his almost unnoticed insistence that for the moment all that was on the menu was the very limited option of the restoration of Grattan's parliament.[31] Parnell often offered audiences Grattan's parliament as the model for Home Rule but he carefully avoided defining what that would mean. Some months after the Cork speech, he told his own Wicklow electors that although it would be impossible to guarantee that Home Rule would not ultimately culminate in separation, the separatist demand was largely a product of misgovernment and would be weakened by Home Rule. He privately presented a Home Rule scheme to Gladstone which, he assured him, did not involve repeal of the Union. While he could not propose such a scheme publicly, he undertook to work for its acceptance.[32]

The Cork formula, the combination of rhetorical flourish with less conspicuous reservation, was used by Parnell throughout his career, but most effectively during the Land War 1879–81 and later in his desperate fight for survival after the split. The apparent extremism of many of his speeches in the period 1890–1 has misled some commentators who read extracts from the speeches rather than the speeches as a whole. This raises the related questions of audience and dissemination. A characteristic feature of Parnell's public speeches is that while they were carefully constructed in terms of balance, they tended to contain accessible and memorable slogans. Stirring rhetoric has less enduring impact on an audience than a catchy phrase constantly repeated. Parnell grasped early the value of the sound bite and the need to ensure dissemination of the message. He took considerable care to facilitate journalists at meetings – for instance, always being accompanied by a journalist on election tours. His career coincided with an upsurge in the number of newspapers in Ireland – the number of nationalist newspapers increased from 41 to 55 between 1880 and 1886 alone.[33]

Parnell was well aware that audiences varied and had different needs: Irish audiences, he felt, needed to be encouraged and lifted up because 'they are oppressed and beaten down'. On the other hand, he felt Irish American audiences, 'require to have cold water thrown upon them'.[34] The latter realisation did not always translate itself into practice, not least on his 1880 visit to the United States when he made a number of extreme speeches more likely to enflame than dampen the enthusiasm of his Irish-American audience. His speech at Cincinnati on 20 February, when Parnell was reported to have declared that he would not rest until he had destroyed the last link which kept Ireland bound to England, proved most controversial. In 1886, when the first Home Rule Bill was being introduced, the speech was resurrected to show that Parnell's new-found moderation was a sham and it was again produced in 1889 at the Special Commission hearings to show a connection between Parnell and Fenianism.

The question of what Parnell did or did not say continues to perplex historians.[35] Parnell told the Special Commission that it was most improbable that he had used the words complained of as they were 'entirely opposed to anything I have ever uttered in any speech during my life'. He insisted that Irish nationhood was compatible with the link with Britain. Parnell produced a report of his speech from the *Cincinnati Daily Gazette* which did not include the offending remarks, nor did they appear in the report published by the *Cincinnati Journal*. In explanation of why the radical *Irish World* newspaper would attribute such words to him, Parnell was inclined to blame it on the animosity of Patrick Ford, the paper's owner, who had indeed publicly criticised Parnell on a number of occasions. However, it transpired that the *Irish World* had simply lifted its report from a third Cincinnati newspaper, the *Cincinnati Commercial Gazette* which, of the four newspapers that reported the meeting, provided the most detailed coverage. The *Commercial Gazette* had no obvious interest in misquoting Parnell.[36]

Thus, it seems likely that Parnell, perhaps as F. S. L. Lyons concludes, carried away by the emotion of the occasion and by his own background, did speak of breaking the link with Britain. Parnell himself offered another possible gloss in 1889: if he had used the words, he thought he must have 'very largely qualified them by another matter', which, I would suggest, is a frank admission of his approach to such speeches.[37] Ultimately, of course, the issue is of only secondary importance as his later disavowal of the views taints the evidence and makes the speech of limited value for the biographer. That did not prevent Barry O'Brien, one of his biographers, from concluding that at Cincinnati, Parnell spoke from the heart and that the more radical version of the Cincinnati speech represented Parnell's true position.[38]

If it is dangerous to rely on newspaper reports of speeches and to take extracts from speeches out of context, it can be equally misleading to choose speeches *à la carte*, out of time. It would be mistaken to assume that a statesman's views or attitude necessarily remain as fixed as the lines on the Parnell monument. His views may develop, be refined or even change completely. In the case of Parnell, the dramatically changing circumstances, from the semi-revolutionary days of the Land War to the pinnacle of the constitutionalist's career in 1886 when his power was at its height and later to the isolation and division of his final years, present peculiar problems in interpreting his statements and divining his real position. There is no doubt that Parnell's views in crucial areas do change or at least are refined as his career proceeds in ways not fully appreciated by some of his biographers.

Probably the best example of this is Parnell's attitude to the Ulster question. The consensus among modern historians is that Parnell knew little about Ulster, that he recklessly disregarded the explosive potential of the problem and that when, after the split, he adopted a more conciliatory tone in a speech in Belfast, that he was guilty of naked opportunism. I have argued, on the contrary, that, while Parnell was initially poorly informed, he developed an instinctive and sophisticated interpretation of the Ulster issue which is best reflected in his speech on the second reading of the Home Rule bill in 1886. Where Bew and Lyons see this speech as belligerent irredentism, I have argued that it is an original, profound and persuasive contribution which is as relevant today as when it was first delivered.

No Sir, we cannot give up a single Irishman. We want the energy, the patriotism, the talent and works of every Irishman to make this great experiment – to ensure that this great experiment shall be successful. The best form of government for a country I believe, to be one that requires that that government shall be the resultant of what forces are in that country. We cannot give away to a second legislature for a section of Ireland any portion of the talent or influence of the Irish Protestants. This class – the Protestant class – will form the most valuable element in the Irish Legislature of the future, constituting as they still will a strong minority and exercising, through the 'First Order', a moderating influence on the making of the untrained legislators in an Irish Parliament. I regard their presence as vitally necessary to the success of this trial. We want, Sir, all creeds and classes in Ireland. We cannot look upon a single Irishman as not belonging to us. However much we recognise their ability, we cannot admit that there is a single one of them too good to take part in this experiment. We do not blame the small proportion of

Protestants who feel any real fear. I admit that there is a small proportion who do. We have been doing our best of late to remove this fear and we shall continue to do so. When this bill becomes an Act we shall not cease to try to conciliate such Irishmen.[39]

So were Bew and Lyons unduly influenced by the political climate of the late 1970s or might I perhaps be accused of wishful thinking? One observer who has written about the debates on the first Home Rule Bill provides some revealing evidence. The debates which stretched over 16 nights, were, in the estimation of John Morley, 'not unworthy of the gravity of the issue, nor the fame of the House of Commons. Only one speaker held the magic secret of Demosthenic oratory. Several others showed themselves masters of the higher arts of parliamentary discussion.'[40] Morley does not specify to whom he was referring. One might assume that it was Gladstone; in fact the evidence suggests Parnell. Elsewhere Morley gives his explicit verdict on Parnell's speech:

> The Irish leader made one of the most masterly speeches that ever fell from him. Whether agreeing with or differing from the policy, every unprejudiced listener felt that this was not the mere dialectic of a party debater, dealing smartly with abstract or verbal or artificial arguments, but the utterance of a statesman with his eye fixed firmly upon the actual circumstances of the nation for whose government this bill would make him responsible. As he dealt with Ulster, with finance, with the supremacy of Parliament, with the loyal minority, with the settlement of education in an Irish legislature, – soberly, steadily, deliberately, with that full, familiar deep insight into the facts of a country, which is only possible to a man who belongs to it and has passed his life in it, the effect of Mr Parnell's speech was to make even able disputants on either side look little better than amateurs.[41]

Demosthenes was the Greek statesman who led the desperate struggle of the Athenians to maintain the freedom of the city-states against the imperialist ambitious of Philip of Macedonia. His speech delivered at his trial in 330 BC is considered by many to be the greatest speech by the ancient world's greatest orator. In the speech which was translated and popularised in the early nineteenth century by the social reformer Lord Brougham, Demosthenes poses the rhetorical question: 'In what circumstances then ought a statesman and an orator to be vehement.' The answer is when the state is in jeopardy. It is precisely at the moments of greatest importance for the nation that Parnell's speeches rise from the mundane to the memorable.[42] Gladstone himself recognised this characteristic: he told a friend that Parnell's speeches reminded him of Lord Palmerston's in their way of expressing exactly what the speaker wanted to say. There was another similarity: Palmerston had a reputation for intense love of constitutional freedom everywhere and for his profound hatred of slavery. When his friend responded that of course Parnell was a pygmy compared to Palmerston, Gladstone's strenuously disagreed.[43]

Another illustration of Parnell's effectiveness on the 'big occasions' is a series of speeches he made in opposition to Gladstone's harsh coercion measure, the Peace Preservation act of 1881. Parnell intervened in this debate on numerous occasions: some of his contributions were points of order or information but on at least two occasions he made speeches of great import and eloquence. In a lengthy speech on the second reading he argued that the government was doing more to separate Ireland and Britain than all the American Fenians from New York to San Francisco. The Land League movement was a constitutional one backed by a united public opinion. In resorting to coercion, the government was helping the separatist movement. They would not get a single Fenian gun. Parnell defended the Fenians:

> I have the greatest respect for many Fenians. I have the greatest respect for men who announce themselves publicly to be Fenians – who believe in the separation of England from Ireland by physical force, and who do not look to constitutional agitation. And although I do not believe they were right, I say the Ministry of today are doing their best to prove that those men are right; they are doing their best to thrust men like myself . . . and others outside the lines of the Constitution.

He continued:

> The more you tyrannise-the more you trifle with the Irish people – the stronger will burn the spirit of nationality, the more they will free themselves from the yoke which renders such things possible. We may have our day – our short day – of persecution. I believe the public opinion of the people of England will, at some day or other, do justice to our motives, even if they do not approve our course.[44]

In his speech on the third reading, Parnell warned the government that they had not only Irish public opinion to contend with, but American public opinion as well. The Irish people in America had had the advantage of a free school system in the country; they had benefited from the educational institutions which were denied to the people of Ireland; and nothing struck him more during his recent visit to America than the superior position of the Irish people there. He dismissed the Home Secretary's characterisation of the Irish-American lobby as supporters of assassination and murder. Everywhere in America he met the Irish as barristers, medical men, merchants, leading men in manufactories, employers of labour, and everywhere he found the intelligent opinion of the Irish people in America was in sympathy with the aims and objects of the Land League in their struggle to free their country from the present [landlord] system. He went on to argue that the people were committed to a great struggle by constitutional means and all that would shake them from that was ill-advised action from the government which would drive them into 'the wild justice of revenge'.[45]

These speeches are classic Parnell speak: rival forces are balanced; Parnell unambiguously espouses a constitutional position yet evokes the spectre of physical force; he occupies an orthodox almost conservative high ground in defence of the constitution and public opinion yet manages to make his message palatable to the hillside men. Either British statesmen engaged with the constitutional movement or they would sooner or later face a less palatable alternative. In fairness, however, Parnell's own position is clear. Parnell was not a separatist although, as P. S. O'Hegarty concluded, a distinction can be made between the man and his impact: Parnell's effect on Irish nationalism was certainly separatist.[46]

As to the wider issues of biography, what conclusions can we draw? On the central question, of course we can use public speeches in establishing what politicians believe, but they require considerable care. The pitfalls identified in this particular case are not new or unexpected; they are part and parcel of the historians' or biographers' first principles in the collection and evaluation of evidence. What is surprising is the regularity with which such principles are transgressed and, even where they are faithfully adhered to, the diversity of interpretations which can still be sustained.

CHAPTER 5

Parnell's Women

Donal McCartney

During her stay at Avondale in 1887 Parnell's mother (then 71) took over the celebrated new cattle-shed (which Parnell had modelled on Brighton's new railway station), evicted the unoffending animals, had a temporary floor laid down and advertised in the *Wicklow Newsletter* as follows:

> Miss Bessie Byrne, the distinguished American actress, assisted by the Gasparro brothers and some local friends, will give a dramatic and musical entertainment at Avondale on Tuesday, the 16th inst. Mrs Delia T. S. Parnell will also give an address.[1]

It appears that Mrs Parnell's famous son was not amused. From England he had tried in vain to retain the shed for its rightful occupants. His mother who often had to be humoured could sometimes be exasperating. A few weeks later he arrived in Avondale and sent this account of the event to Katharine O'Shea:

> Miss B. B. was very old, very ugly, and very vulgar; in fact E [Emily] says, the worst sponge that ever got hold of my mother. She drank nothing but whisky, and took it to bed with her. There was dancing after the theatricals till six in the morning.[2]

Seven years later a reporter in the *Irish Weekly Independent* stated that the decorations and garlands though withered and decayed were still in place in the shed.[3]

The first thing to be emphasised about Parnell's mother is that she was quintessentially American. Her father, Captain (later Commodore, later Rear-Admiral) Charles Stewart, had become famous a year before the birth of his daughter for his capture of two English ships in 1815 – the *Cyane* and the *Levant*. He was celebrated enough to be put forward for the presidency of the United States as Pennsylvania's favourite son in 1838, though he failed to win the nomination.

Stewart's wife, Delia Tudor, belonged to a family long associated with the political, literary and business life of Boston. From the start the temperaments of the Captain and his wife – who had been brought up in the polite society of Boston, Paris and London – were incompatible. When their daughter, Delia, was nine her parents finally separated. Her father, to use the slang term, shacked up with 'a pretty young married country woman'.[4] Though he was never divorced from his wife, he referred to his new partner as Mrs Stewart. Sixty years later his grandson, Charles Stewart Parnell, would cohabit with Mrs O'Shea and address her endearingly as 'Wifie', as if to prove the truth of the Irish adage: Briseann an dúchas tri shúile an chait! [lit. Nature breaks through the eyes of the cat, i.e. Nature will out.]

As a result of the break-up of her parents' marriage Parnell's mother had a very unsettled upbringing. She moved from place to place with her accomplished mother and cultivated grandmother – all three of them called Delia – until settling in Washington where they were accepted in the highest circles. At 19 she married the 22-year-old John Henry Parnell, then on the grand tour of North America. Delia's mother and grandmother wallowed in the thought that their darling, now proudly Mrs Delia Tudor Stewart Parnell, had married into a family that, as they broadcast it, had connections with the nobility of Ireland and England.

But the young American city girl found it very difficult to adjust to life on a country estate in Wicklow. The highlights, which she reported back to mother and grandmother, were the visits to and from the lords and ladies of the county. The hunting, shooting and cricket which her husband and children indulged in did nothing for her. Childbearing became a large part of her life. She gave birth to 12 children (one was stillborn). Then in 1853 after 17 years of marriage she took herself and her girls off to Paris and London for their education and to launch them as debutantes in the expectation of finding suitable husbands for them. From then until John Henry Parnell's death six years later at the age of 48 husband and wife had been virtually separated.

Parnell was only seven when the estrangement began. He was taken to school in England by his father who told the schoolmistress that he was anxious that the child should spend some time 'with someone who would mother him'.[5] Charles was the only member of the family at home when his father died, and apparently the only one of them to attend the funeral. Mrs Parnell did not return from Paris until after the burial. The absent mother's direct influence on her son up to the age of 13 must have been of the slightest.

Following the father's death, mother and daughters moved back to Ireland for a few years before returning to Paris. During this time Charles was at school in England and then at Cambridge. The total number of contact hours between Charles and his mother from the time he was 13 until he entered parliament at 29 would have been, if anything, even slighter than during the first 13 years of his life. What she could have contributed to his direct political formation must have been extremely tenuous. On the other hand, her absences from his life and the deprivation of a mother's attention may very well have influenced the shaping of his pronounced independence of mind and other elements of his personality as well as his hunger for a woman's love.

The myth of the mother's influence on Parnell originated in her own delusions of grandeur. When Parnell was on his political mission to America in 1880, Delia wrote : 'History shows that, as is the mother, so is the son . . . Many a man . . . has surely felt and acknowledged a mother's sacred influence.'[6] And so began her mission to persuade the world that it was she who had formed this brilliant new star in the political firmament.

When Barry O'Brien was gathering material in 1896 for the first complete and most influential biography of Parnell he interviewed Parnell's mother then 80 years old. He was greatly impressed by her calm, determined, self-possessed manner which, he said, had also always distinguished her son. She was a woman of convictions, independent, fearless, indifferent to established conventions and animated by one fixed idea – a rooted hatred of England. O'Brien asked her how it came about that that her son had such antipathy to the English. She replied: 'Why should he not? . . . My grandfather Tudor fought against the English in the War of Independence. My father fought against the English in the War of 1812 . . . It was very natural for Charles to dislike the English.' O'Brien concluded: 'The opinions and sentiments of the mother were certainly the opinions and sentiments of the son.'[7]

To be fair to Mrs Parnell she did quickly add: 'We have no objection to the English people; we object to the English dominion. We would not have it in America. Why should they have it in Ireland?'[8] – as if she had suddenly remembered that she had delighted in invitations for herself and her daughters to Dublin Castle from the Lord Lieutenant; that she had lived happily among the English and was a great admirer of the Queen; and that her patriot son had forfeited all for the love of an English woman.

However, Barry O'Brien's insistence that Parnell had derived his hatred of England from his American mother won general acceptance. F. S. L. Lyons wrote in *Ireland since the famine* (1971) that Mrs Parnell 'duly passed on to her children' her American heritage of 'extreme anti-English feeling'.[9] In his 1976 book, *Charles Stewart Parnell: The Man and his Family*, Roy Foster was right in dismissing Delia's alleged political influence on her son. Several years later, however, in his *Modern Ireland* (1988), Foster inexplicably reverted to the inherited hatred theme describing Parnell as 'half American, inheriting on his mother's side anti-Britishness'.[10]

Less attention has been paid to what that other Mrs Parnell (alias Katharine O'Shea) had to say. She wrote: 'It is a mistake to say that his mother "planted his hatred of England" in him, as she so seldom saw him as a boy'.[11] Nobody

knew Parnell better than Katharine, and no doubt she had received that statement of the actual situation from Parnell himself.

Delia Tudor Stewart Parnell became a celebrity only when her son visited
America in 1880 as President of the Land League. And when her daughter,
Fanny, founded the Ladies' Land League in New York later that year Delia
was appointed titular president. In that capacity she appeared on many public
platforms. It was her children, Charles, Fanny and Anna who bestowed on
her the sentimentalised Irish nationalism that she now loved to proclaim. She
had imbibed whatever anti-English politics she held from them – and not the
other way round.

Although the son's fame reflected on the mother's image, she as a member
of the proud Tudor family of Boston and the daughter of the American hero,
Admiral Stewart, brought to her son's agitation in America an important air
of respectability and a good measure of political and social consequence,
opening doors to him and the Irish cause that might otherwise have remained
closed. And Parnell was clever enough and only too happy to capitalise on
what was Delia Tudor Stewart's substantial contribution.

Most Irish commentators, then and since, have found it hard to come to
grips with this American woman's complex personality. Tim Healy in America
with Parnell wrote home to his brother: 'They are the most extraordinary
family I ever came across. The mother, I think, is a little "off her nut" in some
ways and, for that matter, so are all the rest of them'.[12] And I find it difficult
to accept T. W. Moody's characterisation of her as: 'imperious, headstrong,
selfish and eccentric'.[13] Jane McL. Côté was probably much closer to the truth
when she described her as 'gullible, naive, good-natured, tender-hearted and
easily led'.[14]

Roy Foster's portrait of Delia was anything but flattering. Her speeches,
he said, were confused, pretentious, rambling. She was preoccupied with her
social position; engaged in posturing and at times displayed an overwhelming
snobbery. He spoke of her eccentricity and claimed that: 'like many strong-
minded old women, consistency probably seemed of little account for her'.
He concluded she was 'not unduly likeable'.[15]

I confess to having a much softer spot for her. Her two children who
published reminiscences of the family, Emily and John Howard, described
their mother as charming, accomplished and a brilliant conversationalist.[16]
Katharine Tynan wrote that in old age Mrs Parnell was a flamboyant person,
very American. Tynan added that she was also obviously a handful who must
have been a trial to her grave and dignified son. While it is true that some of
her more flamboyant actions and financial speculations did embarrass Charles,
his filial attachment was never doubted. Even Tim Healy had to admit that
Parnell was 'certainly very fond of his mother'.[17] And Katharine O'Shea confirmed that Parnell was 'most generous and affectionate to his mother'.[18] To

her credit Delia stood loyally by her son during the divorce case and the subsequent split in the party. After Parnell's death Delia comforted Katharine by
blessing their love. And Katharine thanked Delia for her loving letter and the
noble heart and mind that had written it.[19]

If the mother had little direct political influence on Parnell, his younger
sisters, Fanny and Anna, seemed to be extensions of the more radical side of
his nationalism.[20] Fanny was his favourite. And she was also the first of the
family to become associated with the Irish nationalist movement. She read
closely the editorials in the Fenian paper, the *Irish People*, and the verses she
began to write often followed the topics dealt with in these editorials. The first
of her published poems appeared in this paper when she was 16, and this was
followed by a dozen more during the next six months – most of them with
political overtones. Her brother, John Howard, says that he 'used generally to
escort her' to the newspaper's office, but Charles made fun of her poetry and
refused to accompany her to the Fenian stronghold. [21]

In a letter to the *Gaelic American* in 1907,[22] Anna Parnell claimed that
Fanny's teenage poetry in the *Irish People* 'had nothing to do with politics whatever', and 'nothing to do with Ireland'. Roy Foster quotes Anna's comment
to question young Fanny's Fenian sympathies.[23] However, in his earlier book
on the Parnells, Foster instanced Fanny's poetry as showing 'conclusively'
that she was a 'sympathiser with Fenianism'.[24] Jane Côté states that Anna was
mistaken; that of her dozen poems, 'all but two attested to a fervent belief in
Irish independence'.[25]

Charles, in 1864, had as yet shown little interest in politics. If Parnell's
interest in politics originated, as he later claimed, in sympathy with the Fenian
prisoners and martyrs, it was possibly Fanny as much as any other who helped
influence him at this point in his career. Like Anna she was very independent-
minded. But unlike her sister she had the charm and social graces that put her
at her ease with others. Although pursued by many men, especially while
living in Paris with her mother and sisters, she retained a cynical attitude
towards men and never married. She contributed articles of a social nature to
an American journal in Paris – including 'Hints to a Young Lady on Marriage';
'Evil Speaking'; 'Reflections of a Wallflower' which were lighthearted criticism
of the American colony in Paris.

After Delia had inherited the Bordentown, New Jersey, estate of Admiral
Stewart, Fanny and the youngest Parnell girl, Theodosia, moved to America
with their mother. When the *New York Tribune* was critical of Parnell's tactics in November 1879, Fanny wrote a rebuttal which the paper headlined
'A Sister's Defence'. Anna in a newspaper article also came to her brother's
defence. A short time later Parnell began his American mission on behalf
of the Land League. Fanny and Anna worked long hours in the Famine
Relief Fund headquarters in New York, looked after Parnell's neglected

correspondence, and assisted in the organisation of his tour of American cities when it was in danger of becoming something of a mess.

Fanny wrote an article on the Irish land situation for the prestigious *North American Review* (which had been founded by her grand-uncle, William Tudor Jr). The article was published under Charles Stewart Parnell's name.[26] It was a version of this article which Parnell used for his very important address to the US House of Representatives. Granted some of the material was taken from reports of his own earlier speeches, but many of the extended quotations from J. A. Froude, Professor Blackie, Nassau Senior, and references to Sir Robert Kane, the *Boston Globe*, the Old Testament, *et alii* were most likely hers. On this important occasion she had acted both as researcher and speechwriter for the Irish leader.

Fanny also produced at this time a pamphlet, the *Hovels of Ireland*, which was a scathing attack on the landlords. A few months later her Land League ballads began to appear in John Boyle O'Reilly's *Boston Pilot*. Following the rhythm of popular marching songs, these rousing ballads played an important part in the land agitation. They were reprinted in the nationalist newspapers and recited on public platforms in Ireland.

According to Davitt, her poem, 'Hold the Harvest', was 'the *Marseillaise* of the Irish peasant, the trumpet call to the Celtic people to remember the hideous crimes of an odious system'.[27] It was used as evidence of incitement to crime during the state trials of Parnell and the other leading Land Leaguers. It did indeed incorporate some blood-curdling stuff:

> Three hundred years your crops have sprung,
> By murdered corpses fed;
> Your butchered sires, your famished sires,
> For ghastly compost spread;
> Their bones have fertilized your fields,
> Their blood has fall'n like rain;
> They died that ye might eat and live –
> God! Have they died in vain. [28]

Yet, like her brother, she would always claim that what she was preaching was passive resistance, not violence. In her stirring poem against coercion called 'Coercion -Hold the Rent' she wrote:

> Hold your peace and hold your hands – not a finger on them lay, boys!
> Let the pike and rifle stand – we have found a better way, boys.[29]

Despite the heroics of her writing, this shy author suffered from stage-fright when it came to platform speaking. She was content to leave the limelight of the public meeting to her mother who relished such occasions.

Fanny's other notable contribution to the agrarian struggle was the establishment of the Ladies' Land League in America in October 1880. Her health had never been robust, and she died in July 1882 shortly before her 34th birthday. Charles was devastated. Nevertheless he refused to yield to the campaign to have her remains brought back to Ireland, and insisted that she be buried where she had died. Her remains lie to this day in the Tudor vault in Mount Auburn cemetery in Cambridge, Massachusetts.

Fanny's younger sister, Anna, had stayed behind in Dublin and London to attend art school when her mother and sisters had returned to America. She was living in London in the late 1870s when her brother was becoming famous as leader of the obstructionists in parliament. Her interest in art waned as her interest in politics soared. She became a regular visitor to the House of Commons where from the Ladies' Cage she delighted in her brother's performance. Her first real introduction to politics, therefore, was under the influence of Charles in his most radical days. This appealed to her strong, independent spirit, and the radicalism she then espoused, she was never again to abandon.

Like Fanny, she, too, was well read and intelligent, and after rejoining her family in America, she turned to journalism in support of her brother and the Land League. She wrote a series entitled, 'How they do in the House of Commons: Notes from the Ladies Cage' in praise of the obstructionists. With Fanny she threw herself into the work for the Land League, assisting Charles, John Dillon, Healy and Davitt on their visits to America. When, following Fanny's example in America, the Ladies' Land League was formed in Ireland (January 1881), Davitt insisted on putting Anna in charge of the office in Dublin. On her constant excursions around the country more men than women turned out to greet the sister of the Irish leader. To them she was not Anna Parnell, the driving force behind the Ladies' Land League, but Parnell's sister. And though she could do little to change this, it exasperated her strong feminist spirit.

Within six months over 400 branches of the Ladies' Land League had been formed, providing relief for the evicted and the prisoners. With the arrest of Parnell and the other male leaders, more and more of the work fell to the Ladies' League at a time when coercion and crime were on the increase. In the circumstances the women activists attracted much condemnation. 'Capt Moonlight in petticoats' was how F. H. O'Donnell described them.[30]

The compromise between Gladstone and Parnell, known as the Kilmainham Treaty, which ended this phase of the Land War, also lead to the disbandment of the Ladies' Land League. Anna disapproved so strongly of the Treaty that she never spoke to her brother again. Always, however, a defender of minorities, her sympathies were with him in his fight against the majority during the Parnell split. And because she blamed vilification by the majority for his death, she regarded the spectacle of the crowds at his funeral as downright hypocrisy.

Thereafter, although she lived for another twenty years after her brother's death, her life was a sad one, alienated and – except for a few friends – isolated. She suffered bouts of depression, and even a friend (Kate Molony) from Land League days found her at times irritable and quarrelsome. Living in the south of England, there were times when she was so impoverished that she pawned her belongings to find the rent money. In an effort to ease her financial circumstances it was decided to try to publish the poems she had written from time to time. But as a poet she was not in Fanny's league. To his eternal credit, when John Dillon heard of the situation he gave £50 to a publisher to pay her for her poems. Dillon's gesture remained hidden from this proud Parnell who would have scorned the idea of being the recipient of charity.

She became incensed by passages in the *Fall of Feudalism* (1904) by her one time friend and champion, Michael Davitt, which she interpreted as implying that the Ladies' Land League had encouraged crime. The book which she wrote, but found no publisher for in her lifetime, *The Tale of a Great Sham*,[31] was intended to put the record straight on the story of the Land League. Disillusioned by all that had happened in Ireland since 1880, her language had grown, if anything, more intemperate. She wrote of the falsehoods, cowardice and imbecility of the Land League leaders; the landlords were 'a worthless set of human beings'; the Home Rule Party were 'a gang of scoundrels'.[32] And of Irishmen generally she had this to say: 'However long I might live, I knew that it would never again be possible for me to believe that any body of Irishmen meant a word of anything they said.'[33]

In the North Leitrim by-election of 1908 she accepted the invitation to speak on behalf of the Sinn Féin candidate running against the Home Rule man. Privately she explained that if the Sinn Féin candidate had been a Unionist she would have called on the electors to vote for him.

She was living under the assumed name of Miss Cerissa Palmer in a lodging house in the seaside town of Ilfracombe in Devon when she was drowned while swimming. She was then, in 1911, 59. Seven strangers, including her landlady and attendants at the swimming pool followed the hearse to the local cemetery. It was a lonely ending for the woman who had been called the Mademoiselle of the Land War; who had distributed as much as £70,000 to its victims; and who had addressed literally thousands during the 18 months of the Ladies' campaign.

Anna had played a substantial role, but the extent to which she, any more than her mother or sister, Fanny, influenced Charles remains doubtful. Certain it is that her angry protests were unable to prevent his cutting off of the funds to the Ladies' Land League, or his ending of the Land War in favour of concentration on Home Rule. She had commenced her involvement as his fervent admirer, had heroically assisted in the heat of the land struggle, and had ended her days in disillusionment. Although she was never to speak to her brother again, her book has provided his enemies and later critics (as if he had not enough already) with plenty of ammunition (feminist as well as political) to hurl his way.

Long before his startling success in politics, Parnell's good looks and charm had made him attractive to the ladies. Even while still a boy an Italian governess took a great fancy to him; and when at school in England he was said to have had a local sweetheart. Later, as the young master of Avondale, he was a firm favourite among the ladies of Wicklow's genteel society. Historians, however, have dismissed as pure fancy a story about an episode supposed to have happened during his time at Cambridge. According to the story Daisy, a local farmer's daughter, was seduced, became pregnant, was abandoned by Parnell and as a result drowned herself. And, in the most melodramatic style of the Victorian novelette, who should come along the riverbank just as the body was being dragged out but Parnell. Coroners' records, however, show that no girl called Daisy had been drowned in Cambridgeshire or been the subject of any inquest. A 16-year-old girl, Annie Smith, was drowned during Parnell's second year at Cambridge. The verdict was suicide after accidentally setting fire to the curtains in the inn where she had worked as a servant. The post-mortem revealed that she was not pregnant. There is no evidence to connect this unfortunate girl in any way with Parnell.

His first serious love affair was with a wealthy American heiress, fair-haired and vivacious, whom he met while on an extended visit to his uncle in Paris. Parnell, then 24, was smitten. Miss Woods and Charles became, as they say, an item, constantly together and regarded as engaged. He returned to Avondale, it was thought, to prepare it for the expected bride. When she went home to Newport, Rhode Island, he followed her, only to discover that she did not intend to marry him. She married and settled in Newport instead. Ten years later she told Parnell's brother, John, and sister, Theodosia, who had called on her that she regretted not having married their brother because of how happy they would have been.[34]

Later Parnell talked to Katharine O'Shea about her and referred to her great beauty. He admitted that he had met her again while in the USA, when the fact was that he had followed her there. He claimed that while she did not want to live in Ireland, he didn't want to live in America. It was a case of being somewhat economical with the truth.

As a result of the break-up Charles was dejected; and for years afterwards, according to his brother, he was cold and suspicious towards women. By then, too, doubts about the prospects of married bliss were only being reinforced by the disastrous history of marriage in his own family. Grandmother had been abandoned by grandfather Stewart; mother and father had been estranged for years; his older sisters had fared no better – Delia, married to a rich and very jealous husband, had been so unhappy that she had attempted suicide; Emily was very unhappily married to an alcoholic; Sophia at 16 had run away and secretly married the family solicitor. The sisters who were younger than Charles – Fanny and Anna – never married. And although they expressed no desire for spinsterhood, they were more apprehensive of having to live in some unhappy relationship. Like Charles they found sublimation in politics. The youngest, Theodosia, was also unhappy in marriage and disinherited in her husband's will. Parnell's brother, John Howard, waited until he was a sensible 64 before he plucked up the courage to marry a widow. For someone with such a superstitious nature as Charles had, it must have appeared that the dice was mightily loaded against his chances of any normal married relationship.

After the jilting by Miss Woods there is no reference to any love affair in Parnell's life until Mrs O'Shea comes on the scene (July 1880) The O'Shea liaison became known to a number of his colleagues eight months later in somewhat bizarre circumstances. In February 1881 Davitt had been arrested, an angry protest in the House of Commons resulted in the suspension and ejection of 36 Irish MPs, and the government had introduced a draconian coercion bill for the purpose of crushing the land agitation. An emergency meeting of the Land League executive was called to meet in Paris. After a week of waiting for him, Parnell had not shown up. It was decided to open a letter in a woman's hand addressed to him in the hope of finding some clue as to his whereabouts. According to Tim Healy's rather sanctimonious account, Healy handed it to Dillon and Egan stipulating that only those two should know the contents. This was agreed, and Dillon and Egan, in Healy's words, 'mournfully retired with it to another room while the rest awaited the result'.[35]

They returned gloomily and proposed that Biggar and Healy should start for London by the next train to search for Parnell at the address taken from the letter. There they were to set two ex-detectives, Druskovitch and Micklejohn, to trace Parnell. As they were leaving, Parnell arrived. Some time later Healy heard that Biggar, without consulting Healy, had sent a friend to the London address where the forlorn lady lodged. Healy said that he reproached Biggar for this intrusion, but Biggar argued that he feared a scandal if her application for help were left unanswered. She was, according to Healy, Lizzie from Blankshire, and was found in a barely furnished garret in bed with a baby. She had pinned to her bed-cover a newspaper drawing of Parnell. (A Victorian novelette writer was surely lost on our first Governor General of the Irish Free State.) Though in want, Healy assures us, she was staunch to the father of her child and never publicly complained. Her needs were provided for, and she was told where to apply should she require further help. She never did. So Healy assumed that Parnell must have made amends for his temporary neglect.

Healy would have known of the now discredited Emily Dickinson story about 'Daisy' in Parnell's Cambridge days. The fictional Daisy may very well have been the model for Healy's Lizzie. Otherwise we have to believe that Parnell, in the worst landlord tradition, had a weakness for servant girls and barmaids. It is quite possible that Parnell did seduce 'Lizzie'. But the story as told by Healy contains a number of discrepancies for later historians. As F. S. L. Lyons says, Healy's recollections are frequently unreliable'.[36] It was written 50 years after the event when all of the other participants were conveniently dead, and apparently none of those others present in Paris or any of Parnell's lieutenants ever mentioned Lizzie.[37]

And if she were not entirely a figment of Healy's hostile imagination, it was never explained how her address in Holloway could possibly lead to Parnell's whereabouts. Healy, who was then honorary secretary to Parnell, says that Parnell treated him with entire confidence as regards his correspondence. He used to open Parnell's letters daily, yet of late he had without any hint from Parnell reserved for him packets coming in a woman's hand (presumably Mrs O'Shea). Healy pleaded that the decision to open the letter should not be harshly judged, that they were solely animated by concern for the safety of Parnell and the cause of Ireland, and that what was done was done in the national interest.

It is hard, however, not to judge the event as a breach of confidence and a gross invasion of privacy especially at a time when they were objecting to the Post Office opening their own correspondence. Curiosity about the private life of their mysterious leader may have had something to do with it. A possible explanation, however, is that the letter in question had come from Mrs O'Shea. She certainly had Parnell's address in Paris. T. P. O'Connor and Davitt (who were not in Paris but would have heard from those who were) took it that the opened letter had come from Mrs O'Shea. And in her own book Mrs O'Shea stated that 'certain members of the Party opened one of my letters to Parnell'. And she added: 'I make no comment'.[38] It is likely that Katharine's statement goaded Healy into his elaborate account of the episode, and that his Lizzie of Blankshire was really the woman who during the Parnell split he insisted on calling 'Kitty'. 'Lizzie', indeed, would have been one of the mildest names he ever called Katharine in his lifelong bitterness towards the woman he blamed for all the tragedy of the Parnell split.

More recently, Frank Callanan in his detailed biography of Healy gives somewhat more credence to the story than did F. S. L. Lyons.[39] Callanan shows that in the proofs of his book Healy gave further details of the Wellington Hotel, Manchester, where Lizzie – 'a gracious and amiable girl' – worked as a barmaid. And Callanan added that as early as December 1890, at the beginning of the Parnell split, the radical MP, Henry Labouchere, for long an intimate of Healy's, supplied Herbert Gladstone with a version of this story.

Callanan acknowledged, however, that one could readily subscribe to Lyons's distaste for accepting the veracity of an allegation to Parnell's personal life for which Healy was the sole authority. Yet Callanan further added: 'why Healy should have fabricated so intricate an allegation remains to be explained'. And his conclusion was that the matter of the Manchester barmaid remains a mystery.

Katharine belonged to a prominent English family – the kind that Parnell's mother would have loved boasting about. Born in January 1845, she was the youngest of 13 children of Rev. Sir John Page Wood. Seven of the children were alive at the time of Katharine's birth. Like Parnell, she too had grown up largely motherless. She felt that her mother was so absorbed in the affairs of the older children and in her own artistic and literary work, that she had little time for the baby of the family. 'Had it not been for my father', wrote Katharine, 'I should have been a very lonely child'.[40] Katharine would later find in Parnell something of the father-figure she had loved, and he was to find in her something of the motherly attention he had received so little of as a child.

Katharine married Captain William O'Shea in 1867. Whatever spark there may have been initially in this marriage seems to have begun flickering out almost from the start. At one period O'Shea spent 18 months in Spain, never once returning home. Parnell would later claim – though we have to allow for a lover's exaggeration – that out of 23 years of married life O'Shea had spent only forty nights at home.[41]

Yet Katharine was an attractive, warm-hearted woman, with plenty of charm. She enjoyed the attentions of men, was flirtatious, but hardly promiscuous. With O'Shea so often away, she became a bit of a loner, and during solitary walks on the Downs thought about the restrictions of a life with an often absent husband, and with three children and old Aunt Ben demanding her attention.

She was ready for something more exciting in her life when she first met Parnell in the summer of 1880. She was 35 years and six months old and he 34. It was a case of heady mutual attraction. She wrote of their first meeting: 'He looked straight at me smiling, and his curiously burning eyes looked into mine with a wonderful intentness', and she thought: 'This man is wonderful and different.'[42] The bombardment of fervid letters that came from him – he who put so little ever on paper – indicated how smitten he was. There was a hunger that could only have come from two who had been deprived of love for so long.

The torrid love affair thus begun lasted over the next eleven years. They had embarked upon what was destined to be one of the consuming passions of modern history. Two months after their first meeting they were cohabiting, and Parnell had become a semi-resident at her home in Eltham, eight miles from central London. O'Shea was only an occasional visitor.

She fussed over Parnell's health and clothes and appearance. And he, relaxing from the pressures of politics and enjoying the pleasures of home life, perhaps for the first time ever, talked freely in a way that he never did with his parliamentary colleagues. But there was a side to the affair that did not appeal to everyone. It was secretive, and they continued for eleven years the habit of dissimulation with all three of the triangle engaged in some measure of self-deception. Renting love-nests in Brighton and London led Parnell into much duplicity. For cover he used the names of Mr Smith, Mr Stewart, Mr Preston, and Mr Fox. Smith was massively unoriginal; Fox, in the circumstances, most unfortunate. One might well ask what sort of love affair was it that could not become open? Or what sort of marriage was it that could not be ended? The mercenary consideration of Aunt Ben's money clearly had something to do with it. But so, too, did the very defective current divorce laws, especially as they applied to women, also militate against ending the charade.[43] It suited all involved, especially the two O'Sheas, to keep up the pretence – with what disastrous consequences we now know.

Katharine always denied that she was a political woman. Yet she required little encouragement to become involved with O'Shea's political ambitions after his election for Clare in 1880. It was as a hostess promoting the Captain's career in politics that she first sought out Parnell and invited him to dinner.

When Parnell and the other leaders of the Land League were arrested in October 1881, Katharine was five months pregnant with Parnell's first child. The compromise which led to the release of the Land Leaguers resulted in what is known as the Kilmainham Treaty.[44] Katharine claimed that throughout the eleven years of their affair she had not once attempted to influence Parnell's politics except on this one occasion when she had urged him to come to terms with the government in order to obtain his release. Parnell had been released from prison on parole in order to attend the funeral of his nephew in Paris. On his return, he stayed with the O'Sheas at Eltham where the triangle emerged at its most weird. Upstairs Katharine was attending to Parnell's dying child; downstairs Parnell and O'Shea were drawing up the terms of the Kilmainham Treaty. Dismayed by the policies of the agrarian extremists, Katharine threw her whole weight on the side of compromise with the Government. She was convinced that her worries for Parnell's position and safety helped decide him in favour of conciliation. The Captain, too, wanted to be the intermediary offering compromise to the Government. Both O'Sheas, therefore, were exerting pressure on Parnell.

Nonetheless, the details of the treaty were Parnell's own, and these he had discussed already with other leaders of the Party. There were those, however (including Gladstone, F. H. O'Donnell, and Healy), who later believed that it was Mrs O'Shea who had influenced him in the direction of moderation and constitutionalism. There is no doubt that he wished to be out of prison to be

1   Charles Stewart Parnell. Portrait by Sydney Hall. Courtesy National Gallery of Ireland.

2, 3, 4   Fanny Parnell (above left) 1878, Anna Parnell (above right) *c.*1878,
John Howard Parnell (bottom), sisters and brother of Charles Stewart Parnell.

5   Katharine O'Shea
(later Katharine Parnell).

6   Delia Tudor Stewart Parnell
(mother of Charles, Fanny and Anna).

7   'Waiting to see the prisoners: A sketch at Kilmainham Jail, Dublin'.
Illustrated London News, 5 November 1881.

8 'The Irish Land League: Recreation time in Kilmainham Prison'. *Illustrated London News*, 12 November 1881.

9　The grave of Charles Stewart Parnell, Glasnevin Cemetery, Dublin. Photograph: Pauric Travers.

10   The grave of Katharine Parnell,
Littlehampton, Sussex.
Photograph: Pauric Travers.

11   The grave of Claude Sophie O'Shea
(Parnell) Catholic Church, Chislehurst, Kent.
Claude Sophie was born on 16 February 1882
while her father Charles Stewart Parnell
was in Kilmainham. She died on 21 April 1882.
Photograph: Pauric Travers.

12   The grave of Fanny Parnell, Mount Auburn cemetery, Boston, Massachusetts.
Photograph: Brian Coleman.

13   The grave of Anna Parnell, cemetery of Holy Trinity Church, Ilfracombe, Devon.
Photograph: Pauric Travers.

with her. But release from Kilmainham had to be on terms that he would decide were politically honourable and advantageous. Her influence, in so far as it affected the situation, was indirect, and probably a good deal less than she thought. In reality, therefore, her concern for him only confirmed his resolve to bring the Land War to an end so that he could concentrate on Home Rule.

Parnell wanted the 'extremists' and the Ladies' Land League off his back. And in this Katharine was only echoing his views when she described the Ladies' Land League as 'this wild army of mercenaries'. She wrote: 'The fanatic spirit in these ladies was extreme; in Anna Parnell it was abnormal, and Parnell saw no way of saving her, or the country from her folly but by . . . vetoing the payment of another penny to the Ladies' Land League.'[45]

Between the Kilmainham Treaty of 1882 and Gladstone's conversion to Home Rule in 1885 Katharine was the secret and crucial link between Parnell and Gladstone. Gladstone, who had his own right-wing critics to contend with, could not afford to be seen to negotiate openly with Parnell, but he was prepared to consider Parnell's stipulations and submissions presented to him through Katharine. This gave rise to the rather bizarre situation in which Parnell would address a letter to Mrs O'Shea outlining his position; she would enclose the letter for Gladstone, meet him to deliver it, or write apprising him of Parnell's views. Gladstone's response would be in the form of comments made to her. It was not unlike the household in which the parents are not on speaking terms but communicate through the children in each other's presence. Clearly, Gladstone accepted Katharine's claim that Parnell trusted and confided in her alone, and as she said, the GOM always sent her away with the feeling that she was 'a compelling force in the great game of politics' and worthy of the place she held.[46] Essentially, however, she was Parnell's messenger – loyal, efficient and enthusiastic about her role – but still only the messenger.

For very different reasons Katharine was also continuing to work for O'Shea's political ambitions. The Captain was full of his own importance, and of the part he had played in the Kilmainham Treaty and generally in Anglo-Irish relations. Since County Clare would not have him again, he felt that Parnell owed him a safe nationalist seat. But the party leaders were against his nomination since he refused to take the party pledge. Katharine, possibly to keep him busy in politics and away from Eltham, and to ward off the consequences of the political bitterness he was expressing to her about Parnell, pulled every considerable string available to her, to have him returned in the 1885 general election.

For a woman who had claimed to be non-political, she now engaged in the most hectic politicking to have her husband re-elected. Behind all her frenzy, however, one can detect the brain and hand of her lover. Since the Home Rulers did not want to touch O'Shea, the attempt was made by Katharine and Parnell to find him a seat for the Liberals, first in Ulster and then in Liverpool. Katharine badgered Gladstone and the chief whip of the Liberal Party until they consented to recommend O'Shea's nomination. All her determined efforts, however, would not have moved Gladstone and company without the wheeling and dealing about constituencies, and threats about the Irish vote which Parnell had authorised her to make in her approach to the Liberal leaders.

Defeated for Liverpool, but by a very narrow margin, O'Shea next insisted that Parnell support him in the by-election for Galway. Parnell's lieutenants understood that O'Shea was being put forward because he was the husband of Parnell's mistress. Biggar and Healy, however, were the last to hold out against the leader who could now claim to have Home Rule within his grasp. Biggar drafted a telegram to Parnell which said bluntly: 'Mrs O'Shea will be your ruin'.[47] Healy toned it down to read: 'The O'Sheas will be your ruin'. Healy was right. For on her own Mrs O'Shea would have cared nothing about who was elected for Galway, if her husband had not earlier written to her when he felt that Parnell was not doing enough for his re-election that he would 'send a blackguard's reputation into smithereens'.[48] Some of Parnell's colleagues certainly believed that O'Shea was quite capable of political blackmail. Katharine's role in all of this effort to have O'Shea re-elected had Parnell's full backing. They were in on it together in their attempt to neutralise the dangers to both emanating from O'Shea.

Parnell won the battle against his colleagues. O'Shea was returned for Galway and Parnell had shown himself at the peak of his control over the party. But by imposing his lover's husband on Galway, for whatever reason, the war against his leadership was only beginning for Healy and others. Parnell's very private affair with Mrs O'Shea was now seen by his lieutenants to have impinged on his public life, raised questions about his political judgement and the abuse of power, and, if only tentatively for the moment, brought into the reckoning the whole issue of morality in public life.

All of these matters came to a head four years later when the sensational details of the divorce case hit the headlines. Katharine and Charles, in order to be free at last to marry, offered no defence. Parnell was destroyed politically. And Katharine was depicted in England and Ireland as the woman whose fatal attraction had brought about his downfall. She was dubbed 'the were-wolf of Irish politics', and the 'Uncrowned Queen of Ireland'. [49]

A popular novel of Queen Victoria's day was entitled: *She who must be obeyed*. The pronunciation of O'Shea in England was O'Shee. One English journal carried the headline: 'O'Shea who must be obeyed'. [50] Gladstone, who had dealt with Katharine and could claim to have some knowledge of her, remarked on how Parnell was like a bit of wax in the hands of a woman.[51] But Gladstone, like so many contemporaries, was being unfair to Katharine while underestimating Parnell's role. Gladstone was right if all he meant was that Parnell was madly in love with her, and she with him. But he was wrong if what he implied was that she determined his politics. For she had no politics but his on the land question and Home Rule; and they thought and acted as one on all issues relating to politics. It was a unity that had been consolidated over the years of their secret life together. The deep personal relationship between them had at times distracted him from politics; at times, even, made him think of abandoning politics. But whatever her indirect influence, the political decisions were always his – not hers – in the end.

Without regard for chivalry or accuracy, the anti-Parnellites blamed her for everything. For many of them she was 'The Englishwoman' – and that said it all. The name by which she had never been known was grafted on to her: 'Kitty', a nickname for the Victorian woman of easy morals. Tim Healy had a field day. The green flag of Ireland, he said, was to be replaced with a new banner made out of Mrs O'Shea's petticoat.[52] After Parnell and Katharine were married in a registry office, Healy described the marriage as 'legalised concubinage'.[53] But the worst thing he called her was 'a proved British prostitute'.[54] 'What had changed Mr Parnell from the leader Ireland had known to the present despicable specimen of humanity?' he asked. And answered his own question: 'One bad, base, immoral woman?'[55] The animosity he bore her was still palpable nearly 40 years later when, as Governor General of the Irish Free State, he published his *Letters and Leaders of My Day*.[56]

There is no doubt that in Parnell's struggle for political survival, the woman he loved was his Achilles heel. And the scorn and ridicule to which he was subjected on her account were a major weapon in his defeat.

I think it could be said that Parnell had not been particularly blessed among women. On the other hand, tragic or sad endings awaited all of the women whose lives he had closely touched. Delia, aged 82, was sitting alone at a fire after breakfast in Avondale when her clothes caught fire and she died of shock and burns. Fanny, not yet 34, had died at the height of her fame. Anna at 59 living under an assumed name in lodgings and in straitened circumstances in a seaside town in North Devon was drowned and followed to her grave by seven strangers. And Katharine, born into a mansion, passed through periods of deep depression during her long widowhood, and died unknown in a terraced house in Littlehampton.

Delia, Fanny, Anna and Katharine, each in her own way, had contributed to Parnell's political and personal career. From his mother he had received, if not his anti-English feeling, at least his American inheritance which was a highly significant factor both in the formation of his personality and for the advancement of his political career. He was nearest to Fanny in his brand of nationalism, while lacking her poetic romanticism. Anna had all of his political drive, but pushed his radicalism to extremes beyond his own. And

Katharine O'Shea gave him all the domestic comfort and support he needed to sustain his struggle.

All four had supported his Land and Home Rule agitations: the mother by her well-intentioned public appearances; the sisters by their efficient organisation and administration of the Ladies' Land League; and Katharine by being his only trusted and loyal confidante. Their various contributions had been made possible only under the aegis of Parnell's political umbrella. And with Parnell gone their immediate political importance also rapidly declined and disappeared.

But in the long winding road of history they were to escape from underneath Parnell's umbrella, and leave their own significant mark on the feminist future and the liberation of women. Despite my title, they cannot be simply classified as Parnell's women – as mere appendages. They were women who had defied convention; made pioneering inroads into male monopoly of political and public life; and proclaimed their own individual identities. In Anna's case she had defied ecclesiastical condemnation of women operating outside the home; and in Katharine's case of women operating outside marriage. They had upheld the rights of minorities and established themselves as martyrs and role models for later generations. In short, they have deserved to be remembered, not only for their association with Parnell, but for themselves alone. They are especially worthy of being remembered by the Parnell Society.

'Under the Great Comedian's Tomb'

The Funeral of Charles Stewart Parnell

Pauric Travers

Death, Oliver MacDonagh once wrote, is a towering element in Irish life. He was referring among other things to the preoccupation of the nationalist movement with death and the dead generations. For MacDonagh, this was part of a characteristic Irish habit of mind which views the past in a non-linear and inter-active manner as almost continuously present.[1] None of this is unique to Ireland or Irish nationalism. The rise of nationalism throughout Europe from the late eighteenth century is closely associated with the linking of tradition and heritage with the political project of nation building. Building, rediscovering, imagining or inventing the nation required a creative inter-linking of past, present and future in which ceremonials, rituals and commemorations played an important role. The ceremonials, rituals and commemorations which are in question here are those associated with political funerals and, in particular, that of Charles Stewart Parnell.[2]

Parnell died suddenly in Brighton on 6 October 1891 and was buried five days later in Glasnevin. His funeral was one of the largest and most impressive political demonstrations in Ireland in the nineteenth century. The *Irish Times* conceded that Dublin had seen 'a number of monster funeral processions but none which exceeded in significance' that of Parnell or 'left behind impressions more profound'.[3] It was an event of considerable significance in Irish politics but also in Irish social and cultural life. W. B. Yeats who attended the funeral and wrote a moving poem published at the time in *United Ireland* clearly sensed that Parnell after his death would continue to have a significant influence:

> Mourn – and then onward, there is no returning
> He guides you from the tomb;
> His memory now is a tall pillar, burning
> Before us in the gloom.[4]

In his Nobel speech in December 1923, Yeats traced much of the cultural upheaval of the intervening years to Parnell's death.[5] The traumatic experience of the Parnellite split and the fall and death of Parnell climaxed in a funeral which deeply entrenched the psychological impact on the generation which followed. This essay will examine the funeral of Parnell as a public demonstration and will set it in the wider context of similar funerals in the nineteenth century.

The nineteenth-century tradition of public funerals as significant social, cultural and political demonstrations began in Ireland with the interment of Daniel O'Connell. O'Connell's funeral became and remained the prototype for such events including the lying in state and elaborate funeral procession to Prospect Cemetery, Glasnevin via circuitous route and accompanied by rich ceremonial and symbolism. Given that he was a founder of the Dublin Cemeteries Committee and instrumental in the opening of Glasnevin in 1832, it was appropriate that O'Connell should be buried there. Glasnevin quickly became the Catholic necropolis and the Irish equivalent of Westminster Abbey. In its first century, there were over 640,000 burials; more significantly, with few exceptions, major nineteenth-century political figures were buried there. The funerals of O'Connell, Terence Bellew MacManus, Charles Stewart Parnell and Jeremiah O'Donovan Rossa were the most important such occasions which provide an illuminating window on Irish politics and society.[6]

The death of a leader will normally generate private and public grief. It may also unleash other emotions and spark or add fuel to succession or legacy politics in the immediate and long term. The induction of the lost leader into the pantheon of fallen heroes inevitably inaugurates or foreshadows challenges for the right to inherit the mantle and maintain the shrine. Patrick Pearse went to the heart of the matter in his graveside oration at the funeral of O'Donovan Rossa in 1915: 'Life springs from death; and from the graves of patriot men and women spring living nations'.[7] This is a dynamic, iterative and, often, a contested process which is manifest in rituals, ceremonies, processions and subsequent commemorations. All of this is evident in the great public funerals of the nineteenth century and especially Parnell's.

The emotion generated by Parnell's death owed much to intensity of feeling created by the Parnellite split.[8] While Parnell may not have been at the height of his power at the time of the divorce crisis, as he liked to suggest, his leadership of his party and of nationalist Ireland was unchallenged. His vindication by the *Times* commission left him well placed in the event of a liberal return to power. Then, on Christmas Eve, 1889, Captain William O'Shea filed a petition for divorce from his estranged wife, Katharine, citing Parnell as co-respondent. The case which was not defended was finally resolved the following November, with O'Shea being granted his divorce and Parnell stigmatised as the guilty party. Parnell and Katharine were free to marry which they did on 25 June 1891.

In the meantime, Parnell was engaged in a struggle for his political life. The lurid if misleading picture which emerged from the newspaper accounts damaged Parnell's reputation and political standing. Nevertheless a direct challenge to his leadership was slow in coming. The day after the divorce decree (and eleven months after the matter became public) his leadership was warmly endorsed at a meeting of the National League in Dublin. Justin McCarthy, shortly to lead the anti-Parnellite faction, proposed and Timothy Healy seconded a motion declaring that in all political matters Parnell commanded the confidence of the nation. Parnell was unanimously re-elected chairman of the Irish Party on 25 November. The lack of a challenge to Parnell until Gladstone indicated that the Irish Party must choose between Parnell and Home Rule points to the simple conclusion that the Grand Old Man's intervention was decisive.[9] That forced the issue and, all attempts at compromise having failed, culminated in the infamous Committee Room 15 debates of 1–6 December, when the Irish Party split (45 to 27) into anti- and pro-Parnell factions.

The split in the party quickly became a split in the country as Parnell appealed to the grassroots. Most of the senior members of his party deserted Parnell and the full influence of the Catholic Church was also mobilised against him. Parnell commanded strongest support among the young and the working class in the larger towns and cities, especially Dublin – a point of some significance in the context of his funeral. The IRB, the GAA and the incipient cultural nationalist movement rallied to his side. In the course of a spirited but often violent campaign, Parnell sought to mobilise radical opinion. In a manifesto to the Irish people he appealed against being 'thrown to the English wolves now howling for my destruction'. On 16 December, at Castlecomer, he had lime thrown in his eyes by a hostile crowd. In the event, his green card was trumped by a combination of pragmatic, agrarian and clerical politics. Parnellite candidates were defeated in bitter by-election contests in North Kilkenny, Sligo and Carlow. Against the advice of his doctor, Parnell continued an exhausting campaign. At Creggs, on 27 September 1891, in his last public speech, delivered in the pouring rain, he could not conceal the state of his health:

> If I had taken the advice of my doctor, I should have gone to bed when I arrived in Dublin ... but if I had done that my enemies would be throwing up their hats, and announcing that I was dead before I was buried.[10]

Nine days later he died in the arms of his beloved Katharine.

The suddenness of Parnell's death caused a sensation. The *Freeman's Journal* declared that the unexpected news 'fell on Ireland like a stunning blow, producing stupor, amazement and consternation'.[11] Most of his colleagues were unaware that he was ill, leading a Press Association reporter to comment mischievously that he had been in the habit of keeping his affairs to himself.[12] The *Irish Times* reported crowds arguing on every street corner in Dublin and waiting for news outside newspaper offices. A delay in the announcement of the cause of death added to the generally tense atmosphere and provoked considerable speculation. Despite the holding of a post-mortem, rumours persisted. Dr Reginald Jowers who attended Parnell initially refused to comment publicly and then pronounced the cause of death as heart failure due to rheumatic fever. The death certificate signed by his father, F. W. Jowers cited 'rheumatic fever five days, hyperpyrexia, failure of the heart's action'. The Press Association reported a story that Parnell had cancer of the stomach; another rumour suggested that he had committed suicide; while, in the fashion of the fallen hero, it was also widely reported that he was not dead at all but had gone to start a new life.[13]

There was a widespread regret at Parnell's death but that was as far as the agreement extended. The nationalist *Cork Examiner* unavailingly called for no hard words to be spoken or stones cast at the memory of a man who, 'whatever his faults, had been for a number of dreary years our foremost champion in the cause of Ireland and Irishmen'.[14] The liberal *Sheffield Independent* could not resist articulating what good taste prevented other opponents of Parnell from uttering – that it would not 'be deterred by conventionalism from saying that nothing in Mr Parnell's life became him like leaving it. His death . . . is the best service and reparation he could make to his country'.[15] The *Irish Catholic* was even less forgiving and anxious to pronounce the death of Parnellism as well as Parnell:

> How far his name may yet be used as a rallying cry for treachery and for faction it is now impossible to say. The evil that men do lives after them, and the weeds which grow upon the grave of a dead cause are rank and noxious. We have no fear that those which will spring from the tomb of Parnellism will be able to thwart the course of Ireland unto freedom. Her feet are strong enough to tread down the miserable tangles of an unholy and unblessed growth.[16]

The Parnellite *United Ireland* accused his opponents of being responsible for Parnell's death:

> They have killed him – under God today we do solemnly believe that they have killed him, the greatest son of Banba. So far as in us lies we shall burn into their souls morn and night, in good or ill, come weal or woe, that they have driven to his grave, in the strength and glory of his manhood, a son of Ireland, truer than Tone, abler than Grattan, greater than O'Connell, full of love for us as Davis himself.[17]

Nor were these isolated sentiments. At a special meeting of Dublin Corporation called to discuss the funeral arrangements, anti-Parnellites were greeted with loud hisses by the gallery and wisely decided to support a motion of sympathy. John Dillon was accosted near Westland Row station by men shouting 'murderer'. An inquiry by the Press Association as to what might happen if anti-Parnellite MPs attended the funeral evoked the response that it would be 'a very risky thing for them to do. An Irish crowd was apt to be very hasty and the presence on such an occasion of anti-Parnellite members of parliament might lead to scandalous scenes being enacted.' Hardly surprisingly, they chose to stay away, although the appearance of one anti-Parnellite MP in College Green half an hour before the funeral procession passed caused quite a stir. [18]

One of the many wreaths sent to City Hall summed up the mood of some of Parnell's supporters. From the Belfast Parnell Leadership Committee came a 'remarkable work of floral architecture' composed of lilies of the Nile, violets and geraniums in the shape of a shield on which was depicted the red hand of Ulster. On the top, depicted in violets was the word 'Murdered' and on the bottom, in red flowers, the word 'AVENGE'. These words were removed on the instructions of John Redmond. Another wreath, from the Dublin GAA County Board, carried two inscriptions – one bore the message 'In memory of our dear departed Chief'; the other, less conventionally read 'An eye for an eye, a tooth for a tooth.' [19]

Parnell's body was one worth fighting for. As soon as he died, those of his colleagues who were in London, notably John Redmond, Henry Harrison, Joseph Nolan, Pierce O'Mahony and J. J. O'Kelly, rushed to Brighton to take control. They were facilitated by the fact that Katharine Parnell was prostrate with grief and disinclined to make any decisions, while Parnell's family was scattered across two continents. One immediate consequence was that they were able to convey to the press Parnell's dying words, which were, they claimed, 'Give my Love to my Colleagues and to the Irish People'. When Parnell's body lay in state in City Hall in Dublin, the following Sunday, these words were emblazoned on the walls. The message touched the public imagination (as no doubt it was intended to) and quickly found its way on to commemorative wreaths and medallions. Dr Jowers was cited as the source of this dying message but it seems unlikely that Parnell said anything of the sort to a physician who was not a close acquaintance . This was later supported by Katharine who was with Parnell throughout his last hours. Parnell, she said, was incapable of an affectation so complete. Instead, she insisted, his last words were 'Kiss Me, Sweet Wifie, and I will try to sleep a little.'[20]

A more serious dispute arose over where and how Parnell should be buried. Katharine's desire was for a private funeral but she was prevailed upon by his colleagues to allow them to organise a public funeral in Dublin. It was they who chose Glasnevin, because, as they explained, it was there 'so many of the noblest names of Irish history lie buried'. [21] Katharine, who did not attend the funeral, reluctantly agreed. Parnell's mother, Delia, and brother, John Howard, were in the United States and in no position to intervene. His sister Emily (Mrs Dickinson), who travelled to Brighton, acquiesced but later complained bitterly of being prevented by his colleagues from seeing her brother's body. [22] Henry Parnell, three other sisters, Anna, Theodosia (Mrs Paget) and Sophia (Mrs MacDermott) and Sophia's husband favoured Mount Jerome in Harold's Cross as the most appropriate resting place. In a powerful letter to The *Irish Times*, Anna voiced the anger of the Parnell family that their clear preference was ignored. She dismissed the argument of his colleagues that the body belonged to Ireland and that the people of Ireland demanded that Parnell be buried at Glasnevin: she observed acerbically that the claim that her brother's body belonged to the Irish people was true 'only if their having killed him gave them title to it'. [23]

The Parnells did have traditional ties with Mount Jerome – they had a family plot there in which Parnell's father was buried. Also, Thomas Davis was buried in Mount Jerome which meant that it was not without significance for the nationalist movement. However, the main objection to Glasnevin was that it was perceived as being primarily a Catholic cemetery. While this may have been true in theory, provision was made for the burial of non-Catholics and large numbers of Protestants were buried there. Henry Harrison rejected the suggestion that Glasnevin was 'an exclusively sectarian cemetery' and added that it was widely felt that so long as Parnell lay among his own countrymen 'he would not have raised the question of their creed'. [24] The first significant political funeral to Glasnevin was that of John Philpot Curran, leading Protestant patriot and father of Sarah, Emmet's betrothed. Curran died in London in 1817 but, on the initiative of the Cemeteries Committee, his remains were removed to Glasnevin in 1834 and an impressive memorial erected. Later one of Curran's sons became a member of the committee. Nonetheless, Glasnevin continued to be identified as a Catholic cemetery and the decision to bury Parnell there was unusual, not least – and this lay at the root of the family's unease – as the Catholic hierarchy had played a key part in his downfall.

The absence of any formal ceremony in England is remarkable. Parnell's supporters there proposed that a ceremony and procession be organised in London but this was overruled. The organisers were keen to avoid public displays of any sort in England, so around midday on Saturday 10 October the body was moved quietly and more quickly than originally intended by train from Brighton to Clapham Junction and from there to Willesden Junction where it was placed on the 6.30 p.m. Euston to Holyhead boat train. At Clapham, an Irish woman with a baby in her arms approached the funeral party with a little bunch of white flowers which were placed on the coffin alongside the numerous other wreaths. These included a wreath from Katharine with a card carrying the message 'To my love, my dear husband, my king, from his heart-broken wife'. A large crowd gathered at Willesden, mainly London-based supporters of Parnell and representatives of Irish organisations in Britain. Mr Cunninghame-Graham was the only British MP noted as being present. The remains were kept on the train but the top of the wooden case was removed to reveal the coffin and, while John O'Connor MP, Joseph Nolan MP and Henry Harrison MP kept guard at the door, some but not all of the crowd were allowed file through the van.[25] The train then departed for Holyhead. Redmond and his colleagues accompanied by Parnell's brother, H. T. Parnell, and sister, Mrs Dickinson, travelled in a saloon carriage adjoining the remains.

Meanwhile, in Dublin, a number of Parnellite MPs and their supporters made hasty arrangements for what they assumed would be a public funeral to Glasnevin. The agreement of the Corporation was secured for a public lying in state at City Hall – O'Connell, a former Lord Mayor, in contrast had lain in state at the Pro-Cathedral while Bellew MacManus, due to clerical opposition, had lain in state at the Mechanics Institute. It was agreed that the Lord Mayor and those aldermen who wished to do so should attend the funeral in full regalia.[26]

A deputation of Parnellite MPs consisting of Dr J. E. Kenny,[27] Timothy Harrington, Richard Power, J. J. Dalton and Patrick O'Brien was despatched to Glasnevin to choose a suitable plot. This was secured after some initial reticence on the part of the cemetery authorities. Mr Coyle, secretary of the Cemeteries Committee, had promised to place any site they might choose at their disposal but the matter had to be referred to the sub-committee of the Board which met weekly. This in turn found itself unable to authorise the site requested and a special general meeting of the Board had to be summoned for that purpose. The site chosen was a circular mound which had been the 'Poor Ground' and had been used for burial of victims of cholera and, later, of the famine. In the centre of the mound was a fir tree which had to be removed to make room for Parnell's grave. The location was well to the left of the 'new' cemetery entrance and the mortuary chapel and equidistant from the chapel and the original O'Connell circle. O'Connell's remains had been moved in 1869 and re-interred in a crypt at the foot of an imposing larger-than-life size replica round tower at the entrance to the cemetery. In death as in life, Parnell's footsteps were destined to be in the shadow of 'the great comedian'.[28]

On the Friday evening, placards headed 'Funeral of the Irish Chief' appeared throughout Dublin giving details of the arrangements and the order of procession. All persons wishing to participate were enjoined to wear an armlet of crape, fastened with a green ribbon. No other banners were to be carried. There was also an appeal that the procession should be orderly. The

Irish Times reported that over 200 pubs had indicated their intention to close and it was clear that other pubs and shops were expected to follow suit. The IRB was not officially involved in these preparations but Fenians certainly participated in the arrangements made by the Dublin GAA on the Friday before the funeral. A strong statement was issued, condemning the 'miscreants' and 'moral assassins' who opposed Parnell and describing the Chief as the 'only possible constitutional leader of an unconstitutionally governed race'. All GAA members attending the funeral were ordered to carry a draped 'camán' supplied by the County Board. Special trains were organised by the different railway companies to facilitate mourners wishing to travel from the provinces – in some but not all cases a single fare was charged for the return journey.[29]

Parnell's last crossing of the Irish sea was tempestuous – a gale was rising and for most of the journey the deck of the steamer, appropriately named *Ireland*, was at a sharp angle, making it difficult for the passengers to move about. A large crowd, among whom was W. B. Yeats, met the boat at Kingstown, early on Sunday morning, 11 October.[30] The remains were brought by train to Westland Row, arriving at 7.30 a.m. where they were met by a band and a crowd of about a thousand, mainly GAA members, who provided a guard of honour. The coffin of polished oak was removed from the deal case in which it had been placed for the journey[31] and draped in a large green flag. Led by a band playing the Dead March from *Saul*, and flanked by Parnellite MPs, the cortege proceeded through torrential rain to Dame Street. In one of its few original symbolic gestures, it halted at the old Houses of Parliament on College Green.[32] It then moved unexpectedly across the Liffey to St Michan's parish church where a short burial service was conducted by the Rev. Thomas Long, rector, assisted by Rev. George Frye, rector of All Soul's, Manchester. Apparently, it had not initially occurred to the Dublin organisers that the family might wish to have a Protestant religious service. The Parnells had an association with St Michan's – Parnell's grandfather and great grandfather were said to be buried there. It was also the burial place of the Sheares Brothers. Those present at the service were mainly close family members – Parnell's brother Henry, his sister Mrs Dickinson, his brother-in-law Albert McDermott, his nephew, Tudor McDermott and Miss Dickinson and Miss McDermott, nieces.

After the service, the remains were brought back across the Liffey to City Hall where huge crowds awaited. Elaborate preparations had been made. Outside, huge pieces of black fabric were draped across the pillars in imitation of the pantheon in Paris during the funeral of Gambetta.[33] Despite the best efforts of Mr Byrne of Henry Street, who was in charge of decorations, and the Dublin fire brigade who put them up, one observer commented that 'it could hardly be said that the effect was artistic' but it was 'eminently striking'. Inside, the central hall was draped ceiling to floor in black cloth with Parnell's 'last message to Ireland' in white drapery. Most striking of all was a huge floral Celtic cross presented by Parnell's colleagues. Also in a place of honour was a simple ivy wreath sent by a Cork woman as 'the best offering she could afford'. The catafalque was strategically placed in front of a large statue of O'Connell, the base of which was draped with the tattered colours of two regiments of Volunteers from Avondale, yet again linking the two great constitutional nationalist leaders. The body lay in state for just three hours. Organisers estimated that 30,000 people filed past the remains, which seems improbable, although the *Irish Times* did admit that the crowds were so big that most people did not even see the coffin but only the floral cross and O'Connell's statue.[34]

Last respects paid, the hearse moved off, flanked by Parnellite MPs and GAA men with draped hurleys, followed by two family carriages; the officiating clergy; the Fenians James Stephens, John O'Leary and P. N. Fitzgerald; St James Brass Band; the City Marshal, Mr John Carroll, on horseback; the brass band of York Street Working Men's Club; a carriage with Mace and Sword Bearers of the city; the Lord Mayor, Joseph Meade in his robes and chains of office accompanied by his chaplain, Rev Dr Malley, Westland Row; members of the Corporation and other corporations and numerous deputations from the trades, led by the Bridge Street bakers. Immediately behind the hearse was a riderless horse called Home Rule, supposedly Parnell's favourite, led by a groom. In the traditional gesture for a fallen leader, it was saddled with Parnell's riding boots reversed in the stirrups. The number of marchers in the procession was estimated at between 20,000 and 40,000, i.e. roughly the same size as Terence Bellew MacManus's funeral, although the London *Times* claimed that it was the biggest funeral since O'Connell's.[35] It took an hour and three quarters to pass Kingsbridge Station and just over three hours to reach Glasnevin. It was, one observer commented, 'a remarkable demonstration . . . not a straggly crowd after a hearse – it was, for the most part, a six-men-abreast body of followers who marched through a lane, the hedges of which were formed on each side by a multitude wearing mourning badges.'[36] Most newspapers commented on the orderliness of the proceedings and the predominance of ordinary Dublin workers in the procession.

The most noticeable absence was that of Catholic clergy. It was widely claimed that there was not a single priest present, prompting Joseph West Ridgeway, under-secretary for Ireland, to claim that 'Parnell dead has done what Parnell living could not do. He has struck a staggering blow to priestly domination.'[37] The *Irish Ecclesiastical Gazette* boasted that it went without saying that 'no Roman Catholic clergymen were visible on Sunday'.[38] A partial exception was Rev P. J. Ryan of Carlow who telegraphed a message of sympathy: 'My heart is full of sorrow for our own dear brave Chief. God forgive Ireland for her part in the tragedy.'

The circuitous funeral route was in strict accordance with precedents for political funerals, particularly Bellew MacManus. To the accompaniment of bands (33 in all) playing 'Adeste Fidelis', 'Tantum Ergo' and the Dead March from *Saul*, the cortege proceeded along Thomas St stopping at St Catherine's Church on Thomas Street where Robert Emmet was executed – one newspaper explained that it had become 'a kind of Mecca for nationalists' – and at the scene of Lord Edward Fitzgerald's downfall; round by Kingsbridge, along the quays, across Grattan Bridge back along Dame Street where handbills headed 'Murdered' were distributed; across Carlisle bridge, past the impressive O'Connell monument on Sackville Street (another reminder of their shared legacies), past the site of the future Parnell monument, into Cavendish Row and Rutland Square and out to Glasnevin.[39] It was a sombre procession with few banners; as requested, many marchers and onlookers wore mourning badges or armbands. Despite or because of police guards on newspaper offices and other buildings associated with the anti-Parnellites in Prince's Street and Abbey Street, there were no serious incidents. Some interlopers tried to join the head of the procession but they were ejected by the stewards carrying hurleys. All commentators agreed that from beginning to end, 'no hitch occurred, no disturbance took place, no accident happened, and neither jarring note nor word of anger, nor imprecation was heard'.[40]

At the cemetery, such was the size of the crowd that hurleys had to be used to clear a way for the coffin. After the body was deposited, the funeral rites of the Church of Ireland were performed by Rev. Frye who read the first letter of Paul to the Thessalonians and Rev. Vincent, chaplain to the Rotunda. The latter had been asked to officiate by Dr Kenny on behalf of Parnell's family as their 'nearest Protestant neighbour' and did so with the consent of Archbishop Plunkett, Protestant Archbishop of Dublin. Even so, he felt the need to explain his actions to his congregation in terms of his 'Christian duty' adding that if he was chaplain to a jail he might be asked to read the service over the grave of one executed for murder.[41] After the funeral service, wreaths and flowers were placed on the coffin – the first being Katharine Parnell's – the grave was filled in and a final prayer said.

The dramatic impact of the funeral on observers was heightened by the inclement weather. It had rained heavily for most of the day – at Westland Row at 8.00 p.m. the mourners had stood bare headed in the 'pelting rain; at St Michan's, the 'rain poured and the wind blew so violently that it was hardly possible to hold an umbrella in the teeth of the gale'; those who marched behind the hearse on the journey to City Hall were drenched; and it rained intermittently on the final journey to Glasnevin although, by mid-afternoon, the weather had begun to brighten. Night was beginning to fall as the cortege reached the cemetery shortly after 5.15; the sky had cleared, giving way to a still, moonlit night. Shortly before 7.00 p.m. as the burial was concluding, a falling star lit up the night sky. This dramatic conclusion to a dramatic day inspired one of Yeats's greatest poems, 'Parnell's Funeral':[42]

> Under the Great Comedian's Tomb the crowd.
> A bundle of tempestuous cloud is blown
> About the sky; where that is clear of cloud
> Brightness remains; a brighter star shoots down;
> What shudders run through all that animal blood?
> What is this sacrifice? Can someone there
> Recall the Cretan barb that pierced a star?

Nineteenth-century Irish politics was dominated by two great figures, Daniel O'Connell and Charles Stewart Parnell, As Yeats hints, the ghost of Daniel O'Connell stalked Parnell's funeral – at City Hall, the coffin lay at the foot of O'Connell's statue; the procession which passed O'Connell's statue on Sackville Street, by and large followed a template first created for O'Connell's funeral; Parnell was laid to rest in a cemetery effectively established by O'Connell; and, in the ironic words of his biographer, R. Barry O'Brien, 'all that was mortal of Charles Stewart Parnell was laid in the grave, under the shadow of the tower which marks the spot where the greatest Irishman of the century – O'Connell – sleeps'.[43]

Parnell's funeral was impressive but, in many ways, it was more like Bellew MacManus's than O'Connell's, in that it was a sectional and largely secular event. O'Connell's funeral was organised by the Catholic Church and mobilised all sections of liberal, nationalist and Catholic opinion. The funeral and the subsequent commemorations served to assert O'Connell's Catholicism and his opposition to the physical force tradition. Bellew MacManus's re-interment in Glasnevin following his burial in California was a Fenian event condemned by the Church and viewed with unease by some of his former colleagues from the Young Ireland movement and, it would appear, some members of his family. As was intended, it gave an impetus to the Fenian movement. Parnell's funeral was, in effect, boycotted by the clergy and the majority wing of the constitutional nationalist movement. It was organised and attended by an alliance of Parnellites and radical nationalists and gave an impetus to both. However, that alliance did not outlive the reunification of the party in 1900 and Parnell's inheritance would be claimed by both constitutionalists and revolutionaries of all hues in the years that followed.[44] Finally, the funeral helped to enshrine the myth of Parnell as the fallen hero brought down by the bishops, perfidious Albion and disloyal colleagues. It confirmed an anti-clerical stream in Irish nationalist and literary circles and also, paradoxically, a distrust for parliamentarianism which was ultimately to prove fatal for Parnell's successors in the Irish Party.

CHAPTER 7

At the Graveside

Commemorative Orations

Donal McCartney

CHARLES STEWART PARNELL[1]

Anniversaries, like centenaries, can be dangerous occasions – especially in the hands of people who want to do more with them than merely commemorate the event or individual in question. Bodenstown Churchyard, described by Pearse as 'the holiest place in Ireland', holds a grave over which a number of political parties and factions wrangle annually for the bones of Wolfe Tone, each claiming him for its own. And echoes from the Civil War in which Michael Collins died may still be heard once a year in Béal na mBláth. What has been happening annually to Tone and Collins constitutes an abuse of history.

It is, therefore, a matter to be grateful for, and an occasion of congratulation to you, the members of the Parnell Commemoration Committee, that Parnell, at least, has been spared the fate of Tone and Collins. Unlike them, he has not become the plaything of political faction. Thanks to you, faithful Parnellites, who have been gathering round this grave since 1891, Parnell is still remembered for Parnell's sake alone; and not for his alleged paternity of any political faction or policy of today. You have kept his memory green. You have not tried to commandeer him for any party; nor have you contrived to make him fit into any contemporary political mould.

The function which your committee has performed with regard to Parnell is not unlike that which the historian performs for society. The historian has a duty to resist the encroachment of faction on history. To him the past is sacred. It is not a quarry out of which a supply of arguments is to be drawn. Part of the historian's role is to safeguard the past from exploitation by propagandists. Wherever he finds propaganda masquerading as history it is his duty to unmask it. The historian examines the past in the context of the past, for the sake of understanding it; and not for any ulterior political objectives, however close those objectives might be to his own heart.

This commemoration of Parnell, for Parnell's own sake, is therefore only as it should be; for Parnell belongs to the Nation, and not to any single party within it. He is not the grandfather of Fianna Fáil, despite Mr de Valera's sincere admiration for him; or despite his place in Irish history as the inventor of the modern party machine. He is not the grand-uncle of Fine Gael, despite Arthur Griffith's loyalty to him; or despite the essential constitutionalism of his political stance. He is not the ancestor of the Labour Party, despite his successful operation of the boycott and rent-strike, and his championing of the cause of the peasants against the landlords. He is not the godfather of the men of violence, despite Pearse's naming him alongside Tone, Mitchel and Lalor as one of the great 'holy-haters' of the connection with England. He is a man for all Ireland; for it was he, who in the New Departure linked together all the nationalist forces under his own guiding hand.[2]

The year of 1982 produced a rich crop of centenaries: de Valera, Joyce, Sean T. Ó Ceallaigh, Pádraig Ó Conaire. It was also the centenary of the Phoenix Park murders, and of the founding of Parnell's Irish National League. The assassination of Cavendish and Burke in the Phoenix Park on 6 May 1882 was a severe shock to Parnell. It had, in one terrible hour, subdued his spirit in a way that the whole British Administration never had. The weapon which he had used so effectively, namely, the threat of revolutionary violence, which only he could restrain, had exploded in his hands. The manifesto condemning the deed and expressing the feeling of horror which it excited was signed by Parnell, Davitt and Dillon. It called upon the whole Irish people to show the world by their attitude and action that assassination was 'deeply and religiously abhorrent to their every feeling and instinct'.[3] Parnell stood uncompromisingly against violence, despite the attempt of political enemies to identify him with the Invincibles. In a hostile House of Commons, speaking, as he said, on behalf of every Irishman in whatever part of the world he might live, he expressed his 'unqualified detestation of the horrible crime'.[4]

It was this single act of political violence in the Phoenix Park which made Parnell lose his nerve and his sure political touch momentarily, and for the first and only time in his career. And when he had recovered his political balance, he set about the establishment of the Irish National League, the inaugural meeting of which was held one hundred years ago this very month. The Irish National League was Parnell's substitute for the proscribed Land League. It allowed him to detach the national movement from too close a link with secret societies and agrarian revolution and commit it instead to constitutional objectives. The National League provided Parnell with a united and well-disciplined organisation such as the country had never seen before; and it gave him the most formidable parliamentary army that Ireland ever sent into the House of Commons. With his Parliamentary Party of more than eighty members, Parnell so manipulated the political situation at Westminster, that the Liberals committed themselves to Home Rule, and the Tories to the better government of Ireland. Parnell's ascendancy over his party was extraordinary. There had never been anything like it, said Gladstone, in his sixty years of experience in politics.[5]

Parnell, in his all too short career, showed himself to be a constitutional revolutionary. He was the greatest political acrobat in Irish history, performing an amazing balancing act between republican and agrarian revolutionary supporters on the left, and constitutional, conservative supporters on the right. Everything about the 'uncrowned king' was majestic; including the fall. When, eventually, he fell from his tightrope, Samson Agonistes that he was, he brought down the whole edifice with him. The national coalition he had built up split into its elemental parts. They were never to be brought together again. The IRB went its own secret way, only to re-emerge in Easter 1916. The constitutionalists were discredited, and split into Parnellites and anti-Parnellites. The younger generation turned in disgust from politics to Irish-Ireland. Parnell's fall was a tragedy, not only for Ireland, but also for Anglo-Irish relations; and its reverberations were felt throughout the British Empire.

It is a matter of deep satisfaction that no party has ever captured the dead Chief. He remains the historic conscience of our people, ever reminding the doctrinaire among us, that 'no man has the right to set bounds to the march of a nation'. And no party has the right to impose its own limitations on the great, free spirit of Parnell.

KATHARINE PARNELL[6]

Here, in this grave, lie the remains of one who aroused more hatred than perhaps any other woman in the whole of Irish history.

Katharine Wood, to give this woman her maiden name, was the daughter of the Rev. Sir John Page Wood, former chaplain to Queen Caroline.[7] Her mother, Emma Michell, was a novelist, watercolour artist and book illustrator. One of her grandfathers was twice Lord Mayor of London. The other grandfather was Commander-in-Chief of the Portuguese navy during the Napoleonic wars. She had an uncle, Baron Hatherley, who was Lord Chancellor in Gladstone's first ministry. Another uncle was an Admiral in the British navy. One of Katharine's sisters was a prolific popular song writer of the day.[8] Another sister was a novelist.[9] A brother became Field Marshal Sir Evelyn Wood, VC.

Katharine, the youngest of this well-known and highly respected family, was destined to become the most notorious of them all. At 22 she was married to Captain O'Shea. By the time she met Parnell, 13 years later, her marriage to the Captain had long since grown cold; and they were in effect living separate lives. Marriage to one Irishman was a charade. To fall in love with a second Irishman spelt tragedy.

'The O'Sheas will be your ruin' was the warning telegraphed to Parnell by a colleague[10] four years before the O'Shea divorce scandal did indeed dethrone the Uncrowned King of Ireland. The ensuing struggle for political survival cost Parnell his life. The once powerful party which he had controlled was shattered into Parnellites and anti-Parnellites. And Home Rule, which he claimed to have in the hollow of his hand, was destroyed – and destroyed for ever.

To find a scapegoat for the crisis that now engulfed Irish politics, anti-Parnellites fastened ungallantly on the woman at the heart of this hapless triangle. To make the charges stick, she had to be demonised and exhibited as the scarlet woman. On the personal level, she was looked upon as the adulteress – with all of the opprobrium which that word then conveyed in Victorian Britain and Catholic Ireland.

The nationalist press could hardly find words damning enough to express its moral outrage. She was denounced as the faithless wife, a woman of loose morals. 'Degraded', 'disgraced', 'shameless', 'abandoned', 'wretched' were some of the epithets used to describe her.

With Tim Healy vituperation reached its most scurrilous depths. According to him, she was the *mistress* of the party; and her petticoat had become the new flag of Ireland. And it was he who labelled her 'Kitty' – a pet name for the Victorian prostitute – suggesting purring and petting but also sharp hostile claws.[11] Less than a month after Parnell's death he called Parnell's widow 'a proved British prostitute'. And a few days later repeated the charge. There was not then, nor has there been found since, any evidence whatsoever for these outrageous allegations.

On the political level, she was portrayed as the woman who had brought about Parnell's downfall, along with all of its dire consequences for Ireland. Among the more suspicious minded of the anti-Parnellites she was even accusesd of being an English spy. In Healy's eyes she was simply 'a bad woman, who hates Ireland, who cares nothing for Ireland'. And Parnell, he said, had become rotten to the core, worm-eaten by the canker called Kitty O'Shea.

Anti-Parnellite newspapers took up the attack, one of them proclaiming: 'This woman darkened the brightest page of Irish history; she wrecked the career of the most successful of Irish leaders; and plunged a united country into dissension.'[12] Her dark and ominous personality, it was said, lay at the root of all the trouble. Parnell and his Parnellites simply followed the whip of Mrs O'Shea. 'That bitch, that English whore did for him', says a character in Joyce's *Ulysses*.[13] It summed up the distrust and hatred that possessed anti-Parnellites for the woman at the centre of the political storm.[14]

The conviction that she had been a huge and evil influence on Parnell's politics, however widespread among those antagonistic to Parnell, was also very wide of the mark. Of course, during the eleven years of their intense love-affair, she had been his sole confidante. Sometimes, indeed, she was his messenger carrying his proposals to Gladstone. But she was never his political mentor. Ultimately, the political decisions remained always his, and his alone. Or, as he once said to her: 'My life I give to Ireland, but to you I give my love.'[15] And these are the very words you will find on the plaque which we have placed here to commemorate the visit of the Parnell Society to Katharine's grave.

The frenzy of the attacks on her supposed political dominance over Parnell was extraordinary. The language used against her held echoes of the witch-hunts of the past. She was called the English she-wolf; and the were-wolf of Irish politics. And there was reference by a cleric to her 'fatal witchery'.[16] Her registry office marriage to Parnell was called a 'pagan ceremony'; and 'sacrilege added to adultery'. In the words of Bishop O'Donnell: it was the 'climax of brazen horrors'.[17] Uncrowned Queen of Ireland, Katharine never was.

Witch-hunts were never separate from the social and religious context of their time. In late nineteenth-century Ireland sins of the flesh – Thou shalt not commit adultery; Thou shalt not covet thy neighbour's wife – had become an obsession with the clergy, and with our lay spiritual police. In that environment it was easy to regard the fallen woman, with such supposed evil influence on Ireland, as the Witch of Eltham or, in Healy's phrase, the Brighton Banshee. Unfortunately, a peasantry that was involved in the burning of Bridget Cleary in Tipperary as late as 1895 because they believed her to be a fairy changeling could readily be persuaded that Katharine O'Shea was, indeed, some kind of witch or banshee.[18]

Witches, however, were always invented by communities who needed to absolve themselves. The puritanical among Catholics in Ireland and Non-conformists in Britain found their sacrificial lamb in Katharine O'Shea. She was made the scapegoat for the power-struggles, personality clashes and faction-fighting as well as for the social, religious and anti-English prejudices of the political and clerical majority. And she was adapted as the most devastating weapon in the offensive against Parnell.

The viciousness of the assault on Katharine O'Shea's moral character and political motivation is one of the most distasteful episodes in our history. She was, perhaps, no saint. But she was a martyr: a martyr in the sense that she was more the victim of Irish politics than the origin and cause of our political miseries.

In the end, she was also the saddest case of all involved in the Parnell tragedy. She had lost her reputation. She had lost her man in his struggle for political survival. The money left to her by wealthy Aunt Ben she was forced to share with her own avaricious siblings and with Captain O'Shea. She lost Avondale to Parnell's brother. And what money she had left, she lost when she became the victim of embezzlement by a speculating solicitor and through bad investment. Was it any wonder, then, that over her thirty years of widowhood she was periodically to lose her mind too?

She was unfortunate in the era in which she lived. A century later she could have openly accompanied her Irish political leader wherever, and been received the world over as his devoted partner. She who had spent her youth in a mansion of some forty rooms, died in a small rented terraced house, nursed in her last illness by the ever faithful daughter, Norah O'Shea. It was Norah who erected this tombstone. And although Norah, like her father, the Captain, was a Roman Catholic, she, unlike so many in Ireland, most honourably refers to her mother as the widow of Charles Stewart Parnell. Less than two-and-half years later, Norah was interred in this same grave.

I fancy that if Katharine's spirit had a choice of what words might be spoken around her grave she might well choose lines written for her by Parnell himself. One day she was sitting on the doorstep of their new home. Parnell was digging in the garden. Suddenly he stopped and threw himself down beside her. He asked for pencil and paper and wrote the following:

> The grass shall cease to grow,
> The river's stream to run,
> The stars shall ponder in their course,
> No more shall shine the sun;
> The moon shall never wane or grow,
> The tide shall cease to ebb and flow,
> Ere I shall cease to love you.

Not great poetry, perhaps. But the sentiment, she said, meant more to her than anything written by any poet that had ever graced the world with song.

There was a time when the public recognition of Katharine O'Shea by any Irish group would have been unthinkable. I trust that our little ceremony here today goes some small way towards making belated, but sincere amends to Katharine Parnell for the great wrong inflicted on her over the years by her husband's countrymen.

FANNY PARNELL[19]

Fanny Parnell died in July 1882, six weeks short of her 34th birthday. Her brother, Charles, refused permission to have her body shipped back to Ireland for burial. That anyone should be embalmed and moved from one place to another after death was to him, as Mrs O'Shea said, 'unspeakably awful'. And when this was proposed for his favourite, among his six sisters, 'his horror and indignation were extreme'.[20] So she was buried with her mother's people, the Tudors of Boston, in this vault in Mount Auburn.

Early in the new century, another request to have her remains returned to Ireland, was again turned down, and for the same reasons. This time by her sister, Anna.[21] In the 1930s, the question of reburial in Ireland was raised once more: but this also came to nothing.[22] More recently, a participant in one of our Parnell Summer Schools – Denis Foley of Boston, whom we are delighted to have with us again today – reminded some members of our Committee that Fanny Parnell was buried in an unmarked American grave, and that something ought to be done about it. At the time, Jane McL. Côté's book, *Fanny and Anna Parnell*, had aroused considerable interest in Ireland's patriot sisters, as she called them.

And now, we in the Parnell Society have decided that if Fanny Parnell is not to be brought home to her Wicklow Mountains, then a memorial slab of granite, from those same Mountains, and similar to that marking her brother's grave in Glasnevin, should be brought to her. The cost of transporting the stone from Avondale to Mount Auburn was generously and anonymously borne by a member of the sub-committee that planned this trip.[23]

Fanny was never, simply, the sister of her celebrated brother: She deserves to be remembered in her own right. She was still four months short of her 16th birthday when the first of her patriotic poems appeared in the Fenian newspaper, the *Irish People*. John O'Leary, editor of the *Irish People*, described her verses as rhetoric rather than poetry. But, he added, that it was very vigorous and sonorous rhetoric, giving great promise for a girl her age.[24] Whatever the literary merits, what her teenage contributions to the *Irish People* signified was a bright-eyed idealism, a seriousness of purpose, a budding sense of patriotism, an alienation from her own class, and a passion to make Ireland a better place in which to live. When the Fenian leaders were arrested on charges of treason-felony, Fanny attended the trials. And, in the words of her brother, John, 'pictured herself as the next occupant of the dock'.[25]

In her mid-twenties, she settled in America, where Mrs Parnell had inherited the estate of her father, Admiral Stewart. Shortly after this her brother began his meteoric rise in politics. Her personality, cradled in Fenian Ireland, finally came to blossom among the exiles and expatriates in America during the stirring times of the land agitation presided over by her brother. Whenever he was attacked in American newspapers she rushed to his defence. When he established the Famine Relief Fund, she threw herself into its organisation, devoting at least ten hours a day to the work. She arranged for Famine Relief boxes to be placed in post offices all over the USA. She co-ordinated Parnell's hectic mission to some 60 North American cities. She scolded him for not replying to his correspondents, and entreated him to acknowledge subscriptions. She criticised HQ in Dublin for its lack of efficiency. She chaffed about John Dillon because he had left his slippers in one hotel and his nightshirt in another.

Her work rate was frenetic. And those Clan na Gael bosses who felt that the land agitation was diverting people away from pure physical force republicanism, correctly pinpointed 'Miss Fanny' as the leader of those who had defeated their attempts to control Parnell's mission for their own ends.

When Tim Healy arrived in America to attend to Parnell's secretarial problems, he was pleasantly surprised, however, by the young woman who met him. She was thoughtful in providing what he called 'womanly comforts' after his long voyage. He described her as gracious, cheerful, feminine, without a trace of the poetess or bluestocking.[26] And when Davitt and Willie Redmond arrived to continue the work of the Land League, she gave them, also, royal hospitality at the Bordentown estate which she managed efficiently for her mother.

Her pamphlet, *The Hovels of Ireland*, was a hard-hitting attack on landlordism. Two months later, a widely researched, well-written and cogently argued article, entitled 'The Irish Land Question', was published in the prestigious *North American Review* under Charles's name. Apparently, however, it was written by his sister. Her assistance was also evident in the important address which Charles gave to the US House of Representatives.[27]

The Ladies' Land League, first established in New York, was her brainchild. She was never comfortable, however, with public speaking. On one occasion in Boston she had hardly begun to speak when she faltered and said that she had forgotten everything she wanted to say. Patrick Collins, President of the American Land League, and later Mayor of Boston, came to her rescue saying that Miss Parnell: 'has talked, does talk and will continue to talk to the people of two continents in immortal songs which have done more than any speeches to arouse the spirit of Ireland'.[28] He was referring, of course, to her Land League ballads, then being published in John Boyle O'Reilly's *Boston Pilot*, and reprinted in newspapers in Ireland, America, Australia and England. The most famous, 'Hold the Harvest', was described by Michael Davitt as the Marseillaise of the Irish peasant.[29]

> Oh! by the God who made us all
>   The seigneur and the serf –
> Rise up! and swear, this day to hold
> Your own green Irish turf;
> Rise up! and plant your feet as men
> where now you crawl as slaves,
> And make your harvest-fields your camps,
> Or make of them your graves.

Her patriotism has never been in question. Her poetry, though not devoid of literary merit, was never intended to be a contender for the Nobel Prize. It was meant to be, and was, effective propaganda. Her pioneering feminism can be more easily discerned from the present standpoint in history. And what her sister, Anna, foretold has indeed come to pass: 'Perhaps', said Anna, '. . . when we are dead and gone and another generation grown up . . . they will point to us as having set a noble example to all the women of Ireland.'[30] But the patriotism, the poetry, the fervid activity, the propaganda, the feminism were merely the outward expression of her most characteristic virtue: her innate hunger for justice. In the biblical language she loved to cite, she grew up 'as a tender plant, and as a root out of a thirsty land'[31] – a land, as she saw it, thirsting for justice.

She quoted with approval Montalembert on the moral energy which inspires individuals to oppose injustice, and to protest against the abuse of power, even when not directly involved themselves. What inspired her writings, as well as her actions, was this strong social conscience, and an acute awareness of the responsibilities placed upon her by her own privileged position. She reminded her own landlord class that with the accidentals of birth, education, wealth and intelligence go stern duties. That burning sense of *noblesse oblige* which possessed her may also be detected in her siblings, Charles and Anna.

She was one with her friend, John Boyle O'Reilly, when he wrote: 'What is the good of having a republic unless the mass of the people are better off than in a monarchy?'[32] And she agreed with her ally, Michael Davitt, when he said: 'We can afford to put away the harp until we have abolished poverty from Ireland'.

Perhaps the sublimest epitaph written for her came from Francis Sheehy Skeffington – a kindred spirit. He wrote that she was 'the noblest and purest-minded patriot of the Parnell family; and had not her fiery soul "fretted the pigmy body to decay", and brought her to an untimely death, her genius might have won for her a place beside the Maid of Orleans among the liberating heroines of history'.[33]

And so, in Mount Auburn, today, I have an eerie feeling that we mortals are not here alone. There is also present, in the words of one of her poems, a 'jubliant procession'.[34] Among that jubilant host is a contingent of Fenian spirits led by those who first accepted for publicaton her teenage ballads – John O'Leary, Charles Kickham, O'Donovan Rossa. Representatives of the Ladies' Land Leagues of America and Ireland are also here led by her mother, Delia, and sister, Anna. Irish-Americans present include her friends, John Boyle O'Reilly, John Devoy, Patrick Collins. A group from the Irish Parliamentary Party includes Davitt, Dillon, Redmond, with, perhaps, a now sulking Tim Healy in the background.

And if we feel the whisper of a gentle breeze passing through the assembled ranks, we may be sure that it is a tall, handsome, bearded ghost, proudest of all here present, and smiling approvingly that she whom he described as the 'cleverest and most beautiful woman in his family'[35] is here honoured, and her name set in stone.

Undreaming there she will rest and wait,
in the tomb her people make,
Till she hears men's hearts, like the seeds in
Spring, all stirring to be awake,
Till she feels the moving of souls that strain
till the bands around them break;
And then, I think, her dead lips will smile
and her eyes be oped to see,
When the cry goes out to the nations that
the Singer's land is free!

From 'The Dead Singer' by John Boyle O'Reilly

(*in memory of Fanny Parnell*)

AFTER DEATH

Shall mine eyes behold thy glory, O my country?
Shall mine eyes behold thy glory?
Or shall the darkness close around them ere the sunblaze
Break at last upon thy story?
    When the nations ope for thee their queenly circle
As a sweet new sister hail thee,
Shall these lips be sealed in callous death and silence,
That have known but to bewail thee?
    Shall the ear be deaf that only loved thy praises,
When all men their tribute bring thee?
Shall the mouth be clay that sang thee in thy squalor,
When all poets' mouths shall sing thee?
    Oh the harpings and the salvos and the shoutings
Of thy exiled sons returning!
I should hear, tho' dead and mouldered, and the grave-damps
Should not chill my bosom's burning.
    Ah! The tramp of feet victorious! I should hear them
'Mid the shamrock and the mosses.
And my heart should toss within the shroud and quiver,
As a captive dreamer tosses.
    I should turn and rend the cere-clothes round me,
Giant sinews I should borrow –
Crying, O, my brother, I have also loved her
In her loneliness and sorrow!
    Let me join with you the jubilant procession;
Let me chant with you her story;
Then contented I shall go back to the shamrocks,
Now mine eyes have seen her glory!

Fanny Parnell (Written in 1882 – the year of her death)

ANNA PARNELL[36]

Anna Parnell (1852–1911) has still to be assigned the place in history which she had so honourably won – both as a pioneering feminist and an Irish patriot. The second youngest of a family of five boys and six girls, her father died when she was seven. Anna spent her girlhood and impressionable teenage years in the company of her American mother and her talented and politically minded sister, Fanny, who was four years her senior. Almost from the time she left the Avondale nursery (at least after her father's death in 1859) Anna lived with her mother and sisters in the cosmopolitan surroundings of Dublin, Paris, London and America, with only occasional return visits to Avondale.

Her formation as feminist and patriot owed much to Fanny's influence, to her extensive reading and travels, and perhaps most critically of all (while continuing her art studies in London) to her regular attendance at debates in the House of Commons, where from the confinement of the so-called Ladies' Cage she watched in wrapt admiration the obstructionist tactics of her brother, Charles.[37]

Her political convictions were by now becoming firmly grounded. And later she would express them in these words: 'Ireland is a separate country by the act of nature, and therefore cannot be well governed except by herself.'[38] Though believing passionately in the independence of her country, for her there was an even more basic freedom which she stressed when she declared that:

> The best part of independence, the foundation of every other kind, [is] the inde-
> pendence of the mind.[39]

Anna was in America with her mother and sisters when Charles arrived (January 1880) to raise funds for the recently established Land League and for the relief of famine victims in the west of Ireland. On what was clearly a personal note Anna wrote that even to persons not yet born when the Great Famine occurred 'the horrors of those years had a vividness almost as great as active experience of them could produce'.[40] Moved by accounts of the suffering of people at home, and thirsting for political and social justice, Anna and Fanny threw themselves into the work of relieving distress in Ireland. The long hours and energy which they devoted to this humanitarian task amazed many observers.

Returning to Ireland, Anna became the leader and driving force in the organisation and spread of the Ladies' Land League which was launched in January 1881. Not yet 29, she was ready to do battle for her ideals against all establishments – political, agrarian, patriarchal and ecclesiastical. The feminism she now engaged in was pioneering, not only in Ireland but in a much wider international sense. Victorian attitudes to women were not confined to the United Kingdom and Ireland, but were the deeply entrenched culture of the times. And it was to these forces that Anna now found herself opposed.

While it was generally accepted that women might work in charitable organisations and for the relief of famine and distress, their involvement in politics was still taboo. Her sister, Fanny, while organising the original Ladies' Land League in America (founded in October 1880) had written a poem expressing the frustration felt at not being allowed to participate in Irish politics:

> Vain, ah vain is a woman's prayer!
> Vain is a woman's hot despair!
> Nought can she do, nought can she dare –
> I am a woman, I can do nought for thee, Ireland, mother.[41]

The Ladies' Land League, however, under Anna's direction was determined to engage in demonstrations and other political activities especially during the imprisonment of Parnell and the other leaders of the agrarian struggle.

An example of the prejudices Anna was up against found expression in the pastoral of Archbishop McCabe of Dublin condemning the Ladies' Land League. He advised his clergy:

> Do not tolerate in your sodalities the woman who so far disavows her birthright of modesty as to parade herself before the public gaze in a character so unworthy a child of Mary.[42]

And while the Government tried to nullify her efforts even by resorting to the jailing of some of her women colleagues, those who were supposed to be her allies – the leaders of the men's League – were not only reluctant to see the Ladies' organisation established in the first place, but were to remain throughout its existence suspicious of the women's participation in politics even to the point of undermining Anna's position. Undaunted, Anna was ever ready to do battle with what she called 'the dead weight of the majority'.[43]

The woman who took on the combined forces of these establishments was, by most accounts, petite, pale, gentle and ladylike, but also had some of the mystery, aloofness and charm which characterised her famous brother. When provoked, however, by the social and political oppressions in contemporary Ireland, Anna took on the temper of the fearless Fury. In the words of Michael Davitt: 'She was a lady of remarkable ability and energy of character – fragile in form . . . with all her great brother's intense application to any one thing at a time . . . together with a thorough revolutionary spirit.'[44]

Of her primacy in the Ladies' Land League there never was any doubt. Katherine Tynan recalled how on one occasion a lady land leaguer burst into a fellow worker's office late one night with orders from Miss Parnell to leave for Paris to help with the printing of the banned Land League paper, the *United Ireland* – 'Now, tonight, this minute!'[45]

For the 18 months or so during which the Ladies' Land League flourished, she conducted a tireless campaign organising branches, making speeches all over the country, attending and protesting at evictions and everywhere berating the policies of the authorities. All of this work was aimed at the destruction of the landlord system which she held responsile for the poverty and oppression of the people. The *Nation* newspaper described her energy as 'something extraordinary'.[46] She crossed a river on a supporter's back to denounce policemen participating in an eviction. She jumped out before the Lord Lieutenant's carriage in Westmoreland Street to castigate him for obstructing the building of Land League huts intended to shelter evicted tenants.[47]

Her Ladies' Land League was the first movement in Irish history to organise women for political purposes. And if circumstances had been more favourable Anna Parnell might well be honoured today as Ireland's Joan of Arc. She was ahead of her time. She might have been more at home with the women in Maud Gonne's Inghinidhe na hÉireann, or Sheehy Skeffington's feminists and suffragettes, or the republican Cumann na mBan. Indeed, many in these later movements liked to think of themselves as her disciples. From the present standpoint in history we can now appreciate the justice of the claim she made to her colleagues in the Ladies' Land League that history would remember them because of the precedent they set for future generations of Irish women.

Her brother's suppression of the Ladies' Land League so infuriated Anna that she wrote a severe attack on him in a letter intended for publication in the leading nationalist daily, *Freeman's Journal*. Her fury was later expressed in her book, *The Tale of a Great Sham*. The editor of the *Freeman's Journal*, Edward Byrne, has left a graphic account of her visit to his office with her letter, which, wrote Byrne, attacked her brother 'in no measured language'. Byrne continued:

> I remonstrated with her, and endeavoured to dissuade her from seeking its publication. With true Parnell pertinacity she argued the matter for hours through the night, when eventually I prevailed and she consented to withdraw the manuscript. I never had a keener controversy in my life than with that lady, who resembles her great brother in many respects, mentally as well as facially.[48]

After the suppression of the Ladies' Land League and her disillusionment with Irish politics, Anna retired to England; and, as in the days before becoming absorbed in her brother's political causes, she devoted much of her time to painting. She courted anonymity, and was living in a boarding house in the seaside resort of Ilfracombe in Devon in straitened circumstances and under an assumed name, Cerisa Palmer, when she died in a drowning accident in 1911.

Tragedy had haunted the Parnells. Anna's end was perhaps the most tragic of all. The deaths of Charles and Fanny had their own share of tragedy. But their funerals had been occasions of massive political demonstrations and outpourings of national grief. In sad contrast only seven strangers accompanied Anna to her grave. Yet she, too, had served her country and its oppressed tenantry heroically. And in the process she had given initial voice to the women of Ireland. It is only fitting, therefore, that she be remembered for the significant contribution she made to the aspiration for and the development of a more just and caring community.

Her shade will be gratified with the living monument of the presence of so many members of the Parnell Society, their friends and guests and descendants of her youngest sister, Theodosia, round her lonely grave in Ilfracombe. Her fiercely independent and unconquerable spirit will be thrilled that Her Excellency, Mary McAleese, President of Ireland, sent a message to be read at this ceremony, and that the occasion has been further dignified by the presence and address of His Excellency, the Ambassador of the Republic of Ireland. And the young tree from Avondale which we plant here today will be a reminder of a happier childhood, as well as being a promise that her memory will be honoured and kept green for evermore.

CHAPTER 8

In the Footsteps of John Howard Parnell

Memories of an American Journey

Donal McCartney

In April 2001, the Parnell Society undertook an extensive journey exploring the American links of the Parnell family. Our mission to the USA began appropriately enough in Boston, with the Parnells' grandfather, Admiral Charles Stewart. Our first port of call was to the Admiral's ship, the USS *Constitution*, or as it was endearingly nick-named by Americans, *Old Ironsides*, the oldest ship-of-war afloat. We were given, by the enthusiastic guide, an almost blow-by-blow account of how the American naval hero, Charles Stewart, had outmanoeuvred and captured two English warships, the *Cyane* and the *Levant*, off the coast of Portugal on 20 February 1815.

We heard much about his foreign wars; but almost nothing about his domestic arrangements. His parents were Scots-Irish who had emigrated to Philadelphia. He had gone to sea at the age of 12. At the age of 35, two years before his capture of the *Cyane* and *Levant*, a wealthy Captain Stewart, as he now was, having made his money from enterprising commercial shipping, married Delia Tudor from one of Boston's more prominent families. She was nine years younger than the Captain; had been brought up in the polite society of America, France and England; had taken lessons in deportment, in the harp and piano; and had acquired a proficiency in French, Italian, Spanish and German. What expertise in language he had attained had been picked up from sailors or merchants and others in the various ports of call. But true to his family's background, he had no intention of allowing her to squander his hard-earned money on the expensive tastes and affectations she had acquired in the salons of Boston, Paris and London. For him it was a case, perhaps, of lucky in war, unlucky in love.

They were incompatible from the start. And the story in her family was that they quarrelled on the first night of their honeymoon. And for as long as they lived together, they lived unhappily ever after. Her sister's husband summed it up when he said: 'The more they became acquainted, the more distasteful they became to each other.'[1] They had two children, a daughter, Delia Tudor Stewart, the future mother of the Parnells; and a son, Charles Tudor Stewart. When the children were seven and nine respectively their parents separated for good. The Admiral continued to reside on his Bordentown estate with a Mrs Fields (or Field) described as 'a pretty, young countrywoman'. She was already the mother of two daughters and a son. Though never divorced from his wife, the Admiral came to refer to his new partner as Mrs Stewart, and to her children as his step-children. This illicit Stewart–Fields liaison produced another son. A bitter three-year wrangle for the custody of his children with Delia Tudor ended in a settlement, which gave custody of the girl to the mother and of the boy to the father, and secured the mother's and children's rights of inheritance to Stewart's property.

Did the Admiral ever meet his Irish grandchildren, the Parnells? He could have, for he lived long enough. He died in 1869 at the age of 91. And John Howard, on the advice of his uncle, Charles Tudor Stewart – son and heir to the Admiral – had gone to America three years earlier in 1866. Charles and Fanny did not arrive in America until a few years after grandfather's death. Their older sister, Emily, stated that when their father died unexpectedly in 1859 (ten years earlier than the Admiral), 81-year-old grandfather Stewart invited her (then aged 18) to come and live with him. But her aunt and uncle in Ireland – the Wigrams who were Plymouth Brethren – made her a ward of court which meant that she could not be removed from Ireland. This was to save her, as Emily later said, from the questionable moral atmosphere which her uncle 'rightly considered a residence under' her grandad's roof could not fail to be.[2]

John Howard is eloquently silent on whether he or any of his siblings ever met or had anything to do with grandfather Stewart. Indeed, there is one interesting omission from his account of a visit which he and Charles and Fanny made in 1876 to the Centenary of American Independence Exhibition in Philadelphia. He says they spent several days at the Exhibition; that Charles spent most of his time in the Marketing Hall taking special interest in the stone-cutting machinery for possible use at his Avondale quarries; and that he also gave a great deal of attention to the design of the roofs of bridges which he wished to adapt for his sawmills and cattle sheds. John also took him to the Fruit Hall and explained his own system of transporting frozen peaches by rail from Alabama. But there was no mention of grandfather's famous ship, *Ironsides*, which was very much part of this Exhibition. One could be excused for thinking that the Admiral, his love-nest on his Bordentown estate, and his ship constituted one almighty skeleton in the Parnell cupboard; and that the Admiral only became significant for his Irish grandchildren when his name and fame as naval hero against the British were successfully exploited for Irish-American consumption during Parnell's campaign throughout sixty American cities in 1880.

By then, too, Mrs Parnell and her daughters were securely settled on the Bordentown estate which she had inherited following the death of her brother. It was here in Bordentown that Fanny Parnell died suddenly on 20 July 1882. Within a few days of her death, delegates from 35 branches of the Land League of America met in New York. They acknowledged, in their own words, that 'Our dear sister in the cause, the late Fanny Parnell', had 'toiled, lived and died for her native land'; 'for the welfare and prosperity of the Irish people'; for 'the freedom and independence of Ireland'; and that these had been 'the main objects of her labors, hopes and aspirations'. The meeting then passed the following resolution:

> That it is the duty of Irishmen and women the world over, to erect a monument over her remains worthy of the life and character of Fanny Parnell, and to that end a fund should be started to which all may have the pleasure and honor of contributing.[3]

She had to wait 119 years for that monument. The Parnell Society can be justly proud of the part it has played in carrying out the objective of that 1882 resolution by placing a stone of Wicklow granite at her unmarked grave in Mount Auburn Cemetery in April 2001.

The next stage of our journey took us to Bordentown itself. The Admiral's larger, or mansion house no longer stands. We were told, however, by an official associated with the site that Fanny had died in the estate's smaller frame house where we all took several photographs. But on this point the contemporary report of Fanny's death in the local newspaper is ambiguous. It said that she had died at the family residence known as Ironsides. In another section of the newspaper, under the heading, 'Notes on Miss Parnell's Funeral', it had this interesting point to make:

> Commodore Stewart did not die in the same building in which Miss Parnell ended her days, but in the house a short distance from it and now occupied by Mr E. L Stewart.[4]

One would have thought that when the paper said that she had died at Ironsides it referred to the mansion. And this would have meant that the Admiral died in the frame house. Jane McL. Côté claims, though admittedly without giving her sources, that the Admiral had been living for some years in the frame house and died there.[5] This seems quite possible; because, for some time before his death he had been in dispute with the Railway Company which had encroached on his land very close to the mansion. The dispute was settled only after his death when his son and heir, Charles Tudor Stewart, had taken the matter to arbitration.

Now, no doubt, you will already have detected that at the time of Fanny's death the person who was living in the frame house in which the Admiral died 13 years earlier had the same surname as the Admiral. In those days the newspaper was far too discreet to say who Mr E. L. Stewart was. He was, of course, none other than the son of the Admiral with Mrs Fields (Field); and therefore Mrs Parnell's half-brother and Fanny's half-uncle.

At the time of Fanny's death, E. L. Stewart was the father of one little girl of four, and a second was born the year that Fanny died. Reporting on the funeral, the paper noted that Mrs Parnell entered the parlour where the coffin lay 'on the arm of her son, Mr John Parnell', who arrived from Alabama 'just in time to take part in the services'. It also reported that Lieutenant Macaulay of the US Navy, a cousin of Mrs Parnell, was present. The names of the many representatives of the several branches of the American Land League who arrived on the special trains from Trenton, Philadelphia and New York were listed; as were the names of colleagues and family friends who sent elaborate floral designs. Victorian discretion, however, forbade any mention of Fanny's nearest neighbour, Mr E. L. Stewart – half-brother of her mother.

Describing the deceased as someone who was considered in the neighbourhood as very friendly and agreeable to all she met, the newspaper added that in the few leisure hours which Miss Parnell took from her political campaigns, she found time to give garden parties for children. It is inconceivable that E. L. Stewart's four-year-old daughter would have been excluded from these. So, more significant, perhaps, than the question of who died in what house, is the fact that the illegitimate family continued to reside on the estate. This, I believe, was in no small measure due to the graciousness of Fanny's uncle, Charles Tudor Stewart, who seems to have been as kind to his father's second family – among whom, of course, he had spent his own youth – as he was to his Parnell nieces and nephews who had once lived with him in his fine home in Paris.

In the cemetery of the Episcopalian Church in Bordentown we were shown a headstone marking the grave of two sisters: Elizabeth Tudor Stewart (1878–1938), and Frances Stewart (1882–1953). Our hosts in the Bordentown Historical Society asked us to solve the problem of identity of these two sisters. Our first reaction was that they must be related to the Admiral. But then, how come that the older sister, Elizabeth, bore the name of Tudor Stewart? It seemed unlikely that the Admiral would have tolerated 'Tudor', the family name of the wife he hated and from whom he had separated, even in a grandchild.

We then indulged ourselves in a bout of light-hearted, semi-serious conjecture. We recalled the many stories of Charles Stewart Parnell's sexual misadventures, which perhaps Parnellites had dismissed too easily in the past. We also remembered that during his secretive liaison with Mrs O'Shea he sometimes covered his tracks by renting his love-nests under the name of Mr Charles Stewart. Could the two sisters in the cemetery in Bordentown possibly be Parnell's children? If so, we were on to something really sensational. A bit far-fetched, perhaps, but how about the dates?

About two years after Charles had been jilted by the American heiress he had met in Paris, Miss Woods, he and John were back again in Paris (April 1874), this time to help their mother arrange the affairs of her brother, the recently deceased Charles Tudor Stewart. There, at the home of his sister, Emily, he met yet another American beauty, who, according to John, fell violently in love with Charles. To escape her advances he skedaddled back to Ireland. Whether Charles ever met her again we cannot be certain.

He was back in America on a political mission in 1876; and again in 1880 on his famous Land League mission. And at least on the latter occasion there was contact once more with an American lady. Our source this time is the sober Michael Davitt. He wrote:

> Early in 1880 after his [Parnell's] return from the transatlantic mission, a young, accomplished and very wealthy Irish-American girl came to London and Ireland, attracted by the handsome Irish leader and the romance of his public life. There could be no doubt about the trend of her wishes in regard to him. She and her father put up in Morrison's Hotel, where Parnell always had his quarters when in Dublin. Unfortunately there was no response on his part to this delicate but obvious attention. Soon after other eyes only too easily conquered and led him captive into the snares of a fatal affection.[6]

Translated into modern idiom what the rather prudish Davitt seemed to be telling us was that this desirable Irish-American heiress, with her father, had followed Parnell from America to London and from London to Dublin; that she had been smitten by his good looks and the aphrodisiac of political genius; but that he had scampered off into the tragic arms of Mrs O'Shea.

Like grandfather, like grandson? – we asked ourselves. And what if the American beauty in Paris in 1874 and the Irish-American heiress in 1880 were one and the same person? Unfortunately for all this speculation about Parnell's paternity, the dates of birth of the two sisters in Bordentown cemetery, 1878 and 1882 respectively, did not quite match up with his visits to the USA, two years earlier in each case. With no other collaborating evidence the brainstorm passed. And reality dawned. We concluded that the sisters were, of course, the daughters of Mr E. L. Stewart, he who was living in the frame house when Fanny died. Our in-flight poets caught the mood in immortal verse:

In Bordentown's green churchyard
There lies two sisters' grave
And gentle winds caress them
From slander they are saved
Despite futile deductions
And creative use of dates
Of Parnell's misadventures
They were rescued from that fate.[7]

But still the question remained, why was the older one called Elizabeth Tudor Stewart? Probably after Charles Tudor Stewart, her kindly, old bachelor step-uncle. And could it be that the younger daughter, Frances, born the same year as Fanny's death, was named after her friendly, agreeable and famous cousin who had lived in the neighbouring house? Very likely, indeed, I would say. What is not in doubt is that Fanny Parnell, Elizabeth Tudor Stewart and Frances Stewart were all granddaughters of the Admiral. 'Old Ironsides', as the Admiral himself had come to be called, seemed to be haunting us on every step of our journey.

Still in Bordentown, this time in the home of one of our gracious hostesses, Mrs Constance Shields, we were shown a table which had belonged to the Admiral; a blackthorn walking-stick which had belonged to Parnell; and a notebook which had belonged to Fanny. Written in pencil on the inside cover was: 'Fanny Parnell / Fifth Avenue Hotel'. John is here a useful guide. He confirms that he, his mother and Fanny were staying in the Fifth Avenue Hotel when Charles arrived in New York in 1876. Checked against a specimen of Fanny's handwriting, the name and the address were undoubtedly the work of her hand; as were several other pages written in ink elsewhere in the notebook. This was all very exciting. What was disappointing, however, on closer examination, was that the contents did not include any drafts of her poems, or letters, or speeches. What we had was a fair amount of material, apparently transcribed directly from a medical textbook. The detail is more elaborate than one would find today in an ordinary family medical encyclopaedia. The language is often quite technical. And there are few mistakes or corrections over some 48 handwritten pages. This, I believe, indicates transcription rather than dictation or note-taking at a series of lectures.

The material transcribed consists of descriptions and treatment of fractures, dislocations, fevers and therapeutics. We know that during the Franco-Prussian War of 1870, Fanny, then living in Paris with her mother, joined the American Ambulance or Field Hospital. This material does not, however, strike me as first-aid notes written when Paris was about to be attacked. Besides, the notebook had a label which indicated that it was sold by a New York bookseller. And Fanny did not arrive in America until 1874. Of course it is possible that Fanny had acquired the notebook while in Paris in 1870, that she made the transcription there, and that she added her name and address only when staying at the Fifth Avenue Hotel four years later.

What I think to be the more likely is that her experience in the American Ambulance in Paris, and her own deteriorating or indifferent health in America, stimulated her interest in medical matters. I suspect that the transcription was made round about 1876 when she was staying in this hotel. We are unable to say whether she ever intended to take up the professional study of medicine. Certainly from 1880 her time would have been devoted almost entirely to the cause of the Land League.

Later material in the notebook was added by other persons. One used it to write up and paste in recipes. Another scattered basic mathematical calculations haphazardly on to overcrowded pages. Overall, Fanny's notebook was left in a very tattered condition:

with the back cover missing, pages loose and the whole lot barely held together with three pieces of fading sellotape. The notebook was generously presented to the Parnell Society by Mrs Shields.

It might be argued that the biggest discovery of our tour was John Howard Parnell, and the questions posed by his career. It was evident that our hosts in Alabama were far more interested in John than in his more famous brother or sisters. This was understandable: Fanny and Charles were concerned with Ireland and Irish issues; John was involved in the development of peach farming in America. In acreage alone John's stake in America was six times greater than that of his famous American grandfather's. His initial purchase was 1,482 acres; the Admiral's, 225 acres. And he was much longer involved in American affairs than any of his siblings; Fanny had lived there for eight years; Charles visited America on only three occasions; John farmed there for 25 years (1866–91)

Indeed, if we contrast John's profile on one side of the Atlantic with that which he has always had on this side, we might well be talking of two very different persons. The John Howard of Alabama is not the John Howard of Avondale. James Joyce, who with Yeats did so much to invent the god-like myth of the Uncrowned King and dead Chief, also contributed to the damning myth of a weakling brother. Joyce's portrait of John, set in the Dublin of 1904, reads:

There he is: the brother. Image of him. . . . Like a man walking in his sleep. No one knows him. . . . Look at the woebegone walk of him. Eaten a bad egg. . . . Great man's brother: his brother's brother. . . . Drop into the DBC probably for his coffee, play chess there. . . . Eating orange peels in the park. Simon Dedalus said that when they put him in Parliament that Parnell would come back from the grave and lead him out of the House of Commons by the arm.[8]

Reputable historians have tended to confirm this unflattering portrait of Parnell's older brother. F. S. L. Lyons was only being kind when he described John as 'not the man to move mountains'.[9] Roy Foster referred to his 'incorrigible lack of realism'. 'Poor John' was how Foster dubbed him.[10] Referring to the father's will which left Avondale to the younger Charles, Robert Kee says that it was 'a gesture which suggests disappointment with his elder son, John, afflicted as he was with his stammer'.[11] And Jane McL. Côté concurs:

> The beautiful and valuable family estate should have gone to the eldest surviving son . . . But poor John [Note the recurrence of that dismissive phrase] poor John, however, was then and would always be a worthy non-entity.

And as if that dismissal were not harsh enough, Côté adds that John also suffered badly from the Tudor family failing of unproductive speculation.[12]

Perhaps it was because he was determined to disprove his own father's estimate of him – and indeed that of future historians – and of always playing second fiddle to his younger brother, that he decided to make his own way in America. It was on the advice of his uncle, Charles Tudor Stewart, that John went to America in 1866, at the end of the Civil War in which many Southern planters had been ruined, and purchased a property of 1,482 acres for $12,000 in Chattahoochee Valley, Alabama.

He found himself, he said, ' pretty much at home with all the Southern people. I like them very much as they are all real gentlemen and are very hospitable'.[13] And by all accounts they liked him. He had found a new identity among them. He brought over from Wicklow William Merna to be his plantation manager, and Bill's wife, Margaret, to be his housekeeper. Mrs Merna's sister, Mary, according to an interview given by a former neighbour of John's to a local historian, was 'John's concubine'.[14] While John in his memoir of his brother was ready enough to list all of Charles's love affairs, he was remarkably silent about any of his own. But reading between the lines there is one intriguing reference to a woman. Severely injured in a railway accident in October 1872 and confined to a bedroom in a miserable hotel in Birmingham, Alabama, he was nursed tenderly by Charles, and visited by friends. Among these was a Miss Callaghan, who, in his words, 'was a friend of mine'. Could she have been the sister of Mrs Merna?

According to later accounts in local newspapers, John's Sunny South Peach Farm was for years a great success. He added to his original purchase until his estate ran to 1,700 acres, most of it apparently in peach trees. He claimed that his system of transporting frozen peaches attracted considerable attention in the fruit world. (Here surely were echoes of the success of his great-uncle, Frederick Tudor, known as the Ice-King of Boston, who had made a fortune shipping ice to the tropics.) John's peaches were delivered not only to the Southern cities of Atlanta, Montgomery and New Orleans, but further afield, including Ireland. His merchandise was said to have filled 18 freight cars on one occasion. He employed as many as 200 workers – blacks as well as whites – and paid wages at the top rate. Bill Merna and he became skilled in the brewing of cider and wine; at one time storing more than 1,000 barrels in a West Point warehouse.

John did not just arrive in Alabama and achieve all of this on his own. Bill Merna stated that a Mr Samuel Rumph of Fort Valley across the Chattahoochee River in Georgia was a frequent visitor who was especially helpful and attentive. In Chambers County Library we were shown a painting which John had done of his good friends and closest neighbours, the Shank family. Felix Shank gave him expert advice on the quality of the soil, and helped him recruit the workforce.

John's reputation as a successful peach-farmer travelled well beyond Alabama. In 1882, some 15 years after he had established his farm, the New Jersey paper reporting his presence at Fanny's funeral stated:

> He has the credit of being the first one to ship from this country large quantities of peaches in good condition to Europe. He is one of the largest and most successful peach cultivators in the world.[15]

This was high praise indeed – providing the story had not been fed to the reporter by John himself, or by Mrs Parnell who was always capable of making the most extravagant claims for her family.

By then, in any case, John's luck was beginning to run out. In April 1884, a deed transferred his original farm of 1,482 acres to A. M. Eady & Co. A later newspaper account claimed that following a crop failure in 1888, John sold his farm for $8,000. If accurate on dates this presumably could have been the remainder of his 1,700 acres. So what had happened to his once flourishing business?

A single crop failure is hardly the full explanation. John, like all his Tudor relations, had played the stock market. And it would appear that well before he returned to Ireland he had lost more as a speculator than his crops had been worth. Another reason for his downfall was that he had been much too casual in business management and never employed a book-keeper. Despite his ice-barrel, it was also asserted that his venture failed because no proper refrigeration was available in those days. But one of the more interesting commentaries on his failure was provided to a local historian in the 1930s by Mrs Pomp Holt, one of the seven children of Bill and Mrs Merna who had stayed on in America after John's return to Ireland. Because Mrs Holt was the daughter of his overseer this has to be an insider's view.

She ascribed the collapse of his business to his humanitarianism. She said that when the mill in River View burned down that Mr Parnell brought all the workers to his estate, gave them work and built them houses. She also said that in order to assist local farmers who had been suffering financially since the Civil War that John established the Parnell Mercantile Company, the largest store east of Montgomery. Mrs Holt recognised that this humanitarian was, as she phrased it, 'no successful businessman'. But, she added, that he had put 'hundreds of thousands of dollars into circulation throughout the impoverished South'.[16]

The Southerners, towards whom he had shown kindness, were always to remain kind to him and to his memory – as indeed we witnessed for ourselves. If we make the necessary adjustments to the scale: then John was to Chambers Co. what Charles was to Ireland – something of a hero, something of a visionary. And if in the end he failed to achieve his objective, to have failed in a great endeavour was yet a noble failure, one which others subsequently turned to success. The *Industrial News* of Alabama announced on 22 September 1892 that John Howard Parnell, the rich fruit grower, had started back to Ireland after one of his long visits to his American property. It was possible, it continued, that he would never return to America again for any length of time, but that he would go into politics and try to become his brother's successor. Meanwhile the valuable family estate in Wicklow had been entrusted to him and now constituted a large part of his labour.

The mythologising of John Howard Parnell in America, which had begun in his own lifetime, found its most exaggerated expression in the editorial obituary in the *Chattahoochee Valley Times*, 9 May 1923. The banner headline read: 'John Howard Parnell, Father of Commercial Peach Growing in the South is Dead'. It went on to make some rather extravagant claims for him, describing him as 'a man of eminent culture and educational attainments'. The fact is that he had received precious little formal education. He himself acknowledged that the efforts put into the attempt to cure his stammer, under special instruction in Paris, had interfered with other parts of his education. His handwriting, spelling and grammar always remained hopeless. Jane McL. Côté wrote: 'John Howard Parnell's handwriting is a barely legible scrawl, resembling that of a near-illiterate which suggests he may have suffered from dyslexia.'[17] When Charles at 16 was being prepared for the entrance exam for Cambridge, John, though three-and-a-half years older and now attending the same school, was considered capable of receiving only the basics in reading and writing. This, of course, did not mean that he was stupid. After all he was an inveterate and allegedly good chess-player. His talent, like that of his brother, lay not in the academic but in the practical.

It may well be true, as the obituary in the *Chattahoochee Valley Times* also claimed, that he pioneered the export of peaches from America to Europe.

But the claim would be much more convincing if it were authenticated by other than interested Valley, Alabama residents. Until it can be shown that there were no commercial peach farmers in Alabama before his time, and that he did indeed influence the development of the fruit industry in neighbouring Georgia, which has since become famous as the Peach State, the jury must remain out on the question of whether he merits the truly grand title of 'Father of Commercial Peach Growing in the South'.

It will not be denied, however, that his contribution to the industry had its own significance. He had shown that the soil was suited to the crop; that his experiment was not wasted effort. Whether we agree with the writer of the obituary that his soul had burned with a vision of what was possible, we can at least accept the moral which was drawn from his career: that the measure of a man's life lies not in the pile of paltry gold which accrues from his efforts, but in the aspirations of his heart and in the vision which he held before him. In this light, pronounced the *Chattahoochee Valley Times*, we may consider John Howard Parnell a great man.

Apart from this enviable reputation, it was disappointing to find that he had left nothing material behind him after a quarter of a century in America. In Boston Harbour we had walked the decks of his grandfather's 200-year-old frigate. In Mount Auburn we had congregated round the graveside of his sister. In Bordentown we had photographed one of the houses on the estate which his mother had inherited. But in Chambers County there was not even a peach tree that could be said to be the result of his 25 years of labour there. And although there were descendants of the Mernas still living in the vicinity, we were unable to discover whether there had been any offspring of the alleged liaison between John and Bill Merna's sister-in-law.

In contrast to the American obituary, the notices of John's death in the Irish papers were polite but colourless. The explanation for this lies in the fact that during the last thirty years of his life, spent in Ireland, his impact on the commercial or political life of the country was relatively insignificant. He was now, in the wake of the Parnell split, a little fish in a pool swimming with political piranhas. His long life (he died at 81) and marriage at the age of 65 to a widow were the very opposite of Charles's tragically short life and impassioned love- affair. His ineffectiveness as a politician served only to emphasise the much sturdier political virtues and leadership qualities of the dead Chief. His drab performance in Parliament contrasted sharply with the dazzling achievements of his brother. He hardly merited Joyce's dismissive description of him as the brother's brother: he appeared merely as the living ghost to remind the Irish and British public of the towering figure that had been lost.

The will which Charles had made before his marriage, acknowledging his two daughters with Mrs O'Shea, and leaving Avondale to Katharine, turned out to be invalid, because it had not been re-executed after his marriage. John was now heir-at-law to the estate. Some weeks after his brother's death, John visited Katharine to discuss the arrangement of Charles's affairs. He later related how well he got on with Katharine during the week he stayed in Brighton, frequently playing chess with her; and how Parnell's two Irish setters overwhelmed him with caresses; and how the 'Misses O'Shea' as he called them, used to visit him. Typical of John, there was not a word about Parnell's daughters except under the umbrella of 'the Misses O'Shea'.

Also present in Brighton was Parnell's loyal friend and vindicator, Henry Harrison. Harrison had seen the will written in Parnell's own hand upon a double sheet of foolscap. What was important about it, he said, was Parnell's effort to regularise the position of Katharine and their two children and to provide for them. In conversation with John, Harrison hinted broadly how generous and becoming it would be for him to waive his legal rights so as to give effect to his brother's manifest intention. Harrison continued:

> I struck no spark in him. Nor, when I found him vaguely irresponsive, did I persist. I realised . . . that people very seldom do these things, and that if when the idea is presented, the heart does not flash into instant action, with dynamic generosity of impulse, it is merely cruel and useless to urge it further. But that was how it befell that Avondale House, the home of the Parnells, came into the possession of John Howard Parnell and not into that of Parnell's own children.[18]

One could be easily tempted to rush to judgement and say that John, who had shown his humanitarianism in Alabama, had ignored the precept that charity begins at home. Although Katharine lived on in poor mental health for another 30 and John for another 32 years they were never to meet again in all that time. Nor did he ever again mention the 'Misses O'Shea', his nieces.

No doubt he had his own good reasons for wanting to hold on to Avondale. Although the eldest son, he had been given a raw deal in his father's will and left the much less valuable estate, Collure in County Armagh, which was burdened with a heavy annual head-rent to Trinity College and with annuities to his sisters. His sister, Emily, asserted that 'nobody could understand the reason of this apparent act of injustice' which gave Charles 'the place that belonged by moral right to his elder brother'.[19] That John was personally very attached to the home-place was evident in what he later wrote:

> We all loved Avondale, Charley's beautiful home; and to me there is no lovelier spot on earth, and to the end of time my heart will sorrow that it is no longer the home of the Parnells.[20]

On a less altruistic note it has also to be remembered that John's American business had collapsed, and he now saw an opportunity of restoring his financial circumstances.

Those who hold that he had acted badly towards Katharine and his nieces, and who believe in a justice beyond the grave, will be gratified to learn how Charley's ghost reaped vengeance on John. For, the new owner of Avondale was soon to discover that it was indebted for over £50,000, which John maintained he had to clear by selling his beloved Avondale. This, however, he only did nine years later in 1900, and after he, too, had failed to make it profitable. 'It is hard to avoid the conclusion', wrote Roy Foster, 'that John was not cut out for success'.[21]

If anything, John was an even greater loser in politics than he was in business. He fought four parliamentary elections, won one by a margin of less than one per cent, and lost three disastrously, ending up at the bottom of the poll. On a fifth occasion – the general election of 1900 – he had assumed he was unopposed and therefore did not need to submit a deposit. Minutes before nominations closed another nationalist was nominated. John did not have time to complete the formalities and was accordingly disqualified. He could hardly be blamed for regarding this as a shabby trick by colleagues in a so-called reunited party whose members, he complained, had always treated him with contempt and dislike. By any calculation his appears to have been an inglorious political career.

Is there nothing, then, to be said for the five years (1895–1900) that he did serve in Parliament? There were no speeches from this Parnell. But there were a few parliamentary questions. And these were typical of the man's character and practical interests. As MP for Meath South he urged a change in the rail service that would give Kilmessan two mail deliveries a day and speed up the delivery to Navan and Kells.[22] As a Wicklow man, concerned for the environment, he asked the government whether any scheme could be devised and money provided to prevent pollution being pumped into the Avonmore and Avonbeg from the disused Wicklow copper mines. The pollution, he said, was destroying valuable salmon fisheries and injuring the tourist and railway business. And would the Government enquire into whether landlords along the banks of the rivers would give their land free for a separate channel to be made for the polluted waters? The project would provide employment during periods of distress.[23]

As a disciple of his brother, he wanted to know how many evicted tenants were on the roadside; and would the Government consider housing them on one large tract of land?[24] Ever the humanitarian, he proposed that the state should fund poor law unions to enable them to acquire 50 acres in order that technical instruction in farming or market-gardening could be given to able-bodied paupers.[25] 'My son, John', his mother had earlier told Barry O'Brien, 'is full of pity and kindness for everyone'.[26]

As a former exporter of perishable fruit, he asked the government to facilitate the transportation of fruit, flowers and vegetables from Ireland to

London in a large box or basket on wheels, as in the American system. This would have enabled the perishable goods to be wheeled onto railway carriages and ships without the kind of damage that was being done to smaller packages by too much handling. Irish farmers and market-gardeners would thus have been encouraged to increase production.[27]

As an honest businessman himself, who wanted to develop Irish industry to its full potential, he asked the authorities to investigate the sale of liquor in low-class public houses in country districts in Ireland where the liquor was so adulterated as to be dangerous to public health and injurious to one of Ireland's most important industries.[28]

Here, surely, in all these practical proposals was the man we had discovered in Alabama: prolific in ideas, whatever his staying power and his ability to see them through to their profitable conclusion. Of one thing we can be sure. John Howard Parnell would have strongly approved of this year's Summer School theme – Economy and Society. As can be seen from the matters he raised in Parliament, he was concerned – in today's language – with land use, agricultural production and distribution, the economic development of Ireland's natural resources, home industries, protection of the environment, effective transport and communications systems, public health, unemployment and caring for the less fortunate in society. In all of John's concerns with the local and practical side of politics, he was following closely in the footsteps of his more famous brother. Roy Foster has emphasised how Charles was conditioned by his local Wicklow environment; and how sawmills, quarries, mines and the improvement of the harbour facilities at Wicklow and Arklow, and the protection and development of Irish industry were a genuine preoccupation with him.[29]

Our trip to America had turned out to be not only most enjoyable, but also quite instructive. Charles, the Uncrowned King; Fanny and Anna, the patriot sisters; and grandfather, Admiral Stewart, had not been in need of our eulogies. Much had already been written in praise of all of them. John, however, had been almost annihilated from the past. In his own lifetime, and ever since, his star had been dimmed because of the very brightness of his brother's. And recent interest in his famous sisters had only further deepened his obscurity. Our mission in the footsteps of the Parnells, if it had achieved nothing else, had helped to uncover that member of the family who, with all his weaknesses, had been written off too easily as 'Poor John'. This alone would have made our trip worthwhile.

CHAPTER 9

'No turning back'

Anna Parnell, Identity, Memory and Gender

Pauric Travers

Lytton Strachey, in his pioneering *Eminent Victorians* (1918), declared that ignorance was the first requisite for the historian – ignorance which simplifies, clarifies, selects and omits with a placid perfection unattainable by the highest art. While this may seem to reverse the conventional credo of the historian which asserts that history is what the evidence compels us to believe (rather than what ignorance, prejudice or the lack of evidence allows us to assume), it does at least have the merit of emphasising the limitations of the enterprise. In the case of the Parnells, this is appropriate. Notwithstanding a number of family memoirs[1] and the attention of historians over many years, it is striking how much remains unknown, particularly about the Parnell sisters. Enigmatic is the word most commonly used about Charles Stewart Parnell, and that is part of his continuing fascination; but it is a word which applies even more appropriately to his sister, Catherine Maria Anna Mercer Parnell (1852–1911).

Anna Parnell played an important role in the land agitation at a critical moment in its history; she was a pioneering feminist and leader of the Ladies' Land League; and she made a notable if intermittent contribution to the wider nationalist movement. Despite this, until recent decades she was at best a footnote in the pages of Irish history. Anna Parnell and the Ladies' Land League rated only passing mention in general textbooks. How and why her story was downplayed and virtually elided by contemporaries is itself now an indispensable and valuable part of the historical record which carries richer and deeper meaning as a result.

Having written her out of history for almost a century, the last three decades has seen a reverse for which the Parnell Society can claim a little credit. Roy Foster's *Parnell, the Man and his Family* (Sussex, 1976) facilitated the setting of Anna in her wider family context. The belated publication of Anna Parnell's own account of the Ladies' Land League, *The Tale of A Great Sham* (Dublin, 1986) both reflected and contributed to this revival of interest.

Jane McL. Coté's *Fanny and Anna Parnell: Ireland's Patriot Sisters* (Dublin, 1991), despite some limitations, represented a significant contribution to the rehabilitation of Anna Parnell. It contains a useful account of the Ladies' Land League which complements those in Dana Hearne's introduction to *The Tale* and Marie O'Neill's *From Parnell to De Valera: A Biography of Jennie Wyse Power* (Dublin, 1991).[2]

Despite this resurgence in interest, significant gaps remain: we lack a full-scale history of the Ladies' Land League and our knowledge of Anna's life after 1882 is episodic and incomplete. The absence of any substantial collection of personal papers and a characteristic reticence on Anna's part to promote herself rather than her politics have complicated the task of producing a comprehensive assessment of her life and career. Such 'ignorance' may be the first requisite for the historian, as Lytton Strachey would have it, but it does inhibit a full understanding of Anna Parnell and the complexity of her identity. For all her fortrightness, fundamental questions remain about her outlook which will be explored here through a discussion of her family life, her public career and her poetry.

The Parnell family identity was nourished by Irish, American and English roots. While historians have argued about the relative importance of each, their English heritage has been understated. The American background of the family and its importance has received a great deal of attention, but the significance of their English heritage has not, perhaps for understandable reasons. Michael Davitt described Charles Stewart Parnell as an 'Englishman of the strongest type moulded for an Irish purpose'.[3] He was unmistakably Anglo-Irish; he went to school and university in England and lived for long stretches there. Likewise Anna studied painting in London and lived in England almost continuously from 1886 until her death in 1911. L. C. B. Seaman has pointed out that Charles Stewart Parnell and Oscar Wilde were two of the few major figures whose life and careers fall completely within the Victorian period.[4] Anna Parnell lived on into a new era and rejected many aspects of contemporary Britain including its monarchy; but she fits more comfortably than one might expect into a Victorian mould.

The Parnells came to Ireland from Congleton in Cheshire after the Restoration in 1660. They were typical of the 'middling sort of people' who were the mainstay of the parliamentary cause during the English civil war. Thomas Parnell was a merchant and mayor of Congleton in the early seventeenth century; his son Richard also became mayor. Richard's brother Tobias was a gilder and painter. It was Tobias's son Thomas who brought the Parnell name to Ireland when he bought an estate in Queen's County. The association with Avondale and Wicklow commenced more than a century later.[5] The Avondale estate of *c*.4,000 acres acquired by the Parnells at the end of the eighteenth century was relatively modest even in Wicklow but it confirmed their status as landlords and 'middling gentry'.[6] They formed part of a Liberal Protestant tradition associated in some manifestations in the late eighteenth century and again in the 1870s and 1880s with 'settler nationalism'. Many of the pioneers of the women's suffrage movement also sprang from this class.

Superimposed on this background and a significant element in shaping of the consciousness of Anna, Fanny and Charles was their American mother, Delia. Frances Power Cobbe, recalled in her autobiography that Anna's grand-aunt, Mrs Evans, *née* Sophia Parnell, had often spoken to her about Delia and the Parnells and 'more than once' said

> There is mischief brewing! I am troubled at what is going on in Avondale. My nephew's wife [Delia Tudor] has a hatred of England and is educating my nephew, like a little Hannibal, to hate it too.[7]

Cobbe (1822–1904) was a pioneering Victorian feminist and member of the well-known Cobbe family from Newbridge House, Donabate and Kildare. Although most of her career was spent in England and she was hostile to Home Rule, it is certain that Anna was familiar with her and her work.

The Parnell's American antecedents, the Tudors and the Stewarts, were exceptionally well connected – Admiral Charles Stewart, Anna's grandfather was an American naval hero who had captured two British ships in a daring encounter during the 1812 war. Jane Côté has argued persuasively that the American family background was much more conventional and conformist than Irish historians have assumed.[8] However, it does continue to provide a plausible partial explanation for the unconventional political odyssey of some members of the family which carried them beyond the conventional bounds of the Wicklow landlord class. In his classic *Democracy in America* published in 1835 and 1840, Alexis de Tocqueville pointed to significant differences between young women in the United States and Europe which are apposite in the case of the Parnell sisters who enjoyed unusual freedom of movement and expression:

> In almost all Protestant nations girls are much more in control of their own behaviour than among Catholic ones . . . In the United States, Protestant teaching is combined with a very free constitution and a very democratic society and in no other country is a girl left so soon or so completely to look after herself. Long before the young American woman has reached marriageable age, the process of freeing her from her mother's care has started stage by stage. Before she has completely left childhood behind she already thinks for herself, speaks freely and acts on her own. All the doings of the world are ever plain for her to see; far from trying to keep this from her sight, she is continuously shown more and more of it and taught to look thereon with firm and quiet gaze. So the vices and dangers of society

are soon plain to her, and seeing them clearly she judges them without illusion and faces them without fear, for she is full of confidence in her own powers.[9]

We know that Anna read de Tocqueville's work which was hailed by J. S. Mill as the first philosophical book ever written on democracy. De Tocqueville was writing in a transitionary period in which European aristocracy was in decline and the movement for equality seemed irresistible. In America he saw the future. He also identified dangers, the best known of which was the 'tyranny of majority' – an idea echoed by Anna Parnell both in her 'Notes from Women's Cage' and her introduction to Jennie Wyse Power's *Words of the Dead Chief* published in 1892, in which she wrote that 'the humblest minority owed no allegiance to the proudest majority on a point of principle'.[10] More fundamentally, de Tocqueville spoke for a declining elite at a time when they had to renegotiate their own position in a democratic state – traces of that dilemma are detectable in the careers of both Anna and Charles Stewart Parnell.

Anna Parnell was born at Avondale in 1852, the second youngest of eleven Parnell children. While Fanny was close to Charles, Anna was closer to Theodosia, Henry Tudor and, later, Fanny.[11] Growing up in Wicklow, the social and political tensions of post-famine Ireland were inescapable and they deeply influenced the Parnell sisters. Their family life was fractured and fragile too. Ostensibly well to do, their circumstances were sometimes precarious. Their parents were estranged from 1853 with Delia living way from Avondale for long spells in London and Paris. When her father died in 1859, the family was moved; they lived in turn in Dalkey, Kingstown and in Temple Street in Dublin. Anna also lived for periods in London, Paris, New York and Bordentown. She was educated privately and at the Royal Dublin Academy of Art and the Heatherley School of Art in London where she excelled in painting.

In appearance, Anna was considered by contemporaries and historians as 'somewhat bony faced' and plainer than her sisters who were 'beauties' who 'attracted considerable attention whenever they were displayed'[12] – one suspects Anna had little patience at being 'displayed'. Her brother John Howard describes her as 'dark haired, with dark eyes, slight, of medium height, and delicate in constitution'. Her strength of character belied that constitution and was widely attested, if sometimes in terms which were double-edged; Jules Abels said she had the 'steel-like resolve of a Lady Macbeth'.[13] The celebrated occasion in 1882 when she grabbed the reins of the Lord Lieutenant's carriage in the streets of Dublin to berate him for preventing the erection of huts for evicted tenants demonstrated her commitment to what she believed in. Similarly when public opinion recoiled in horror at the Phoenix Park murders which were fortrightly condemned by her brother, she wrote to the London *Times* pointing to outrages committed by the police in Ireland and suggesting that they should not be surprised 'that the assassins arm was not idle'.[14]

When he first met Anna and Fanny in New York, Tim Healy wrote to his brother Maurice: 'the Parnell girls are their brother's sisters'. Notwithstanding their later quarrels, Healy considered Anna 'an unyielding and courageous soul'.[15] She possessed a passionate commitment to the poor and marginalised and, as her own account of the Ladies' Land League demonstrates, a great loathing for hypocrisy. Less frequently commented on was a genuine kindness which she displayed throughout her career. While she had a difficult relationship with her mother, she rushed to her side in 1884 when she was injured in an incident at Bordentown. She spent liberally to support those in need, often to her own disadvantage.[16]

Money was a recurrent problem. In *Tale of a Great Sham*, she attacked the practice of landlords of leaving nearly all of their property to their sons and virtually nothing to their daughters: 'If the Irish landlords had not deserved extermination for anything else, they would have deserved it for their treatment of their own women.'[17] During her adult life, she lived on an annuity from her father of £100 *per annum* secured on the Collure estate in County Armagh. This was administered by John Howard, was irregularly paid and eventually dried up – leaving her near destitution in her later years. Fiercely proud she refused assistance from friends, so much so that to assist her a subterfuge was resorted to – money was secretly donated to pay for publication of a volume of her poetry.[18] In 1910, the year before she died, Anna's financial problems were eased when she came into a small inheritance probably from her mother's estate.

Anna Parnell's introduction to politics followed and was directly related to her brother's but she quickly carved out a distinctive role. She wrote a short series of articles as a parliamentary correspondent for the Irish-American monthly, *Celtic Monthly*.[19] Her firm commitment to women's rights issues was clear: she reminded her American readers that American women did not suffer under the same restrictions as their European sisters. The difficulties besetting women in public life were manifold: unable to vote or to stand for parliament, most women took little part in politics. If they attended political meetings they were expected to sit in the gallery. From the late eighteenth century, they were allowed sit in the visitors' gallery in the House of Commons in London but, as a result of an incident in the 1830s, a grill was installed at the front of the special gallery which became known as the Ladies' Cage. Anna Parnell's 'How they do in the House of Commons: Notes from the Ladies' Cage' was an innovative piece of journalism – irreverent and sometimes witty and amusing – which gives insight into both the observer and the observed. She recorded much of the obstruction campaign of 1877–9 but also commented on other issues.

Anna's initiation into direct political activism was inspired by the harvest failure of 1878–9 when she helped to organise a famine relief fund. With her sister Fanny, she travelled to New York where she worked tirelessly on behalf of the Land League Famine Relief Fund and to promote the Land League generally. She worked closely with Michael Davitt who formed a high opinion of her passion and ability which he retained despite later differences between them over the Ladies' Land League. William O'Brien concluded that she was 'in more than one respect, little removed in genius from her brother'.[20]

Her name is inextricably linked with the Ladies' Land League which was one of the first political associations for Irish women and which made a significant contribution to the history of the land struggle in Ireland before being suppressed in 1882.[21] Its short and controversial history is a revealing case study of some of the realities of gender politics. In October 1880, the Ladies' Land League of New York was founded by Fanny Parnell to collect funds for Irish tenants. Its first president was Fanny's mother, Delia Parnell. Fanny Parnell suggested that a women's land league should be established in Ireland. Her brother Charles who was president of the Land League was doubtful, but Michael Davitt was enthusiastic because he knew that the male leaders of the Land League would soon be arrested. The first meeting of the Ladies' League in Dublin was held on 31 January 1881. At Michael Davitt's suggestion, Anna Parnell was given charge of the new organisation. [22]

Inevitably the new organisation which had its headquarters in Sackville Street in Dublin was largely middle class in leadership; not enough is known in relation to local branches to be certain but it is likely that this was true too in the localities. These women were quickly propelled from a welfare to a central political role by the arrest of the leaders of the Land League. As well as leading a campaign to support the prisoners, the Ladies' League provided a ready-made structure for the continuance of the land agitation. It organised fund-raising for the prisoners and helped evicted tenants by providing food and accommodation. Instructions were issued that no one should rent a farm from which a tenant had been evicted and that 'land grabbers' were to be boycotted. Detailed information was collected about evictions. Anna Parnell displayed enormous almost frantic energy: she kept in contact with branches of the Land League in all parts of the country and toured Ireland and Britain. Her organisational acumen and her intimate knowledge of land issues was commented on by many contemporaries. There were some criticisms too and indications that she was not universally popular whether because of her manner or because, as the person making most of the decisions in relation to which families should receive aid and how much, she was in a position where she was likely to offend as many supplicants as she pleased.[23]

Andrew Kettle, secretary of the Land League, was initially dubious about Davitt's wisdom in involving women in 'such a rough and tumble business'. However, when he had the opportunity of making Anna Parnell's acquaintance, he 'became even more enthusiastic about it than Mr Davitt.'. She had also succeeded in assembling around her 'a surprising number of really talented women'. As a north Dublin farmer, Kettle's assessment of Anna is revealing and worth quoting at some length:

> I found she had a better knowledge of the lights and shades of Irish peasant life, of the real economic conditions of the country, and of the social and political forces which had to be acted upon to work out the freedom of Ireland than any person, man or woman I have ever met. It was a knowledge that reminded me very much of my own mother. It was simple, masterful and profound. Ignorance of the ethics of the real condition of Ireland has, in my opinion, been the chief cause of the failure of all our movements and our leaders in their efforts to work out the redemption of the country. Anna Parnell would have worked the Land League revolution to a much better conclusion than her great brother.[24]

When Kettle spoke in these terms to Charles, he responded that his sister knew 'all about Irish politics. She is never at a loss and never is mistaken in her judgement.'

The Ladies' Land League proved very popular with 400 branches at its height, distributing over £60,000 in aid and waging a successful campaign on behalf of the prisoners and the wider aims of the land agitation. It soon attracted attention from the police who tried to put an end to its activities by dispersing meetings and arresting and imprisoning its members. Anna Parnell later claimed that the conditions in which the female prisoners were held were much stricter than those of the men.[25] William O'Brien described the Ladies' Land League as 'as truly heroic a band of women as ever a country had the happiness to possess in an hour of stress. They unquestionably deserve the largest share of credit for breaking Mr. Forster's power in a winter when even pretty resolute men's hearts beat low.'[26]

The attendant notoriety inevitably attracted attention from clerical and other critics of their activities. Archbishop McCabe attacked the involvement of women while his colleague, Archbishop Croke, came to their defence. McCabe condemned the Ladies' Land League in a letter read at all Catholic churches in Dublin:

> The modesty of her daughters was the ancient glory of Ireland . . . Ireland shone out more brightly by the chastity of her daughters . . . like Mary their place was the seclusion of the home. If charity threw them out of doors, their work was done with speed, their voices were not heard in the world's thoroughfare . . . But all this was to be laid aside and the daughters of our Catholic people, be they matrons or virgins, are called forth, under the flimsy pretext of charity, to take their stand in the noisy streets of life. The pretext of charity is merely assumed . . . They are asked to forget the modesty of their sex and the high dignity of their womanhood by leaders who seem reckless of consequences, and who by that recklessness have brought misery

on many families. God grant that they may not have brought defeat on the cause which they appeared to advocate. . . . This attempt at degrading the women of Ireland comes very appropriately from men who have drawn the country into the present terribly deplorable condition.[27]

Despite such disapproval, the women involved threw themselves whole-heartedly into the struggle. In the process they displayed an enthusiasm, organisational ability and radicalism which at first impressed and then alarmed their male counterparts. Some felt it unseemly for women to be publicly involved in political agitation and opposed the Ladies' League from the start. Others felt that once a political compromise had been reached between Parnell and Gladstone (in the Kilmainham Treaty) which brought the release of the prisoners, the Ladies' League had served its purpose. They felt that the women should quietly leave the political stage. Much to the disgust of Anna, her brother Charles took this view. Shortly after his release from Kilmainham, he confided to Davitt that he thought the Ladies' League had harmed the movement. He persuaded T. M. Healy to speak out against Ladies' League which he did in the *Boston Republic* for which he was a correspondent. An outraged Anna rushed to his lodgings, demanding to know who had put him up to it and probably suspecting it was her brother.[28] She believed that the Ladies' League was being victimised for its temerity in pursuing an inde-pendent course.[29] This is probably true but Charles's view was consistent with his attitude to the Land League itself. Critics of his suppression of the Ladies' League tend to forget that he suppressed both organisations. As described above,[30] his policy was to scale down the land agitation and refocus the move-ment which he led in a political direction. Not that that was any consolation to Anna: her radicalism and his conservatism extended beyond gender issues. While he believed that the Land League had served its purpose, she favoured an even more active campaign. She was unwilling to allow the Ladies' Land League to revert to a secondary role, preferring instead to wind it up.

The precarious financial position of the Ladies' Land League was used as a device to facilitate its suppression. The organisation was seriously in debt arising from its active assistance to evicted tenants. Its critics attributed the debt to maladministration rather than the reluctance of the Land League to release money from central funds to pay for these activities. Charles Parnell initially refused pleas to pay off the overdraft of £5,000 but then agreed on condition that the Ladies' League would disband. This was agreed. Anna acquiesced because of her disillusionment with the wider policy – she preferred dissolution in the belief that nothing could be achieved as the land campaign had sold out; she concluded that it would be better to pack up rather than maintain a pretence. She had grown dissatisfied with the male leaders including her brother whom she considered too weak and compromising.

The suppression of the Ladies' Land League was both an act of deep symbolic importance and a watershed in the life and career of Anna Parnell. It provoked a serious breach between Anna and Charles which never fully healed. Katharine O'Shea claimed that

> Anna Parnell never forgave her brother for this act, and to the last day of his life refused to hold any communication with him again. Parnell had much family affection and many times made overtures of peace to his sister, of whom he was really fond, and for whose strength of mind and will he had much respect. On two occasions he met her accidentally and tried to speak to her, but she resolutely turned from him and refused any reply to the letters he wrote.[31]

Parnell told William O'Brien something similar and O'Brien claimed they never met again.[32] It is true that relations were strained as a result, but in 1891, when Healy alleged that brother and sister had not spoken for nine years, Anna wrote to the press specifically to deny it. She wrote and spoke in defence of her brother during the split and introduced a collection of his speeches after his death.[33]

The suppression of the Ladies' Land League and what she saw as the betrayal of the land agitation had a profoundly disillusioning impact on Anna Parnell. This was intensified by the coincidence of the death of her sister Fanny in July 1882 which deeply affected her. It is interesting that in the case of both Anna and Charles, their political and personal lives were inextricably enmeshed in these crucial months in a way which shaped their decisions and their future lives. The Kilmainham Treaty was deeply influenced by the circumstances of Charles' relationship with Katharine, while Anna's spirit was shattered by a combination of political and personal misfortune.[34]

After 1882, Anna was in many ways a rebel with a number of causes but no clear focus. She was dogged by personal ill health and led a peripatetic existence, often living under an assumed name. She continued to paint and write sporadically and occasionally reappeared on the public stage to support radical platforms. In 1885, she spoke at a meeting in Camberwell in support of Helen Taylor who was seeking a parliamentary nomination for the Radical Liberals.[35] She supported Inghinidhe na hÉireann, the nationalist women's organisation founded by Maud Gonne which had a number of personal links with the Ladies' Land League – notably Jennie Wyse Power.[36] She subscribed £1 to the Patriotic Children's Treat Committee and telegraphed support for the movement to oppose the visit of King Edward VII in 1903. During the 1908 North Leitrim by-election, she campaigned briefly on behalf of C. J. Dolan, a former nationalist MP who stood for Sinn Féin. Jennie Wyse Power was a member of the executive of the new Sinn Féin party and Anna was sympathetic to their cause. She had worked closely with Wyse Power in the Ladies'

Land League and although they differed on the issue of its suppression, she wrote an introduction to her collection of Parnell's speeches in which she strongly argued the case of a more independent, self-reliant nationalist movement. In their efforts to assist evicted tenants, the Ladies' Land League had become involved in the establishment of cottage industries for example in Connemara, initiatives which foreshadowed later Sinn Féin policies.[37] In Leitrim, Anna attacked the Irish Party as 'humbugs' and called for voters to cast their votes not for Dolan's sake, 'not for the sake of Sinn Féin, but for my sake and for the recollection of old times'.[38] Unfortunately, recollection of old times was not a priority in a campaign which was nasty and violent. When she attempted to address a meeting in Drumkeerin, rotten eggs were thrown at the platform and a pail of water was thrown over her. To add insult to injury, Dolan was defeated. The mistreatment of Parnell's sister became a matter of public comment particularly in the Sinn Féin press which claimed to be the real inheritors of the Parnell legacy.

> When down to County Leitrim
> They marched the other day
> Who but the sister of Parnell
> Should cross them on their way
> Those heroes, nothing daunted.
> When she came on the scene
> Fired rotten 'spuds' and eggs at her
> For the wearing of the green
> An' they're peltin' filth like heroes
> For the wearing of the green[39]

Her last known cameo appearance in political affairs was in 1911, not long before her death. She paid the fine of Helena Molony who had been imprisoned for one month for non payment of a 40s fine imposed for throwing stones at a picture of George V during the royal visit in July.[40] Molony was editing Anna's memoir of the Ladies' Land League at the time. Two months later, on 20 September, Anna drowned while swimming at Ilfracombe.[41]

Long after her death, Anna Parnell made another (posthumous) contribution to Irish history. Although the *Tale of a Great Sham*, her account of the Ladies' Land League, was completed in 1907 it was not finally published in book-form until 1986, in spite of numerous attempts before and after her death.[42] It is in many ways an extraordinary book, detailed, dense and painstaking. It was written in response to the account of the Ladies' League contained in Davitt's *The Fall of Feudalism in Ireland*, published in 1904, which Anna considered misleading on both the origins of the women's' movement and its impact. Unfortunately it contains little direct testimony about Anna herself or the other leading figures, including Davitt and her brother Charles. This may reflect both her wider view of political affairs and her attitude to the cult of personality associated with 'the Chief', before and since his death. She confided to a friend that she 'avoided personalities as much as possible there as I consider the actions of particular individuals are unimportant in history, while the actions of groups, classes etc of persons are most important because the former are not met with again while the latter are'.[43]

Reflecting on the experience of the Ladies' Land League and politics generally, Anna Parnell concluded that England and the British empire were in terminal decline and that Ireland, debilitated by the effects of prolonged colonisation, stood in need of transformation. It was this analysis which attracted her to the Sinn Féin movement. She rejected Home Rule as a compromise that was no longer relevant in favour of self-government. She predicted that 'in spite of its poor prospects, armed rebellion seems likely to be the next thing either tried or played at here'. In relation to Ulster unionism, she pointed out that not all of Ulster was anti-nationalist and suggested that the north-east corner could be allowed choose whether it wished to be part of an independent country or remain part of Britain. She did not think it would choose the latter but, if it did, 'it would soon change its mind'.[44]

In her view, debilitation permeated social, cultural and political life and gender relations. Her conclusion that men could never be trusted, as they would always bargain and compromise raises interesting questions about gender and politics.[45] St John Ervine in his biography of Parnell drew hostile parallels between the uncompromising stance of the Ladies' Land League and the part played by women in the War of Independence and Treaty split when, in his view, Dublin was 'full of hysterical women'. 'Irish women', he commented, 'when they take to politics, have a capacity for fanaticism which is almost inhuman.' A more balanced weighing of the scales as between pragmatism and principle in both cases might as plausibly suggest the opposite verdict – male inconstancy as opposed to female intransigence.[46]

The Tale of a Great Sham is an indispensable account of the Ladies' Land League from a unique perspective; but it is disappointing as a mirror to the soul of Anna Parnell. This makes the insights to be gained from her other writings, and particularly her poetry, all the more important. Anna Parnell's poetry has been largely dismissed or ignored by historians: Fanny is remembered as a poet patriot and Anna as a single-minded organiser with a talent for painting. This is understandable. Anna painted actively at various times in her life while her poetic output is relatively limited. Most of the poems in her one published collection, *Old Tales and New*,[47] have been dismissed by Jane Côté as, 'in a word, execrable'. Anna's gift was 'for writing clean, spare and unambiguous prose, except when it came to explaining or justifying her own actions. The allusive nature of poetic expression escaped her entirely.'[48] This is a somewhat harsh verdict. While she was not an accomplished poet, many of the 17 poems in this slim volume have artistic merit and they all, without exception, offer insights into the outlook and sensibility of their author. The language is unrestrained and 'unmeasured' at times but it is arresting and powerful. There is a strong mood of darkness and despair about the collection but there is also occasional lightness, levity, irony and humour.

In 'the Legal World', Anna turns her pen on the legal fraternity and pokes fun at their clothes, pretension and hypocrisy.

> So things are very strange, you see
> Within the legal world
> For donkeys there wear horse's hair,
> Upon their foreheads curled . . .
>
> And Bench and Bar can walk and talk
> And wear both silk and stuff,
> And ermine too, for well we know
> Their suits they cost enough.

Several of the poems are overtly political and reveal much about the poet's enduring concerns. Katharine O'Shea recounts an incident at Eltham on Guy Fawkes night in November 1880 at the height of the Land War when an effigy of Anna Parnell was burned alongside that of the Pope. The anecdote is interesting for her brother's revealing response – apart from the fact that it was Anna's rather than Charles's effigy which was burned: 'Poor Anna! Her pride in being burnt, as a menace to England, would be so drowned in horror at her company that it could put the fire out.'[49] Although she spent almost half her life in England, Anna retained a strong anglophobia. This was increasingly concentrated in a hostility to the Crown and to the British empire which is evident in her poetry. Two poems in *Old Tales and New* are outspoken attacks on Queen Victoria while a number of others attack the empire. '22nd January 1897' marked the sixtieth anniversary of Victoria's coronation with a fierce denunciation of a throne 'all stained, by filth ingrained, and the blood that cries to heaven' and an empire 'built on the blackest silt'. Four years later, in '22nd January 1901' she returned to the attack: the 'Famine queen' has now passed away 'and that dread form will never more be seen, in pomp of fancied glory and of pride, or humbled, scorned defeated as she died'.

A number of these poems were prompted by the Boer War – Anna shared the Irish nationalist sympathy for the Boer cause and a general contempt for empire. 'To Field-Marshal Earl Roberts' (with apologies to Dion Boucicault) lampoons British military setbacks to the tune of a popular music hall ditty:

> Oh Bobby dear and did you hear
> The news that's going round?
> They say you lost your prestige, sir,
> Upon South Afric's ground . . .
>
> For that's the most distressful country
> He ever yet has seen,
> No hanging and no burning there
> Will make them save the Queen.

The tone in 'the British Empire' is less light-hearted and more passionate:

> The red wind sweeps from North to South
> From West to the burning East,
> And where it blows no good thing grows;
> But man, and woman and beast
> All wither and pine, and bodies and souls
> are blighted and slain,
> And the things that thrive are dull despair,
> Disease and vice, and sorrow and care,
> And want and hate, and grief and pain.

'With Apologies to Bishop Heber' takes up the same theme but with a more universal canvas embracing empires everywhere and adding a significant additional dimension.[50] The poem links religion and the spread of empire through 'bullet, lash and chain':

> Oppression foul – starvation –
> We'll do our best to spread
> Till each remotest nation
> Messiah's name will dread.

It is clear that Anna Parnell's target is not confined to the British Empire. She explains that 'Cuba' was written in anticipation of Cuba's being granted her freedom but this did not happen owing to 'the petty meanness of the United States'.[51] Although the poem deals with Cuba, it articulates with great clarity Anna Parnell's aspirations for all nations, including Ireland:

> Oh glad is the day when Victory's crown
> Rests on the brow of those who have fought
> For a nation's right, and counted as nought
> Tyranny's might and tyranny's frown.

In 'the Iron Horse', she uses the metaphor of the train to comment on the social impact of technology and change. She also reveals some of her own sense of dislocation:

> You can make the shrivelled toiler in the grimy city herds
> Think of leafy trees and many coloured fields and singing birds;
> You can touch chord within the weary exile's yawning breast
> That speaks of home and country, of friends and kin and peace and rest.

Anna reflects gloomily on life's journey in 'Middle Age', using the metaphor of a day. She has borne the 'morning chill' and the 'noon day' heat and has learned that 'hope is a phantom guide' so she would gladly leave out afternoon and evening.

> I am longing to be gone,
> Though my years are not two score,
> Though my course is but half-run,
> I've no wish to travel more.

In a later poem, entitled 'the Journey', Anna Parnell returns to this metaphor and theme. The mood is even more despairing. The poet reflects on her life's journey which began with a firm and light step but quite early in the day a band of thieves beset her and rob her. Since then she has 'crawled a cripple blind with tears'. In a moving and prophetic conclusion, she predicts that she would die alone in the cold and darkness. This is not an original motif and it needs to be borne in mind that some of these poems were written at a time when Anna was destitute and alone which may partially explain the intensity of the despair. However it is clear that she suffered greatly from depression and longed for release. The 'Geraldine' is a long poem about a woman who was swept out by a wave and drowned. It dwells in detail on the 'charms of the dream that men call dying' and contemplates with unusual equanimity death by drowning:

> When a bridegroom has felt his sea-bride's kiss
> He knows no grief again.
> No want, no care, no sorrow and no pain,
> Nor even aught save bliss.

Given the circumstances of Anna's own death, the last verse has an eerie foreboding:

Some children who saw it said next day
That nothing was ever clear,
The great wave must have swept her away
The time when she went so near.

The later years of Anna Parnell's life were ones of sadness, illness, disillusionment and betrayal. There is a sense in which she lived too long or too short. Had her life been confined to the Victorian era, like Charles and Fanny, she would have died closer to the period of intense activity which was her greatest achievement; had she lived a decade longer, she would have seen greater progress in relation to the causes she passionately believed in and championed – national regeneration, self-government, the decline of empire, the achievement of women's suffrage and the advance of women's rights. As it was, she contributed to progress in all of these areas. The experience of the Ladies' Land League politicised many Irish women and radicalised some. Although it only lasted a short time, Anna hoped that the Land League had set an example for future generations of women. There is no better testament than her own words: 'Perhaps when we are dead and gone and another generation grown up . . . they will point to us as having set a noble example to all the women of Ireland.'[52]

THE JOURNEY

When I first began my journey
My step was firm and light,
And I hoped to reach a shelter
Before the fall of night.

But a band of thieves beset me
Quite early in the day;
They robbed me and then they cast me
All bleeding by the way.

And since that hour I have crawled
A cripple blind with tears
While each step I've made has cost me
The pain and strain of years.

I've no shelter from the storm,
No screen against the heat;
The sun has beat against my head,
The shards have cut my feet.

My fellow-travellers on the road
Bound for the self-same goal
With purse and staff and scrip equipped
And limbs and raiment whole,

All point at me with scorn, and say:
'Why does he choose to roam?
For travelling he is not fit;
Cripples should stay at home'.

Alas they do not know that I
Was once as fit as they
And that there is no turning back
For those who go this way.

The long dark shadows of the night
Are closing on me now,
And its clammy dews are lying
Heavily on my brow.

I see the light of the City
Where I may never win,
And I know there's warmth and comfort
For those who are within;

And alone in the cold and darkness
I know that I must die
And unburied in the desert
My bones will always lie.

Anna Parnell

CHAPTER 10

'The Thurible as a Weapon of War'

Ivy Day at Glasnevin, 1891–1991

Pauric Travers

With only the faintest of encouragement, Mr Hynes, one of the characters in James Joyce's classic story Ivy Day at the Committee Room, took off his hat, cleared his throat and recited all eleven verses of his own poem 'The Death of Parnell: 6 October 1891':

> They had their way: they laid him low,
> But Erin, list, his spirit may
> Rise, like the Phoenix from the flames
> When breaks the dawning of the day,
>
> The day that brings us freedom's reign
> And on that day may Erin well
> Pledge in the cup she lifts to Joy
> One grief – the memory of Parnell.[1]

For good and ill, the memory of Ivy Day has been immortalised in Joyce's story in which the small time petty politics of Joyce's day is contrasted with the glory days of Parnell – good, because it is a memory worth perpetuating and, paradoxically, ill because it has deflected attention away from and trivialised Ivy Day itself and the significant role it played in the social and political life of Dublin especially in the decade after the death of Parnell.

This essay examines the origins and development of the Ivy Day commemorations and their contribution to the shaping of the Parnell myth.[2] Much of the discussion of the Parnell myth has focused on the impact of writers such as Joyce, Yeats and O'Casey and how the literary imagination has shaped and re-shaped versions of Parnell and, in the process, shaped and re-shaped the public perceptions of the 'lost leader'. However, the literary view of Parnell is not the concern here: other than to suggest that intellectuals are inclined to overrate the impact of literature in shaping popular consciousness.

While the commemoration of Parnell took many forms – including GAA clubs[3] named in his honour, street names[4] and statues[5] – the focus here is on the public procession and other ceremonials associated with the commemoration of the anniversary of his death. The Parnell monument unveiled in 1911 and the marking of Parnell's grave with a stone of granite in the 1930s will be dealt with but mainly in the context of their relationship with Ivy Day. If, as has been argued in the introduction to this collection, commemorative ceremonies and rituals are 'a kind of language' which, when we learn to decode it, reveals much about the society which produced them, what can we learn from the rise and decline of Ivy Day? That is the central question posed in this essay.

Parnell's funeral to Glasnevin on 11 October 1891 was the occasion of high drama, grief and emotion, all the more intense because of the bitterness of the split in the nationalist movement.[6] As we have seen, the choice of Glasnevin rather than the Parnell family plot in Mount Jerome emphasised the extent to which the event was self-consciously designed to be a political demonstration. The largest funeral in Dublin since O'Connell's, it followed the precedents set by great funerals including the Liberator and Terence Bellew MacManus, with huge crowds, formal lying-in-state, elaborate rituals and symbols and extensive procession through the streets to Glasnevin via circuitous but meaningful route.[7] It also set the pattern for the annual commemorations which followed.

There were some precedents for an annual procession which took the form of an ersatz funeral and sought to recapture and channel some of the emotion which the original had generated, notably the 'Manchester Martyrs' commemorative marches.[8] William Allen and Michael O'Brien from Cork and Michael Larkin from Offaly were hanged at Manchester prison on 23 November 1867 for their part in the rescue of two Fenian prisoners during which a policeman was killed. The executions caused an outcry among Irish nationalists and for many years commemorative events were organised in different parts of Ireland, Britain and the United States. The largest of these was an annual march to the Manchester Martyrs' memorial erected in 1868 in Glasnevin. Although this was an initiative of the IRB, it attracted support from across the nationalist spectrum, not least, in the 1880s and 1890s from Parnellites. It seems reasonable to assume that the form of the Ivy Day commemoration owed much to the Manchester Martyr demonstrations; nor was this inappropriate given that Parnell's first notable contribution in the House of Commons was an interjection to insist that the executed men had not been guilty of murder and that this had first drawn him to the attention of the Fenians, thus beginning an informal relationship which was to be of enormous significance to both.[9]

Many of the marchers at Manchester Martyr demonstrations wore green ribbons; through accident or design, those promoting the commemoration of

Parnell seized upon an even more potent and evocative symbol: the ivy leaf. The reasons for the choice of the ivy have been the subject of debate. In a place of honour, beside Parnell's remains as they lay in state in City Hall, was a simple ivy wreath from a Cork woman 'as the best offering she could afford'.[10] Later at Glasnevin, as the multitudes filed into Glasnevin, some ordinary Dubliners took ivy leaves from the walls of the cemetery and put them in their lapels. The origins of the tradition of wearing ivy to commemorate Parnell may lie in either or neither of these events. What is clear is that the 'tradition' began almost immediately and that it was astutely promoted by Parnell's supporters and particularly by the *Irish Daily Independent*. In the days before the first anniversary of Parnell's death, the *Independent* carried an advertisement inviting Parnellites to wear the ivy in token of their fidelity to the lost leader's independent principles. Ivy leaves were available from the Ladies' Parnell Committee or from the offices of the *Independent* or the *Evening Herald*. Anticipating a shortage, friends in the country were urged to send packages of ivy to Dublin.[11] In an editorial, the *Independent* declared that

> the ivy worn in the button-hole will be regarded as . . . plain and determined evidence of devotion to the Independent principles which must always be associated with the name of 'the Chief'. To give such evidence, quietly but impressively, is now every man's duty, and the display of that meaningful sprig of ivy is simply a confession of political faith in the face of the enemy. Today will be inaugurated an annual custom as significant as it is pretty, and it is to be hoped that every Parnellite in the country will support it and that its initiation will be successful.'

William Michael Murphy in his book *The Parnell Myth and Irish Politics 1891–1956* (New York, Peter Lang, 1986) attributes the initiative of wearing the ivy to the *Independent*, while the *Irish Times* gives the credit to the Parnell Anniversary Committee.[12] Either way, it is clear that what was to become an 'annual custom' owed more to self-conscious manufacture than to spontaneity.

There was no inevitability in the adoption of the ivy leaf as the Parnellite symbol. For some years there was a lively market in officially endorsed and commercial badges and mementoes. In 1892, the Parnell Anniversary Committee endorsed an official commemorative badge with a vignette portrait of Parnell lithographed in white satin between two black bars with the words 'Died October 1891' underneath.[13] The badge was worn by many marchers that year but its popularity proved short-lived, presumably because it was relatively expensive and lacked the simplicity and symbolism of the ivy leaf. In the 1892 procession marchers wore green sashes and various tokens including black badges. Some wore ribbons with the motto: 'Done to death'. On the second anniversary, the portrait badges at 1*d*, 3*d* or 6*d* for a superior style, were reported to have had a 'bad market' with the trade 'badly depressed' by the sale of pewter 'army' medals engraved with Parnell's last words as reported by his colleagues.[14]

The portrait badge was still being worn prominently in 1894; it and other Parnell badges retailed in later years for a penny each.[15] However, it was the simple ivy leaf which caught the public imagination and became the enduring symbol. Despite Parnell's reputed horror for the colour green, it was the national colour and the clinging ivy symbolised fidelity to Parnell's independent principles. Lest there be any doubt about that, on 7 October 1892 the *Independent* published in full a poem entitled 'the Green Ivy', written by Katharine Tynan:

> O'er many an Irish castle, great and hoary
> The Irish ivy trails;
> And o'er grey fanes that catch the sun's last gilding
> See the last sails
> An o'er the round towers that forget their building,
> The Irish ivy trails
> And because you were our Tower, our Castle
> Tall in the landscape grey,
> Though all the lights were out, and over wassail,
> And night usurps the day.
> And since – our sorrow – in the grave you're sleeping,
> The ivy you shall have,
> Wrapping your towering height in tender keeping,
> Kissing your grave
> All your splendour shall the ivy cover
> With dew and rain-drops wet,
> And ever greener as the years go over,
> Closer and greener get.

The self-conscious attempt to achieve through the commemoration of Parnell what he had failed to achieve in life was viewed with some unease by his political opponents. Tim Healy attacked the 'ivy boys' and contemptuously dismissed the 'child's play with ivy' as perpetuating dissension.[16] In a battle of the poems, the *Freeman* produced a poetic answer to Katharine Tynan:

> Fit Symbol of those parasitic minds,
> That clung, destructive, to the stately tree,
> With grip that drags to earth whate'er it binds,
> Whether the hoary oak or noble pile it be.
> The clinging ivy, emblem of decay,
> Of ruined shrine, or leafless trunk, of ill
> To all it grapples, sapping life away,
> Thou art not Erin's badge, she wears her shamrock still!

Healy alleged that 'child's play with the ivy leaves' was 'borrowed from the British primroses', that is the British Primrose League.[17] This allegation was a petty attempt to impugn the independent nationalist credentials of the Parnellites by associating them with the Tories, but it may not have been completely wide of the mark. The Primrose League was established in 1883 by a group of Tories including Randolph Churchill to promote the maintenance of religion, of the estates of the realm and the unity of the empire. It was named in memory of Benjamin Disraeli, Earl of Beaconsfield. On the erroneous assumption that his favourite flower was the primrose, the anniversary of Disraeli's death on 19 April 1881 was termed Primrose Day and members of the League wore primroses. A tradition developed of laying primrose wreaths on his grave and later at his statue in Parliament Square. The League spread rapidly and claimed more than a million members in 1891, including many in Ireland and Australia.[18] However, if Primrose Day offered a precedent for Ivy Day, it is interesting that no attempt was made to move beyond commemorative activity to create an Ivy League as a political movement.

Whatever its origins, Ivy Day proved an immediate success in Dublin and throughout Ireland. By the first anniversary of Parnell's death, the 'tradition' of wearing the ivy had been well established. The *Morning Post* reported that 'nearly every man in the great crowd was to be seen wearing an ivy leaf.' The *Daily Telegraph* predicted that there would be a long series of Ivy Sundays in the future. The *Dublin Evening Mail* noted that 'groups of boys, in most cases decorated with ivy . . . proceeded through the streets, cheering for Parnell and groaning for T. M. Healy'. The *Irish Times* gave the most vivid account of what it conceded was an imposing procession and reported that 'a large trade was done in the sale of bunches of ivy':

> by noon the thoroughfares were thronged with men and women wearing green sashes or mourning badges bearing a picture of Mr Parnell, or green rosettes, and all having a modest leaf of ivy in the buttonhole or on the breast. Large numbers of ladies wore the same token of commemoration on their bosoms or in their hats. Little boys wore it, and numbers of the drivers of vehicles – some of them for politic as well as political reasons – wore it also, and had their horses decked with the little green leaf. It was a strange sight, and the enormous display of the green emblem must have been some answer to those of a different section of Nationalists who have been asserting in a confident manner that Parnellism is a thing of the past.[19]

The following year, the *Daily Chronicle* reported that the practice had spread to London with the ivy leaf 'in strong evidence in buttonholes, and, perhaps, even more in bonnets'.[20] By 1894, the ivy leaf was ubiquitous, as even the *Freeman's Journal* grudgingly conceded but with Tim Healy adding, in an exasperated editorial:

How long is this thing to last? Is the ivy leaf to take its place for all times beside the orange lily as the new type of a dissentient minority. Is the Liffey to rival the Boyne? Is dissension to be perpetuated to all time?

The *Freeman* was inclined to blame moral pressure and intimidation for the undoubted popularity of the ivy. It highlighted a 'regrettable incident' at the cemetery gates where a man observed not to be wearing an ivy leaf was set upon by members of the procession and beaten until police intervened. [21]

Again in 1895 and 1896, there was consensus in the newspaper reports that all the processionists and many of the spectators wore ivy leaves.[22] By 1896, the fifth anniversary of Parnell's death, the wearing of the ivy had become so commonplace as to be taken for granted. The ivy continued to be an essential feature of subsequent processions but it caused less comment.[23]

While the ivy leaf was the great original symbol of the Parnell commemorations, there were numerous other symbols and rituals in abundance. The order and form of procession, the wreaths, floral tributes and banners, the bands and the music the funeral route itself – all were richly textured acts and symbols with layers of meaning and precedent.

The assembly point for the procession was St Stephen's Green, a suitable site for practical reasons. From 1898, the foundation stone of the Wolfe Tone memorial opposite the top of Grafton Street provided a practical and symbolically useful starting point.[24] From St Stephen's Green, the route of the procession was down Grafton Street, along College Green past the Old Parliament Buildings and City hall where Parnell had lain in state, down Parliament Street, across the Liffey, along the Quays into Sackville Street, past O'Connell's statue and out to Glasnevin. This route was in part the route taken by Parnell's funeral which in turn followed well established precedents for nineteenth-century political funerals.[25] From 1896, the route was shortened with the procession moving more directly from St Stephen's Green to O'Connell Street. Later still, when numbers participating dwindled, the assembly point became the Parnell monument on O'Connell Street, unveiled in 1911, with a short procession to Glasnevin. In more recent times, the procession was abandoned in favour of the simple wreath laying at Glasnevin.[26]

On the first anniversary of Parnell's death, the procession was headed by the York Street band followed by a memorial car drawn by six black horses and guarded on either side by six 'Gaels' or GAA members. The York Street club was the largest working men's club in Dublin and was closely associated with radical nationalist politics. The band played a leading part in Parnell's funeral and, along with several other such bands from Dublin and Cork, participated annually in the Ivy Day parade for many years.[27] The memorial car was literally covered with wreaths and it was followed by a second car similarly laden. In 1894, among the wreaths were noted two of ivy and roses which bore the poignant inscriptions 'With Clara's love from Mrs CS Parnell's Clara' and 'With Katie's love. From Mrs CS Parnell's Katie.'[28] Clare and Katie were Charles's daughters. Next in the procession came a long line of carriages with various dignatories, including the Lord Mayor and members of the corporation in full regalia, members of other corporations and colleagues of Parnell. One of the carriages carried Parnell's brother, John Howard, and his sister Mrs Dickinson who attended the parade on a number of subsequent occasions. In 1896, the wreaths included one from Katharine Parnell with the inscription 'With undying love to the memory of my husband. K Parnell' and another – a cross of Ivy from Avondale – from Delia, John Howard Parnell and Mrs Dickinson.[29] Delia Parnell, Parnell's mother, attended for the first time that year, joining the procession at Eccles Street with her daughter Emily (Mrs Dickinson).[30] This added an element of intense emotion especially when she was assisted on to the mound at her son's grave.

After the carriages came a vast array of Dublin trade organisations – the Plasterers' Society, the Regular House-painters, the Brassfounders, the Amalgamated Carpenters, the Operative Stonecutters, the Bacon Curers, the Pork Butchers' Friendly Society and numerous contingents of political and trade groups from all over the country with their own banners and their own bands.

Despite its solemn and funereal origins, the parade quickly took on more of the aspect of a pageant, fete or carnival. The railway companies organised special trains from all parts of the country and offered excursion fares. Large numbers of people travelled to Dublin as much for the spectacle and the social occasion as for the procession. Ivy Day was a day for an excursion to Dublin. In 1892, one excursionist was killed when he fell on to the tracks while waiting in a large crowd for his return train. In 1896 there was a similar accident at Kingsbridge when a railway employee fell in front of the train.[31]

Plunkett Kenny who attended the parade in 1894 recorded his impression of the spectacle:

> As a fete, it was distinctly a success . . . From the 'member' in frock coat and tall hat to the ragamuffin selling matches, all seemed to take an innocent pride in the badge of ivy. Young ladies in point, picture hats, and feathers abounded. That both lace and wearer were imitations rather than originals distracted little from the *coup d'oeil* and nothing from the intrinsic worth of the lady. [32]

Hundreds of boys from the Parnell Boys' Brigade marched in the early years; later, in response to the need for enhanced spectacle, came pikemen from Wicklow and Wexford and the Irish National Foresters in uniforms including Robert Emmet costumes. In the early years, the bands played the Dead March and other melancholy tunes and the procession moved at 'slow military funeral pace'. In 1897, a formal decision seems to have been taken by the organisers to play down the funereal aspect and to brighten the proceedings. The bands played lively airs and the pace of the procession was more rapid. From 1898, the music included the Marseillaise and 1798 airs. The presence of the Dublin Fire Brigade added a significant note of colour.

While it increasingly took on the elements of pageant, fete and carnival, Ivy Day began and remained until at least 1911 a political demonstration. The anti-Parnellite irritation about the ivy leaf reflected a deeper concern in relation to the popularity of Parnell in death. In the early years, the crowds attracted to the commemoration – to march or to spectate – were enormous. The first procession was variously described as 'enormous', 'imposing', 'immense', 'striking', and 'impressive'. The London *Times*, no friend of Parnell, observed that 'the Irish capital, which refused a few days ago to offer the slightest recognition to Mr Gladstone's Lord Lieutenant, poured out its thousands to do honour to the memory of Mr. Parnell . . . no doubt can hang over the reality of Sunday's demonstration as the expression of Irish "national" feeling in the anti-English sense'. The *Daily Telegraph* judged the event a success not merely from the point of view of the promoters but 'a very memorable and significant demonstration on the part of Dublin, Cork, and other important cities, of the honour, gratitude, and affection with which the name of the departed leader is still regarded.'[33]

In the three subsequent years, the commemoration was equally impressive. Estimates of numbers attending varied, depending on the political disposition of the source and whether those who spectated were included. The *Freeman's Journal* consistently played down the attendance, commenting in 1893 that while large numbers took part and it took the greater portion of an hour to pass a given point, the processionists walked only three abreast and at a slow pace. The *Irish Times* offered a more dispassionate view:

> The enthusiasm and the allegiance of the followers of the late Mr Charles Stewart Parnell do not appear to have abated in the slightest, to judge from the nature of the demonstration which passed through the streets of Dublin yesterday. . . . Last year . . . the mass of people who walked to the grave was of vast dimensions . . . yesterday . . . the dimensions of the crowd who joined the celebration was as great as ever.

With eleven excursion trains from the South and a similar number from North and West; 'the city was crowded in an almost unprecedented fashion'. There were 2,500 excursionists from Cork alone and another 1,200 left behind. The throng of people on the streets was 'remarkable'. The procession departed St Stephen's Green at 1.30 p.m. and arrived at Glasnevin at 3.45 p.m. At some points, the streets were 'practically impassable'. In the cemetery, 'so great was the rush and so lively was the enthusiasm . . . that they failed to keep back the surging crowd from the graveside, or even to preserve a passage'.[34]

In 1894, the *Irish Times* concluded that there was no diminution either in numbers or enthusiasm while the *Freeman* conceded that it could not deny the magnitude of the procession. The *Irish Times* put the number of marchers at 7,500 and the number of spectators at 30,000. [35] In 1895, opinion divided along predictable lines as to whether the crowd was larger or smaller; while, in 1896, it was agreed that there was some falling off. Nonetheless, it was commented that the day seemed to have 'taken a place permanently in the Irish national calendar'.[36] Again in 1897, 1898 and 1899, there was some falling off in numbers processing but the crowds of spectators filling the streets remained large, in 1897 'unprecedentedly large'. In 1899, while contingents from the country had fallen, the congestion in Grafton Street in particular was 'the greatest ever seen'. This may be explained by the fact that the foundation stone of the Parnell monument was paraded through the streets and laid in Sackville Street.[37]

The laying of the foundation stone for the monument marked the beginning of the end of the heyday of the Ivy Day processions; thereafter numbers declined significantly, with occasional periods of revival. The parade had served its purpose as a rallying point for the anti-Parnellite cause. Following a decade of division, the constitutional movement reunited in 1900 under the leadership of the Parnellite, John Redmond. It was expected that this might result in a revival of interest in 1901 but this did not occur although crowds in the city for Ivy Day remained large. In 1902 again the procession was small but crowds in the city 'very large'. By 1905, the Dublin Metropolitan Police reported a parade of five bands and 300 persons adding that 'no person of importance attended the gathering at Rutland Square or marched in the procession to Glasnevin and few seemed interested in the proceedings which most people are of the opinion should be dropped'.[38] The police reports on the procession in subsequent years strike a similar note with five bands and 400 marchers noted in 1907, six bands and 300 marchers in 1909, and four bands and 300 marchers in 1910.[39]

The decline in the scale and intensity of the Ivy Day commemoration owed much to the passage of time but also to the changing political environment of which it was inextricably part. The emotion and enthusiasm generated by what was in effect an annual political demonstration gave an impetus to the Parnellite movement which was grasped eagerly and skilfully to win hearts and minds and gain a propaganda victory.

Whereas the living Parnell fought a losing battle after the split, the dead Parnell helped reverse the fortunes of his supporters; at least in terms of rhetoric, ideology and public perception, the Parnellites lost the battle but won the war. As the anti-Parnellite majority fragmented into a number of factions, the pro-Parnellite minority in parliament remained relatively cohesive. The continuing stridency of anti-Parnell invective from the *Freeman's Journal*, Tim Healy and others was itself an acknowledgement of the way the pendulum was swinging. While the Parnellites offered the ivy leaf as a national symbol, Healy berated them as a faction who 'cannot count a single man whom, on his own merits, the smallest section of his countrymen could follow and trust as leader. That is why they fasten like leeches on the reputation of Mr. Parnell, whose great name covers their littleness. That is why they would make his grave the camping ground of faction.'[40] Frank Callanan has described Healy at this time as wielding the funeral thurible as a weapon of war but his opponents proved even more adept in mobilising the memory of the dead in support of their cause.[41]

The funeral oration delivered at the 1892 commemoration by J. J. O'Kelly comprised a spirited attack on the anti-Parnellites and a restatement of Parnell's independent principles. Successive commemorations provided the occasion to wrap the mantle of Parnell around his successors and for a rallying call to a new generation. But who were Parnell's real successors? The Parnell inheritance was one worth fighting for. Even the anti-Parnellites could not afford to and did not completely dissociate themselves from Parnell's earlier achievements. They lauded 'Parnell of the good old days', Parnell the preserver not 'Parnell the destroyer'. Healy in full vitriolic flow still paused to assert that it was the Parnell of 'that last wild year of his life' they objected to. The worst enemies of Parnell's memory, he said, were those 'who fix attention on his last year and set aside the teachings of the rest of his lifetime'.[42] This subtle distinction allowed the anti-Parnellite's some room for manoeuvre and facilitated a reasonable smooth reunification in 1900. Not that this resulted in anti-Parnellite MPs participating in Ivy Day ceremonies thereafter. In fact, the number of MPs of any description participating dwindled.

The decision to nominate J. J. O'Kelly to give the oration in 1892 was viewed by some as the culmination of a division within the ranks of the Parnellites between the 'non-kid-glove types' and the 'snobbish element'. In more conventional terms, O'Kelly was seen as representing the 'hillside section'.[43] It is certainly true that his oration emphasised the more radical side of Parnell's career and his independent principles.

It also looked to the time when Parnell's stand would be retrospectively vindicated by posterity: there would surely come a time, he said, 'when in every house in Ireland there will be a picture of Parnell'. In response, the *Pall Mall Gazette* ran a perceptive editorial entitled 'the Parnell legend' which warned that legends do not always grow spontaneously; they are sometimes manufactured. Is Mr Parnell to be depicted as a moderate or as an extremist, it asked. Answering its own question, the *Gazette* predicted that Parnell would be enshrined in memory as an extremist.[44] After 1892, the oration at Glasnevin was dispensed with, either because O'Kelly's oration had been completely inaudible to the crowds or to circumvent any possibility of a radical hijack.[45] Thereafter, a separate political meeting was held, usually at the Rotunda. This became in effect the end-of-year meeting of the Parnellite party.[46]

The contest for the Parnell legacy was not simply a bilateral one between the rival wings of the parliamentary movement. Parnell, especially the later Parnell, was closely identified with the separatist tradition. Members of the GAA and IRB provided a guard of honour at his funeral and both participated in the Ivy Day commemorations. GAA contingents were conspicuous in the procession each year, while the police consistently reported the participation of IRB suspects who used the cover of the parade to travel to Dublin and attend secret meetings.[47] James Stephens and P. N. Fitzgerald who attended Parnell's funeral[48] and subsequent Ivy Day events were closely associated with the Manchester Martyrs' parade held each year in late November; the two parades were frequented by many of the same people and, especially in the early years, there was a considerable overlap between the two organising groups. Participants in Martyrs' Day very often placed a wreath on Parnell's grave as well as at the Martyrs' cenotaph nearby. On Martyrs' Day in 1893, a wreath was placed on Parnell's grave with the inscription 'he too, like Allen, Larkin and O'Brien, was sacrificed to English hate and prejudice'.[49] During the 1890s, Ivy Day supplanted Martyrs' Day as the end-of-year rallying point for advanced nationalism. With the parliamentary movement divided, Ivy Day became an expression of independence. Parnellites and, later, members of the United Irish League (the new constitutional nationalist organisation), dominated the Martyrs' demonstration to the annoyance of some republicans. However, with the revival of interest in republicanism and Wolfe Tone generated by the centenary of 1798 and, later, the reunification of the Irish Party under Redmond in 1900, it became increasingly difficult to sustain the uneasy alliance of Parnellites and separatists.

The cracks in the alliance of moderate Parnellites and the hillside men emerged gradually. By 1894, public figures associated with the IRB were publicly castigating some Parnellites for failing to live up to their radical rhetoric.[50] The cracks became even more public in 1898 during the 1798 centenary celebrations. On 15 August, the foundation stone of the Wolfe Tone monument was laid at St Stephen's Green in an event organised by the IRB but publicly dominated by Irish Party MPs.[51] The following year, a decision by the Corporation to permit the laying of the foundation stone for the Parnell monument and to proceed with this project before the completion of the Wolfe Tone statue caused outrage and forced many separatists to choose between the two heroes: there is here, one observer commented with relish, 'a split' – between those who preferred Wolfe Tone to Parnell and those who preferred Parnell to Wolfe Tone. This was made 'vociferously abundant' during the 1899 procession when the Lord Mayor's carriage was jeered and booed. The subsequent speeches at the site of the proposed monument were delivered 'amid a scene of some disorder' with scuffles, shouts of 'Up the Boers' and attempts by young men to scale the platform. When Captain Toole of Waterford declared that he stood there in the name of Parnell and added that he 'did not care for Archbishop Walsh, nor for Dr Croke, nor for the pope of Rome himself' he was roundly booed and drowned out with shouts of 'withdraw' and 'sit down'. The Lord Mayor who was presented with an address acknowledging his efforts in relation to the Parnell monument was barracked throughout his short speech and required a police escort as he beat a hasty retreat to the Mansion House. In his address, John Redmond indignantly repudiated the suggestion that the monument project was motivated by party motive and stressed that it should become a symbol of unity. By way of appeasing the radical element, he expressed the hope that the gallant republic of South Africa might be able to maintain its liberty intact – there had been a very sizeable anti-war demonstration in Dublin the previous week.[52]

It would be wrong to overstate the significance of these fissures; James Stephens was the guest of honour at the ceremony and many Fenians participated. In his speech, J. K. Bracken reasserted the links between Parnell and the separatist position: 'they came here every October', he said, 'to proclaim their faith in Parnell's principles, and they would come again, to tell the British Government and the West Britons in Ireland that though Parnell was laid to rest they would continue to fight on the same lines until they made this old land of theirs a nation once again.[53] However, it is evident that as the split between the two wings of the parliamentary movement began to heal, cracks began to appear in the broad coalition of Parnellites and separatists who had shaped the commemoration of Parnell throughout the 1890s.[54] Ivy Day increasingly became the preserve of Parnell's old parliamentary comrades while the Martyrs' commemoration was more closely associated with separatist nationalism. Nonetheless, as late as 1911, the decoration of the Martyrs' cenotaph and the graves of Parnell, John O'Leary and James Stephens was undertaken by the Parnell Memorial Committee. In the same year, W. A. Redmond MP gave the address at the Martyrs' parade in Manchester. His words emphasise the dangers of an unduly schematised categorisation of the various wings of the nationalist movement and the speed with which retrospective legitimisation was achieved:

> I offer no apology for the actions, aims and objects of Irish Fenians. I am yet a young man, but I solemnly declare if I had been alive in Ireland in those sad and turbulent times I would not have hesitated to fight for my native land.[55]

The initiative for erecting a statue to Parnell in the centre of Dublin to rival that of O'Connell came from John Redmond and was inextricably linked with the movement towards creation of a reunified constitutional nationalist movement. In the Autumn of 1898, a committee was established to solicit subscriptions and obtain a site from the Corporation, chaired by the Lord Mayor, Daniel Tallon, and comprising Redmond, Dr J. E. Kenny MP, Edward Blake MP, Thomas Baker from the *Irish Independent* and Count Plunkett. The project was dogged with problems from the outset. The Corporation refused to sanction the preferred location which would have involved moving the Thomas Moore statue; instead a site beside the Rotunda was agreed. The unseemly rows at the laying of the foundation stone helped to alienate both republican and anti-Parnellite factions. The choice of the Irish-American sculptor, Augustus Saint-Gaudens, was designed to facilitate fund-raising in the United States but the response from both Ireland and America was lukewarm. Redmond was forced to tour America to drum up support. Just under £6,000 was raised initially, far short of the sum required and further appeals for funds were required over the next decade. In 1904, a fire at Saint-Gaudens studio destroyed a scale model of the monument and in 1907, shortly after the statue was delivered to Ireland, Saint-Gaudens died and alternative arrangements had to be made for supervising the erection of the monument.[56] When finally completed, the impressive monument, built of Shantalla and Barna granite, was an obelisk triangular in plan, rising to a height of 57 feet above street level crowned with a bronze tripod eight feet high, and fronted on an elevated pedestal by a bronze statue of Parnell eight feet high.[57]

The unveiling of the completed monument on 1 October 1911 marked a watershed in the Ivy Day commemorations which had been in gradual decline for some years. According to a contemporary police report, the procession was the largest seen in Dublin for many years, with close on 70 bands, numerous representative bodies and trades societies taking part.[58] The unveiling became in effect the Ivy Day commemoration that year – the Ivy Day procession the following week was a more muted affair marked only by the nine-foot high wreath from the Parnell Commemoration Association.[59] In his address at the unveiling ceremony, John Redmond posed the rhetorical question, where were the belittlers of Parnell's greatness now? The polite response from the *Freeman* was an editorial arguing that it was only now possible to estimate what Parnell had done for Ireland: the figure of Parnell grew in magnitude and the importance of his work became more and more apparent as time passed on. It concluded that 'if we are on the threshold of Home Rule, no man is more accountable for that than Parnell.' A more succinct answer, from Arthur Griffith and *Sinn Féin*, was that the enemies of Parnell were behind Redmond on the platform.[60]

After 1911, the Ivy Day commemoration was on a more modest scale. The revival of Home Rule after 1911 and the radicalisation of Irish opinion after 1914 ensured that the Parnell legacy would continue to be disputed. Home

Rulers and Republicans continued to claim rights of succession but it was hardly surprising that the Ivy Day commemoration was more muted. It is significant that in the aftermath of the 1916 Rising, Redmond chose the 25th anniversary of Parnell's death for an important speech on Home Rule – but the speech was, of necessity, not delivered at Glasnevin, but in Waterford.[61] In October 1921 the Parnell monument was decorated with ivy and a low-key ceremony was organised at Glasnevin by the Parnell Commemoration Committee. That set the tone for later years.[62]

In the late 1930s there was a slight revival of interest associated with the establishment of a committee by Niall Harrington and H. P. Boland in 1937 to mark Parnell's grave more fittingly.[63] Paradoxically, despite the annual Ivy Day parade to his grave, Parnell's last resting place had not been marked by any significant memorial. It had been intended that the grave would become the centre of a Parnell circle to rival the O'Connell circle, in which would be buried Parnell's comrades and family but this did not happen. Only Parnell's mother Delia was buried in the Parnell circle alongside her son (in 1898). After Parnell's funeral, the grave was tended by a ladies' committee led by Mrs J. J. Clancy, Mrs Wyse Power and Miss Fottrell. The grave was re-sodded with shamrock sods and the surroundings planted – attempts to grow ivy at the head of the grave proved futile because of the constant taking of the shoots by visitors. For over a year, the large floral cross presented by his colleagues was maintained and freshly dressed, but eventually this became impractical and it was replaced by an Irish cross of iron in which was placed an evergreen wreath. The words 'Parnell' were maintained in evergreens at the foot of the grave. In 1893, Thomas Fagan of Great Brunswick Street was contracted to place an iron railing around the circle enclosing the grave at a cost of £360, raised mainly by the ladies' committee.[64] Set in limestone, these railings are decorated with ivy leaf and shamrock motifs.

The attention to Parnell's grave in the early years was not unusual or unprecedented. In 1892, Decoration Day was instigated by the IRB, partly in response to the plethora of patriot graves but also by way of staking a claim to all the patriot dead. Based on American patriotic practice, this foreshadowed to a limited extent the contemporary day of national remembrance by designating a common day on which nationalists of whatever hue who had died for Ireland, could be commemorated. In effect the occasion which was held in November, the month of the dead, generally on the same day as the Martyrs' commemoration, was an occasion when graves were visited, decorated and wreaths laid. It endured for about 25 years. It would appear that Parnellites used this occasion mainly as an extension of Ivy Day.[65]

Inevitably, John Redmond's initiative to erect a monument on O'Connell Street diverted attention away from the grave and the need for a more lasting memorial at Glasnevin. By the time St Gaudens' monument was completed, the moment had passed. There matters rested until 1937 when a new initiative was taken by Boland and Harrington. Boland was a brother of Ambassador Freddy Boland while Captain Harrington was a son of Timothy Harrington MP, secretary of the Land League and, later, Lord Mayor of Dublin. When Boland inquired about the commemoration of Parnell and the trustees of the grave, Leon O'Broin put him in contact with Harrington who was involved with the Parnell Commemoration Committee which organised Ivy Day.[66] Following a public meeting in April 1938, it was decided to establish a committee and launch a public appeal for subscriptions with a view to placing a permanent name-stone on the grave and to provide for the care of the grave plot in perpetuity.[67]

The launch produced a rebuke from 'Siobhan Bean An Paoraigh' (Jennie Wyse Power), a member of the original ladies' committee which had long since disbanded. She had taken offence on behalf of her colleagues at the impression conveyed that the grave had been neglected. Fortunately for the new committee, as a split is never far from the surface in Parnellite politics, they were able to point out that one of their number, Charles Clancy, was the son of Mrs J. J. Clancy, President of the ladies' committee.[68] The other members of the new committee were mainly old Parnellites or their children, with no motive other than the preservation of Parnell's memory. Clancy, John P. Hayden, ex MP (Mullingar), J. J. Horgan (Cork), and Mrs W.A. Redmond TD, Waterford, were trustees and Boland and Harrington were joint secretaries. The other members of the committee were Captain Henry Harrison, Dr Mark Ryan, Alderman L. Walsh TD, Mayor of Drogheda, Alderman P. Doyle TD, Dublin, Dr Lorcan Sherlock, fomer Lord Mayor of Dublin, James Montgomery and W. Barry, Mullingar. George P. Sheridan, architect to the Cemeteries Committee, agreed to act as adviser.

The committee was anxious to emphasise that it was a non-political group, unconnected with other organisations, even the Parnell Commemoration Committee. With Fianna Fáil in the ascendant, a perceived association of the rump of the Redmondite Party with Cumann na nGaedheal was not conducive to successful fund-raising. Harrington for his part was keen to play down his own role as he was a serving army officer.[69] It was estimated that £500 would be required to complete their task. The organisers quickly concluded that 'they would not get much help from the general public' – an indication of the extent to which Parnell's memory had faded by the 1930s – and concentrated instead on targeting individual subscriptions.[70] While some money was raised in Cork and Mullingar, Boland wrote to Harrington in May 1938 that it seemed likely that 'Dublin, as it did in 1890' would be the mainstay of the movement.[71] Within weeks, he was reporting that 'steam was drying up' and that it would be necessary to seek support in Britain and the USA. A circular to TDs and senators had produced 'a solitary guinea' when a general election was called and the prospect of further support from that quarter vanished.[72] In desperation contact was made with Mr Dunphy, the President's secretary, asking him to bring the scheme to his notice. Boland urged Harrington:

> We don't want one more added to the list of abortive memorial subscription schemes – like Wolfe Tone's, the Land League Mon'mt in Co. Mayo, the Parnell one in Wicklow and so on. I often think these abortions were the result of the procrastinators always counselling delay, to which our people in general need no encouragement.[73]

By September, a sum of £237 had been raised from 138 subscribers including Douglas Hyde, President, and Eamon de Valera, Taoiseach, who each subscribed £10. The largest single donation was £25.[74] Fund-raising efforts continued to make slow progress until the fund finally reached £328. Arising from a combination of the simplicity of what was proposed and the prudence of Boland and Harrington, the cost of the memorial came to a modest £126. A small portion of the balance was used to place a plaque on the former Morrison's Hotel on Dawson Street where Parnell was arrested in 1882 and the remainder was donated to the Cemeteries Committee to provide for the care of the grave in perpetuity.

Whether as a throwback to the complexities of Parnell politics or as a product of Harrington's and Boland's temperaments, they structured their project in almost Byzantine fashion with a general committee, an executive committee and a sub-committee to deal with the memorial itself. After some division within the sub-committee, a simple but striking monument was decided upon: a great boulder of Wicklow granite. After some investigation, a suitable stone almost eight tons in weight was located at Poulaphuca and inscribed with the name Parnell. The owner of the field agreed to accept £5 and the cost of transportation to Glasnevin was estimated at £25. Removal, erection and inscribing of the boulder were undertaken by stone-cutters from Ballyknocken supervised by Pierce Purcell, an engineer whose father had been a Parnellite.[75] The Parnell circle was cleared of trees and shrubs which were now overgrown and the opening in the original railings were closed. A small slab was laid inside the circle indicating that the stone was of Wicklow granite and that Parnell's mother Delia lies beside him.[76]

Although it was not directly related, the memorial project gave a new focus to the Ivy Day commemorations; but there was no revival. In 1937, the commemoration attracted notoriety because of a decision by the cemetery authorities to prohibit an oration, citing an obscure byelaw. H. P. Boland had agreed to give the oration but withdrew when the authorities announced the ban. Following the customary procession from the Parnell monument,

P. J. MacDonnell, secretary of the Commemoration Association, laid the wreath and read a short prepared statement explaining the absence of an oration and P. J. Mathews, chairman, thanked the small crowd of republicans and Parnellites who attended.[77] In 1938 it was estimated that no more than two score people attended the commemoration; in 1939 the numbers were estimated at 50 and, in 1940, even smaller. On all three occasions, orations were delivered at the Parnell monument before marching to Glasnevin for the wreath laying. In 1938, P. J. Mathews emphasised Parnell's separatism and his championing of the working classes while in 1940 Mr T. Bannon spoke of the efforts to have Fanny Parnell's remains returned to Ireland.[78]

The fiftieth anniversary of Parnell's death was marked by a very significant commemoration. A full week of activities were organised in Dublin and in Wicklow. While the Commemoration Association organised Ivy Day, the other events were organised and co-ordinated by the Dublin Wicklowmen's Association. This lent a non-party dimension and facilitated an impressive celebration. Events included a public lecture by Henry Harrison and an exhibition of sixty sketches illustrating Land League and Home Rule struggles at the Municipal Gallery. The green flag which draped Parnell's coffin was displayed by the Irish Tourist association. On Monday 6 October, the anniversary of the death, de Valera placed a tricoloured wreath on the grave while John Hayden MP laid a wreath of ivy. In his speech before a crowd of about a hundred mainly elderly men and women, de Valera praised those like Parnell who had sown the seeds of independence, on behalf of the living generation who had reaped the harvest, and praised his fearless leadership of the land struggle.

On Ivy Day, the following Sunday, thousands lined the streets to watch a colourful procession from St Stephen's Green to Glasnevin. Nineteen bands participated as well as a contingent of pike-men from Wicklow and an honour guard of IRB men. Set against the background of international war, there was a decidedly military tone. Among those who observed the procession were Sir John Maffey, representative of the British government, Mr Gray, the United States representative and the secretaries of the German, French and Italian legations. Hundreds of police and LDF men were on duty regulating traffic. Some of the spectators seeking better vantage points stood on the roof of an air-raid shelter near the Parnell monument. The speeches stressed Irish independence and self-determination. Giolla Chriost O'Brien declared that if Parnell were alive he would be fighting for the complete freedom of Ireland. There was a large attendance of senior government ministers. A letter was received from Basil Brooke, Northern Minister for agriculture politely declining an invitation to attend. At Glasnevin, wreaths were laid, a yew tree from Avondale was planted and a volley of shots was fired by a party representing various army battalions.[79]

Since 1941, Ivy Day has continued as a small, dignified, low-key occasion organised by the Parnell Commemoration Association. In the 1970s, efforts were made to reinvigorate the association by opening membership at an annual subscription of 50 pence. The aims were defined as being 'to perpetuate the memory of Charles Stewart Parnell by initiating or assisting in all lawful means aimed at that purpose'. The association was 'non political and non-sectarian'. As well as the annual wreath laying, occasional lectures were organised with speakers including T. W. Moody, R. Dudley Edwards and Conor Cruise O'Brien and a successful campaign was initiated to have Avondale opened to the public. The long-time secretary and later President was Niall Harrington.[80]

As the centenary of Parnell's death approached, Mr John Bruton TD, put down a Dáil question for the Taoiseach asking about plans to commemorate Parnell and whether he would take steps to encourage members of the Oireachtas to attend Ivy Day in Glasnevin. Mr Haughey replied:

It gives me great pleasure, for once, to acknowledge a very good suggestion from the Deputy. I think we both agree on our admiration for Parnell.

In the exchanges which followed, Deputy Jim Mitchell, Fine Gael, interjected that Parnell 'was a closet Fianna Fáiler'. Later that year, in answer to another question, the Taoiseach stated that the question of government representation at the ceremony would be considered in due course.[81] In the event, a full range of commemorations took place in Wicklow and at the Parnell monument – the Ivy Day ceremony at Glasnevin was along now traditional lines. A crowd of about 200 attended the wreath laying and heard the historian Robert Kee deliver a short oration.[82]

What had been in its first decade a major potent symbolic political and social event excited only occasional interest thereafter. As the *Irish Times* commented in 1939, in the spray above the recent cascades of political history, new patriots had appeared.[83] Each brought with him his own sacred sites and places of pilgrimage. While all the parties in the state, including Sinn Féin, could claim a share in the legacy of Parnell, in no case did that go to the heart of their identity. At the end of the Second World War, *The Bell* pointed to the obvious truth that with every Ivy Day that passes, the 'reality that the few survivors knew grows more blurred while the myth becomes more distinct and rigid'.[84] Parnell and Ivy Day has passed from memory into history.

CHAPTER II

From Politics to History

The Changing Image of Parnell

Donal McCartney

'"I was at Parnell's funeral", shall be a proud yet melancholy boast in years to come . . . No greater upheaval of emotion had ever been witnessed in Ireland.' So said the *Freeman's Journal* (12 October 1891) reporting the event. Yet, no Catholic clergyman nor anti-Parnellite MP was present.

The vilification to which he had been exposed in the last year of his life did not dissolve with his death; but raged throughout the ten-year split of the 1890s; survived the reunification of the party in 1900; and remained palpable throughout the years of the first Free State government. Opposition to Parnell, and to the commemoration of his memory, was both political and moralistic. But what was political and what was moral could hardly be separated: the rhetoric of both was the same. And anti-Parnellism became a measure of the extent to which Nationalism and Catholicism had fused by the late nineteenth century.

Michael Davitt was the first of the lieutenants to repudiate Parnell. Three days after the verdict of the divorce court, he wrote to Archbishops Walsh of Dublin and Croke of Cashel (20 November 1890): 'Are we going to allow Parnell to wreck the Irish cause in the interests of the strumpet for whom he has all but sacrificed us already?'[1] Without waiting for their response, he publicly condemned the continuation of Parnell's leadership on moral as well as on political grounds; and complained that not a single bishop or priest had spoken out against Parnell.[2]

Croke and Walsh were agreed that had silence been observed in the immediate aftermath of the divorce verdict, a reasonable compromise might have been negotiated. 'Davitt', said Croke, 'though substantially right, was as usual precipitate'. How Croke felt privately about Parnell was expressed in a letter to Walsh. He wrote (22 November 1890): 'I have flung him away forever. His bust which for some time has held a prominent place in my hall, I kicked out yesterday.'[3]

Guided by William Walsh, the shrewd Archbishop of Dublin, the bishops had been slow to issue any public condemnations of Parnell, though they were under pressure to do so. As Dr Walsh explained in reply to Cardinal Manning's urgings, he had adopted the line of private communication because he was convinced that such a course was more likely to be effective than that of public declarations. So, while he restrained the more impetuous among his colleagues, he privately urged the politicians to achieve Parnell's retirement from the leadership. He was aware that too hasty a public denunciation by the bishops would be open to the charge of clerical interference in politics. Then, while the party was still discussing the crisis in committee room 15, the Hierarchy issued a statement declaring: 'Surely Catholic Ireland so eminently conspicuous for its virtue and the purity of its social life, will not accept as its leader a man thus dishonoured, and wholly unworthy of Christian confidence.'[4]

It was one thing to condemn Parnell on moral grounds, it was quite another for the clergy to become actively engaged in anti-Parnellite politics. There was more than a grain of truth in the comment by the *Tablet*: 'The motive of the Irish bishops for opposing Parnell', it said, 'was a combination of the love of purity and a fear of political damnation in the next general election.'[5]

Under the Household Franchise Act of 1884, the number of voters in Ireland had been increased from a quarter of a million to three quarters of a million. The influence of the clergy on the new voters, especially in the rural parishes, became apparent in the three by-elections that took place during the last year of Parnell's lifetime.

The first of these was in North Kilkenny. The Bishop of Ossory, Dr Brownrigg, wrote to Archbishop Croke (11 December): 'Here, we are doing all that men can do to win. We are organising election committees and opening subscriptions.'[6] He invited Croke to join him on an election platform in Kilkenny with Michael Davitt. (A cynic would later remark that when Our Lord was crucified it was between two thieves; but when anti-Parnellites stood on the hustings they were supported by two bishops).[7] And the bishop boasted that victory was due: 'not to politics, nor to morality, nor to the Irish Party; but purely and simply to the influence . . . of the priesthood.'[8]

It was precisely this kind of involvement that resulted in the allegation that the anti-Parnellites were 'the Bishops' Party'. For the anti-Parnellites needed the bishops; and the bishops needed the anti-Parnellites. After Kilkenny, when William O'Brien and Dillon tried to negotiate some sort of settlement with Parnell, the intransigence of Healy and Davitt was matched on the episcopal side by Croke: 'So far . . . as I am concerned' wrote Croke, 'no truce, no compromise shall be entered into. Parnell *must* retire.'[9] And he directed a confidential circular to the clergy of Cashel: 'Organise your parish as soon and as effectively as possible . . . Reconstruct the League in your parish . . . so as to be under legitimate control . . . in defence of truth, honour, religion and country.'[10]

North Sligo was the second of these by-elections. Four dioceses overlapped the county. The Bishops of three – Elphin, Ardagh, and Achonry – supported the anti-Parnellite candidate. The Bishop of Killala (Conway), old and ill, wished to remain neutral. He came under intense pressure from his fellow bishops, one of whom charitably described him as 'hazy and stupid' and 'not fully aware of what was going on'.[11] A government supporter reported that the extravagant efforts made by the priests to control, or perhaps even to intimidate the ignorant peasants, had succeeded.

Carlow was the last of the three by-elections held before Parnell's death. The Bishop of Kildare and Leighlin and his coadjutor nominated the anti-Parnellite. A few days before polling, Parnell was married to Katharine O'Shea in a registry office. That same day in Maynooth the Hierarchy passed a resolution which, far from being a wedding present, declared that 'by his public misconduct' he had 'utterly disqualified himself' from being leader of the Irish people, and called upon the people to repudiate his leadership.[12] Clerical influence had helped to defeat all three of Parnell's candidates. Then, in the general elections, the clerical-backed anti-Parnellites overwhelmed the Parnellites by 70 seats to 9 in 1892, and by 70 seats to 11 in 1895.

What steps the bishops had been prepared to take in their campaign is illustrated in the role they played in the setting up of an anti-Parnellite daily newspaper. Archbishop Walsh encouraged and aided the establishment of this viciously anti-Parnell publication, called the *National Press*. It was controlled by Tim Healy. Logue of Armagh reported to Rome that the bishops had received a written guarantee which would secure its soundness. 'Of course', he added, 'this is private, as the knowledge of it might be made a handle to ruin the influence of the new paper.'[13]

Moral condemnation of Parnell by the bishops had been followed by their blatant political opposition, which, combined with Tim Healy's scurrilous attacks, created the demonic image of Parnell that pervaded the 1890s. He was now described as 'this arch-enemy of religion'. Bishop O'Doherty of Derry compared him to Lucifer.[14] Archbishop Logue believed that the Parnellites were educating the people into undisguised anti-clericalism and a hatred of Church authority.[15] An editorial in the *Irish Catholic* (1 August 1891) declared Parnellism a Satanic revolt . . . an anti-Christian movement whose objective is the deification of immorality . . . A war between Christ and anti-Christ.[16] Nor in its report of Parnell's death did the *Irish Catholic* mollify its anathemas. 'Death has come upon him in a house of sin', it reported. He is linked forever with a woman whose presence seemed to forbid all thought of his repentance. The light of hope shines not, and there is nought but darkness, drear and horrid.'[17] In brief, he was condemned to Hell.

Bishop Nulty's pastoral, read in all the churches of the diocese of Meath during the general election of 1892, described Parnellism as having sprung from the foul root of sensualism and sin. 'Parnellism, like Paganism', it continued, 'impedes, obstructs and cripples the efficiency, and blights the fruitfulness of the preaching of the Gospel and the diffusion of that Divine knowledge without which our people cannot be saved.'[18] The natural tendency and inevitable result of Parnellism, it claimed, would be the extirpation of the Catholic religion. Preaching at Trim, the Bishop said that he would approach the deathbed of a drunkard or a profligate with greater confidence as to his salvation than that of a Parnellite. And when the *Westmeath Examiner* supported the Parnellites he proclaimed it a sin to read it, and declared the person who continued to read it unfit for the Sacraments. It seemed as if all the hounds of the Lord were hot on the scent of Parnell.

Nor was the Satanic image of Parnell likely to disappear in the new century. The bishops most scathing in their condemnations survived well into the twentieth century, and not one retracted his censures. Although Parnell retained support among a few of the lower clergy, the hierarchy to a man had lined up against him. That the bishops were seen to have taken so powerful a scalp as Parnell's was ominous. A hierarchy that had been publicly divided on the land agitation had now solidly and solemnly reunited in its denunciation of Parnell's adultery and his fitness for leadership. And a united hierarchy could proceed in greater confidence, arrogance and influence into a half-century or so following its role in the bringing down of the Uncrowned King. The part played by the bishops was bolstered and underwritten by the lay politicians who had been Parnell's erstwhile lieutenants.

Davitt's influential book, *The Fall of Feudalism in Ireland*, was published in 1904. And though he acknowledged the good Parnell had done in the Land League, he remained as critical as ever of the liaison with Mrs O'Shea, and of the Parnell who in his view had wrecked Home Rule, split the party, and betrayed the people by his deliberate and insane refusal to retire.

Tim Healy's *Letters and Leaders of My Day* was published in 1928. He was even less indulgent than Davitt: it was extraordinary how much of the bitterness and scurrility of almost 40 years earlier had been retained. Healy and William Martin Murphy, leading the clericalist party, represented that right-wing conservative Catholic nationalism which had surfaced with the fall of Parnell. It survived the republican nationalism of 1916–21. And was still clearly in evidence in the Free State of 1922–32. The clear sign that Parnellism had been vanquished was in the appointment of Tim Healy as first Governor-General of the Free State, on the unanimous recommendation of the Free State's Executive Council. There could be no reinstatement of Parnell in such circumstances; and no official commemoration of his achievements.

Much more congenial to the spirit of the times were the celebrations in 1929 of the centenary of Catholic Emancipation, and in 1932 of the Eucharistic Congress. Lenten pastorals encouraged the people to participate in commemorating the achievement of O'Connell – not O'Connell the Repealer, but O'Connell the Liberator. Celebrations were held in a number of places throughout the country. A quarter of a million assembled for Pontifical Mass in the Phoenix Park. This was a dress rehearsal for the Eucharistic Congress, for which a state reception was held in Dublin Castle, and a garden party in the grounds of Blackrock College with 14,000 guests. The open-air Mass in the Phoenix Park drew one million people. And a procession of the Blessed Sacrament ended appropriately at the O'Connell monument on O'Connell Bridge. Not simply a religious ceremony, it was also a monster demonstration of Irish Catholic nationalism. Faith and Fatherland were inseparably one. And O'Connell's Catholic Ireland had come to dominate over Parnellism as surely as the O'Connell round tower in Glasnevin towered over Parnell's modest grave.

By contrast with the official celebration of O'Connell, the Liberator, the much smaller, non-official commemorations at Parnell's grave could still be seen as fanning the flames of dissension and keeping alive the animosities of the split. Healy had ridiculed these gatherings by those he had labelled the 'Ivy-boys'; and he had called Parnell's grave 'the camping ground of faction'.[19] The foundation stone of the Parnell monument had been laid in October 1899, with Redmond's express purpose of putting an end to what he called the 'national ingratitude' of the Irish people to Parnell.[20] But anti-Parnellite MPs and clergy had once again boycotted the ceremony. Yet, Redmond had persevered; and money collected in America paid for the statue which was transported to Ireland eventually in 1907. Late in 1909, Tim Harrington, that stalwart Parnellite, had to make a further appeal in the national press for the petty sum still required for the pedestal. It was remarked that either Parnell was forgotten, or Irishmen were still miserably afraid of the bishops. When the monument was finally unveiled in 1911, the *Irish Catholic* commented that the structure bore a pagan aspect, and the appearance of bleakness, darkness and desolation.[21]

A pamphlet addressed to Archbishop Walsh by F. H. O'Donnell, the former Home Rule MP, taunted the Archbishop, declaring that a semi-pagan phallic pillar had been erected in the most conspicuous street of the Archdiocese. He added: 'It may not be complimentary to the Cathedral City, but it was painfully adequate to the subject commemorated.'[22]

When that was written in 1914, the whole political environment was changing radically. And with it the satanic image of Parnell, created by the bishops and Healy, was also losing its appeal. A major contribution to the softening of the image of Parnell was Barry O'Brien's *Life of Parnell*, first published in 1898, reissued in a popular edition in 1910, and made available, as John Redmond said in his preface, 'to the masses of our people in Ireland and overseas'.[23] A great admirer of Parnell, O'Brien gave flesh and blood to his hero. And he gave credibility to his portrait by getting Gladstone to testify that Parnell possessed extraordinary political skills and leadership qualities, and was the most remarkable and interesting man that he had ever met in his 60 years in parliament. The man who had brought down Parnell, by insisting there could be no Home Rule while Parnell remained leader, had now, in O'Brien's biography, proclaimed Parnell the greatest Irish political figure of the nineteenth century.[24]

It was in the year following the publication of the cheap edition of O'Brien's biography that the monument was unveiled. About 50 MPs (including old rivals) and some clergy were now present. But significantly, also in attendance were Countess Markievicz's Fianna under their banner with Tone's rallying cry: 'To break the connection with England'. And there also was the enemy of Wm. M. Murphy – Jim Larkin and his trade union. It was a sign that republicanism and radicalism were on the march in Dublin, and carrying, as it were, the banner of Parnell.

Then, at Christmas 1915, Pearse issued his famous pamphlet, *Ghosts*. It began: 'There has been nothing more terrible in Irish history than the failure of the last generation . . . The men who have led Ireland for twenty-five years [i.e. since they destroyed Parnell] have done evil, and they are bankrupt . . .' (This was a sentiment that the IRB, Sinn Féin, Connolly and many in the literary movement could empathise with.) Pearse continued: 'One finds oneself wondering what sin these men have been guilty of that so great a shame could come upon them. . . . does the ghost of Parnell hunt them to their damnation?' Not only did Pearse place Parnell in the pantheon of Irish patriots, but portrayed him alongside Tone, Davis, Lalor and Mitchel as a Separatist. 'His instinct', he wrote, 'was a Separatist instinct'.[25] And Pearse's writings, his heroes and his deed were about to have a profound influence on the subsequent half-century of Ireland's history. And so Parnell, the demon of the bishops, transfigured once more into the Uncrowned King by Barry O'Brien's biography, had now become, in Pearse's portrait, the crypto-Fenian.

Further metamorphoses still awaited him. In the writings of the two greatest names in Anglo-Irish literature, Joyce and Yeats, he was commemorated – mythologised and immortalised – as the romantic hero brought down by his own people who proved themselves unworthy of him. Joyce wrote:

> May everlasting shame consume
> The memory of those who tried
> To befoul and smear the exalted name
> Of one who spurned them in his pride.[26]

But in Catholic Ireland there still remained the scandal of the O'Shea affair. Parnell and Mrs O'Shea had decided not to offer any defence in the divorce action, since a decree in favour of Captain O'Shea would leave them free to marry. And Parnell's explanation was never heard. That is, not until his colleague, Henry Harrison, published his book *Parnell Vindicated* (1931).

The book was dedicated 'not less to those that were misled, than to those that stood true'. The intention was to save Parnell's name from the slur that had been left upon it by the undefended divorce action. Harrison showed that the O'Sheas had been virtually separated for years during which time Parnell and Mrs O'Shea had been living in harmonious partnership equivalent, in their view, to honourable marriage; and that dishonour and discredit were on the husband's side and not on Parnell's.

Harrison later visited Yeats and begged him to write something to convince all Parnellites that Parnell had nothing to be ashamed of in his love for Katharine O'Shea. Yeats responded with the ballad: 'Come gather round me Parnellites / And praise our chosen man' (1936). All are familiar with the last verse:

> The Bishops and the Party
> That tragic story made,
> A husband that had sold his wife
> And after that betrayed;
> But stories that live longest
> Are sung above the glass,
> And Parnell loved his country
> And Parnell loved his lass.[27]

Loving his country and loving his lass had become equally virtuous in Yeats's portrait of Parnell.

During the Kilkenny by-election in 1890, it was claimed that 'the only power in Ireland that can stand up to Parnell is the Church, and the only power that can stand up to the Church is Fenianism'.[28] By the 1930s, the Church and what now passed for the Fenian or Republican tradition were no longer at war with each other. Fianna Fáil, the Republican Party, had come to power. And de Valera was able on the one hand to participate fully in the Eucharistic Congress, and on the other to honour Parnell officially in 1941, fifty years after his death, and again in 1946, the centenary of his birth.

Harrison's book had been the final shot fired by either Parnellite or anti-Parnellite. And with it Parnell finally passed from politics into history. Academically trained historians began to approach Parnell, no longer from the standpoint of bitter partisanship, but in the interest of historical explanation. There followed studies on various aspects of the Parnell phenomenon from historians such as T. W. Moody, C. C. O'Brien, F. S. L. Lyons, Emmet Larkin, Roy Foster, Paul Bew, Frank Callanan, Robert Kee. They did not always agree on emphasis or interpretation. But they were no longer bitter partisans. Their work amounted to yet another way of commemorating Parnell's enduring fascination.[29]

And that brings us right down to the late and much beloved Máire Tobin, who died on 2 June 2004. Máire, with a few friends, was founder, secretary and for nearly twenty years the inspiration of the Parnell Society. The daughter of Liam Tobin of the IRB, one of Collins's squad, she was herself a staunch republican. She had been actively involved in a Fianna Fáil Cumann in Greystones, until, as some might say, she saw the light. But she remained republican; participated in Ivy-Day ceremonies; was keenly aware of Fenian loyalty to Parnell; was pleased that Parnell had won approval from the later Republicans; rejoiced in the heroic image created by Joyce and Yeats, and eagerly read the more sober analyses made by the professional historians. Putting all of these elements together, she initiated what was first called: the County Wicklow Parnell Commemorative Group.

I received a letter from Máire, secretary of this group, dated 9 December 1985, inviting me to give a lecture at a seminar which they planned to hold in Avondale in the Spring of 1986, the centenary of the first Home Rule Bill. Her letter said that the group was formed to stimulate interest in C. S. Parnell – his life, his work and times; and also to promote Avondale so that it would more fully reflect its connection with Parnell and his family.

There were probably more syllables in the original name of this County Wicklow Parnell Commemorative Group than members. So the name was changed to the more manageable 'Parnell Society', and a third aim was added: 'To explore the relevance of Parnell and the politics of his era to modern Ireland.' From that tiny seed-bed, so lovingly tended by Máire, there developed a Spring Day, then an Autumn Weekend, and since 1991, the Summer School, which so far has resulted in the publication of a couple of books of lectures that were delivered on those occasions. She also organised Christmas at Avondale, and trips to Fanny Parnell's grave at Mount Auburn outside Boston, to Anna's at Ilfracombe, in Devon, and to Katharine's at Littlehampton, in Sussex. Altogether, she has generated much pleasure, some tolerance for different points of view, and not a little knowledge. Máire Tobin's name is now linked forevermore with the commemoration of C. S. Parnell. This book of essays is dedicated to her cherished memory.

Notes

INTRODUCTION

1   For a good overview of the debate on revisionism, see Ciaran Brady (ed.), *Interpreting Irish History: The Debate on Historical Revisionism* (Dublin, 1994).

2   The commemoration of the famine was spread over three years from 1995 to 1997. The themes of the Parnell Summer School in those years were 'the Famine', 'Emigration' and 'Land'.

3   Tim Carey, *Hanged for Ireland: The Forgotten Ten Executed 1920–1921* (Dublin, 2001), p. 199. Interestingly, RTÉ experienced difficulty in getting a historian to participate in the extended television coverage.

4   Tom Dunne, *Rebellions: Memoir, Memory and 1798* (Dublin, 2004), pp. 130–50.

5   Roy Foster, *The Irish Story: Telling Tales and Making It Up in Ireland* (London, 2001), pp. 211–34.

6   For a concise summary of the development of the commemorations, see Brian Walker, *Past and Present: History, Identity and Politics in Ireland* (Belfast, 2000), pp. 92–4; Rosemary Ryan et al., 'Commemorating 1916', *Retrospect* (Journal of Irish History Students' Association) (1984), pp. 59–62.

7   Ryan, 'Commemorating 1916', p. 61.

8   Ibid.

9   *Irish Times*, 28 Jan. 2006.

10   For a short discussion of commemoration see Pauric Travers, 'Our Fenian dead: Glasnevin cemetery and the genesis of the republican funeral', in U. MacGearailt and J. Kelly, *Dublin and Dubliners* (Dublin 1989), pp. 52–3. For more recent elaborations on similar themes, see Ian McBride (ed.), *History and Memory in Modern Ireland* (Cambridge, 2001); and Brian Walker, *Past and Present*.

11   Michael Davitt, *The Fall of Feudalism in Ireland* (London, 1904), p. 110.

CHAPTER I   PARNELL: NATIONALISM AND ROMANCE

Delivered at the Parnell Summer School, 19 August 2003. The theme of the Summer School was 'Reflections on Romantic Nationalism'.

1   The extravagant conjectures and wild claims of misty romanticism are to be found in the publications of men like Charles Vallancey, Sylvester O'Halloran, Patrick Lynch and Rev. Charles O'Connor.

2 From Thomas Davis's poem ,'Ireland', which begins 'She is a rich and rare land'.

3 Gladstone to R. Barry O'Brien, 11 Dec. 1895. R. Barry O'Brien, *The Life of Charles Stewart Parnell* (London, 1910 edn [1898]), p. 554.

4 Ibid., p. 536.

5 See excerpts from Croke's letter in Mark Tierney, *Croke of Cashel* (Dublin, 1976), p. 195; also T. F. O'Sullivan, *The Story of the GAA* (Dublin, 1916), pp. 9–10.

6 *Gaelic Journal* 4 (July 1892), p. 156.

7 Ibid., pp. 157–60.

8 William O'Brien, *The Parnell of Real Life* (London, 1926), pp. 38–9.

9 Barry O'Brien, *Life of Charles Stewart Parnell*, p. 146

10 Ibid.

11 F. S. L. Lyons, *Charles Stewart Parnell* (London, 1978), pp. 260–1; for a discussion of Parnell's meaning, see also Oliver MacDonagh, *States of Mind: A Study of Anglo-Irish Conflict, 1780–1980* (London, 1983), pp. 59–61; for the Cincinnati speech, see below pp. 51, 63.

12 William O'Brien, *Parnell of Real Life*, p. 39.

13 Ibid., p. 12.

14 *Brighton Gazette*, 20 Nov. 1890.

15 Barry O'Brien, *Life of Charles Stewart Parnell*, p. 556.

16 William O'Brien, *Parnell of Real Life*, p. 69.

17 Ibid., p. 69.

18 R. F. Foster, *Charles Stewart Parnell: The Man and his Family* (Sussex, 1976), p. 46; Barry O'Brien, *Life of Charles Stewart Parnell*, p. 36.

19 Katharine O'Shea, *Charles Stewart Parnell*, 2 vols (London, 1914), I, p. 188; II, p. 85.

20 C. S. Parnell to Mrs O'Shea, 4 Dec. 1880. Katharine O'Shea, *Charles Stewart Parnell*, I, p. 163.

21 O'Shea, *Charles Stewart Parnell*, I, p. 163.

22 T.M. Healy, *Letters and Leaders of My Day*, 2 vols (London, 1928), I, pp. 326–7.

23 O'Shea, *Charles Stewart Parnell*, II, p. 63.

24 Ibid., II, p. 203.

25 Ibid., II, p. 183.

CHAPTER 2   THE BLACKBIRD OF AVONDALE

Delivered at Parnell Society Spring day, at Kilmainham Jail, 6 October 2001.

1 George Denis Zimmermann, *Songs of the Irish Rebellion: Irish Political Street Ballads and Rebel Songs, 1790–1900* (Geneva, 1966; Dublin, 2002), pp. 277–8. Parnell assured Katharine O'Shea that his cell which faced south was the best in Kilmainham. Parnell to Katharine O'Shea, 14 and 17 Oct. 1881. Katharine O'Shea, *Charles Stewart Parnell: His Love Story and Political Life* (1 vol. edn [1914] Dublin, 2005 edn), p. 126.

2   *Freeman's Journal,* 9 June 1879; Michael Davitt, *The Fall of Feudalism in Ireland* (London, 1904), pp. 147–54.

3   Parnell had already dismissed dual ownership, arguing that in good times it might be workable but that in times of crisis it would be the tenant who would be squeezed. Speeches at Kilkenny, 2 Oct. 1880; Belleek, 9 Nov. 1880. Shorthand record by Alfred Frederick Mill and Spencer C. Harry respectively, reprinted in *Queen versus C. S. Parnell and Others: Report of the Trials for Conspiracy* (Dublin, 1881), pp. 147–50; 236–7.

4   C. Cruise O'Brien, *Parnell and his Party 1880–1890* (Oxford, 1964), pp. 65–79; Pauric Travers, *Settlements and Divisions* (Dublin, 1988), pp. 14–23.

5   John Morley, *The Life of William Ewart Gladstone,* 3 vols (London, 1903), III, pp. 60–1.

6   Jennie Wyse-Power, *Words of the Dead Chief* (Dublin, 1892), pp. 56–7.

7   *Irish Times,* 13 Oct. 1881.

8   Memoranda by W. E. Forster, NLI, MS 8167.

9   Morley, *Life of Gladstone,* III, p. 62.

10   *Irish Times* 14 Oct. 1881.

11   R. Barry O'Brien, *The Life of Charles Stewart Parnell,* 2 vols (London, 1898), I, pp. 311–12.

12   Tighe Hopkins, *Kilmainham Memories: The Story of the Greatest Political Crime of the Century* (London, 1896), p. 24.

13   O'Shea, *Charles Stewart Parnell,* I vol. edn, p. 123. Anna Parnell subsequently reached a similar conclusion arguing that incarceration saved the leaders from being confronted with the failure of the League. Anna Parnell, *The Tale of a Great Sham* (Dublin, 1986), p. 104.

14   Travers, *Settlements and Divisions,* pp. 110–11.

15   *Irish Times,* 14 Oct. 1881. For the response in Dublin, see Barry O'Brien, *Life of Charles Stewart Parnell,* I, pp. 317–18.

16   Zimmermann, *Songs of the Irish Rebellion,* pp. 277–8. One farmer whose eviction had been the subject of a ballad was reported to be quite reconciled to the loss of his farm but 'kilt entirely' by having been 'scandalised through the whole civilised world in a ballad'. Letter from Dennis Hannigan from Kilmainham, 4 Apr. 1881. NLI, MS 10,700.

17   St John Ervine, *Parnell* (London, 1925), pp. 165–6. For the authorship of this ballad see Sir John Ross, *The Years of My Pilgrimage* (London, 1924), p. 10 and *Pilgrim Scrip: More Random Reminiscences* (London, 1927), pp. 62–3. I am indebted to Dr Patrick Maume for his assistance in resolving this issue.

18   William O'Brien, *Recollections* (London, 1905), p. 401; Hopkins, *Kilmainham Memories,* p. 26.

19   Harrington to Mahon, 29 Nov. 1881, Land League Papers, F. S. Bourke Collection, NLI, MS 10,700.

20   Address to Anna Parnell, 16–17 Nov. 1881, NLI, MS 17,701(5).

21   Ervine, *Parnell,* p. 165.

22   NLI, MS 17,701.

23   Quinn to O'Toole, n.d; Harrington to O'Toole, 9 Nov. 1881; unknown prisoner to O'Toole, 11 Nov. 1881, NLI, MS 17,700. The books collected by the Ladies' Land League

later became a source of contention between Anna Parnell and the National Land League. Anna Parnell to Quinn, 2 May 1884. Quinn papers, NLI, MS 5930.

24 Maggie Lynch to Anna Parnell, 15 Nov. 1881; Dublin citizen to Anna Parnell, 9 Nov. 1881, NLI, MS 17,701(3).

25 Hopkins, *Kilmainham Memories*, pp. 14–15, 20. Hopkins's pamphlet was written originally for an American audience. The crime referred to in the title was the Phoenix Park murders. Coincidentally, given Hopkins's reference to Mr Gilbert, when Parnell and Dillon visited the offices of the Ladies' Land League on Sackville Street shortly after their release from Kilmainham, they were greeted by a group of ladies who serenaded them with 'Twenty love-sick maidens we' from the Gilbert and Sullivan opera *Patience*. O'Brien, *Recollections*, p. 465.

26 NLI, MS 26,742 (1). Marked by Anna Parnell 'Answered Nov. 3' – with a note saying 'drink and pudding when no soup and meat or fish and meat. Cocoa an option, do cheese, sardines, eggs, bacon, marmalade, preserves, cold meat at tea, potatoes and veg and bread at dinner'.

27 O'Brien, *Recollections*, pp. 393–4.

28 T. J. O'Dempsey diary, NLI, MS351, p. 1.

29 Kilmainham Prison Register 13 Oct. 1881–31 July 1883, Register no. 1003, NAI, V16/6/5

30 Outside Kilmainham, there was some cynicism in certain quarters about the alleged misuse of funds raised for evicted tenants and the lifestyle of the leaders of the League. Richard Pigott, *A History of Fenianism: Personal Recollections of an Irish National Journalist* (Dublin, 1882; Cork, 1979), pp. 424–8.

31 O'Dempsey diary, p. 2.

32 Ibid., p. 4

33 Ibid., pp. 8–9, 13–14; Anna Parnell, *The Tale*, p. 126.

34 Parnell to Katharine O'Shea, 24 Dec. 1881. O'Shea, *Charles Stewart Parnell* (2005 edn), p. 134.

35 Ibid., 5, 12, 29 Nov., 9, 14, 22, 24 Dec. 1881. O'Shea, *Charles Stewart Parnell*, pp. 126–34; F. S. L. Lyons, *Charles Stewart Parnell* (London, 1978), pp. 186–7.

36 Ibid., p. 9.

37 *Irish Times*, 13 Oct. 1881.

38 *The Memoirs of Andrew J Kettle*, ed. Laurence J. Kettle (Dublin 1958), p. 57.

39 R. Barry O'Brien interview with Gladstone. Barry O'Brien, *Life of Charles Stewart Parnell*, II, pp. 360–1. Kenny was later Parnellite MP for College Green.

40 J. B. Lyons, 'Charles Stewart Parnell and his doctors', in Donal McCartney (ed.), *Parnell, The Politics of Power* (Dublin, 1991), p. 172.

41 F. S. L. Lyons, *John Dillon: A Biography* (London, 1968), pp. 61–3.

42 Emily Monroe Dickinson, *A Patriot's Mistake: Reminiscences of the Parnell Family* (Dublin 1905), pp. 107–8. This view was shared by John Howard Parnell and other members of the Parnell family. John Howard Parnell, *Charles Stewart Parnell: A Memoir* (London, 1916), p. 198.

43 For Kenny's reports see NAI, CSO, RP 1881/4027/6; 1881/4046/1; 1882/2104/0; see also Lyons, *Parnell*, pp. 183–6.

44 J. B. Lyons, 'Parnell and his doctors', p. 172.

45 Parnell to Katharine O'Shea, 21 Oct. and 1 Nov. 1881, O'Shea, *Charles Stewart Parnell*, pp. 127–8.

46 Ibid., 5 Nov. 1881. O'Shea, *Charles Stewart Parnell*, pp. 128–9.

47 Parnell to Katharine O'Shea, 9 Dec. 1881. O'Shea, *Charles Stewart Parnell*, p. 132.

48 Parnell to Katharine O'Shea, 17 Oct. 1881. O'Shea, *Charles Stewart Parnell*, p. 126.

49 Cited in F. S. L. Lyons, *Parnell*, p. 183. For contemporary accounts of the prison regime, see *Nation*, 22 Oct. and 17 Dec.; account by W. H. Duignan who visited Parnell, in C. D. H. Howard, 'The man on a tricycle: W. H. Duignan and Ireland 1881–5', *IHS* XIV, no. 55 (Mar. 1965), pp. 246–60.

50 Dickinson, *A Patriot's Mistake*, p. 107.

51 Barry O'Brien, *Life of Charles Stewart Parnell*, I, p. 323.

52 William O'Brien, *Recollections*, pp. 395–6; Parnell to Katharine O'Shea, 17 Oct. 1881. O'Shea, *Charles Stewart Parnell*, p. 126.

53 F. S. L. Lyons, *Parnell*, p. 182; Dickinson, *A Patriot's Mistake*, p. 109.

54 Hopkins, *Kilmainham Memories*, p. 20.

55 'Dennie Hannigan' 4 April 1881. NLI, MS 10,700. Denis Hannigan, a farmer from Drumcollogher, County Limerick was in prison for 'intimidating persons to quit their farms'. Kilmainham Prison Register, 1881. NAI, v16/6/4.

56 O'Shea, *Charles Stewart Parnell*, p. 123.

57 Ibid., pp. 132–3, 138.

58 Dickinson, *A Patriot's Mistake*, p. 19.

59 *Freeman's Journal*, 16 May 1882; Anon., *The Kilmainham ——— [Compact]* (Edinburgh, London, 1883); Barry O'Brien, *Life of Charles Stewart Parnell*, I, pp. 339–50; Cruise O'Brien, *Parnell and his Party*, pp. 72–9; F. S. L. Lyons, *Parnell*, pp. 189–207. For Chamberlain's role, see C. H. D. Howard (ed.), *Joseph Chamberlain: A Political Memoir* (London, 1953), ch. 2.

60 Barry O'Brien, *Life of Charles Stewart Parnell*, I, p. 350; T. M. Healy, *Letters and Leaders of My Day*, 2 vols (London, 1928), II, p. 410

61 Cruise O'Brien, *Parnell and his Party*, p. 78.

62 Gladstone to Forster, 12 April 1882. Quoted in Morley, *Gladstone*, III, pp. 58–9.

63 Parnell to Captain O'Shea, 28 Apr. 1882. Howard, *Joseph Chamberlain*, pp. 49–50.

64 R. Barry O'Brien interview with Gladstone. Barry O'Brien, *Life of Charles Stewart Parnell*, II, p. 361; Morley, *Gladstone*, III, p. 64;

65 Morley, *Gladstone*, III, p. 66

66 Barry O'Brien, *Life of Charles Stewart Parnell*, I, p. 318.

CHAPTER 3   PARNELL AND THE AMERICAN CONNECTION

An extended version of a lecture delivered at the Parnell Summer School, 18 August 1996.

1   I am indebted to Jane McL. Côté, *Fanny and Anna Parnell* (Dublin 1991), for this abridged account of the Tudor family of Boston.

2   John D. Fair and Cordelia C. Humphrey, 'The Alabama dimension to the political thought of Charles Stewart Parnell', *Alabama Review* 52, no. 1 (Jan. 1999), have shown

from contemporary events in Alabama that Parnell's visit must have taken place in 1872, not in 1871 as stated in John Howard Parnell's memoir of his brother and followed by all subsequent biographers.

3   For an account of Parnell's first visit to America, see John Howard Parnell, *Charles Stewart Parnell: A Memoir* (London, 1916), pp. 82–109.

4   Extracts from his Liverpool address are given in the biographies of Parnell by R. Barry O'Brien, *The Life of Charles Stewart Parnell*, 2 vols (London, 1910 [1898]), pp. 83–5; F. S. L. Lyons, *Charles Stewart Parnell* (London, 1978), p. 57; and Robert Kee, *The Laurel and the Ivy: The Story of Charles Stewart Parnell and Irish Nationalism* (London, 1993), pp. 126–7.

5   J. J. O'Kelly to John Devoy, 5 Aug. 1877, in *Devoy's Postbag*, ed. William O'Brien and Desmond Ryan, 2 vols (Dublin 1948, 1953), I, pp. 267–8.

6   O'Kelly to Devoy, 21 Aug. 1877, ibid., pp. 269–70.

7   W. B. Yeats, 'Remorse for Intemperate Speech' from *The Winding Stair and Other Poems* (1933).

8   *Irish World*, 13 Nov. 1880, quoted in Thomas N. Brown, *Irish-American Nationalism* (Philadelphia and New York, 1966).

9   For the above account of the Irish in America I am indebted to Thomas N. Brown, *Irish-American Nationalism*.

10   Quoted in Kee, *The Laurel and the Ivy*, p. 222.

11   For a more detailed discussion of Parnell as orator, see below chapter 4; also Alan O'Day, 'Parnell: orator and speaker' in D. George Boyce and Alan O'Day (eds), *Parnell in Perspective* (London, 1991), pp. 193–210.

12   *United Ireland*, 8 Oct. 1891, quoted in Edward Byrne, *Parnell: A Memoir*, ed. Frank Callanan (Dublin 1991), p. 43.

13   A 'rough diary' of Parnell's tour, with his address before Congress and quotations from some of the other speeches, are given in Michael Davitt, *The Fall of Feudalism in Ireland* (London, 1904), pp. 193–210.

14   Quoted in Kee, *The Laurel and the Ivy*, p. 219.

15   Kee, *The Laurel and the Ivy*, p. 217.

16   The 'last link' phrase was reported in some of the newspaper accounts of the speech though not in others. For a discussion of the problem of the divergent reports see below, pp. 63–4 and Lyons, *Parnell*, pp. 111–12.

17   Barry O'Brien, *Parnell*, p. 160.

18   Kee, *The Laurel and the Ivy*, p. 219.

19   Barry O'Brien, *Parnell*, pp. 160–1.

20   Davitt, *Fall of Feudalism*, p. 205

21   Ibid., p. 207.

22   Ibid., p. 208.

23   Ibid.

24   Ibid., p. 637.

25   Quoted in C. Cruise O'Brien, *Parnell and his Party 1880–1890* (Oxford, 1964), p. 161.

CHAPTER 4   READING BETWEEN THE LINES

This paper was originally published in *Studia Hibernica* XXXI (2000–1), pp. 243–56.

1   There is as yet no comprehensive published collection of Parnell's speeches. For a highly abbreviated selection see Jennie Wyse Power, *Words of the Dead Chief: Extracts from the Public Speeches and Other Pronouncements of Charles Stewart Parnell* (Dublin, 1892). For a recent assessment of some of the issues involved in discourse analysis and public oratory, see Christina Schäffner (ed.), *Analysing Political Speeches* (Clevedon, 1997). For a comparative perspective, see Thomas W Benson (ed.), *Rhetoric and Political Culture in Nineteenth Century America* (Michigan, 1997).

2   F. S. L. Lyons, 'The economic ideas of Parnell', in M. Roberts (ed.), *Historical Studies* II (1959), p. 61.

3   Alan O'Day, 'Parnell: orator and speaker', in D. George Boyce and Alan O'Day (eds), *Parnell in Perspective* (London, 1991), p. 203.

4   See above, pp. 12, 21.

5   John Howard Parnell, *Charles Stewart Parnell: A Memoir* (London, 1916), p. 175.

6   John Morley, *The Life of William Ewart Gladstone*, 3 vols (London, 1903), III, p. 399.

7   R. Barry O'Brien, *The Life of Charles Stewart Parnell*, 2 vols (London, 1898), p. 137.

8   For an analysis of this speech, see R. Post, 'Charles Stewart Parnell before Congress', *Quarterly Journal of Speech* 51 (Dec. 1965), pp. 419–25.

9   Cited in *Nation*, 22 Jan. 1881.

10   Richard Pigott, *Personal Recollections of an Irish National Journalist* (Dublin, 1882; Cork, 1979), p. 349.

11   John Morley, *Recollections* (London, 1917), I, p. 241. Michael Davitt described Parnell as a 'sober, unemotional speaker who never quoted an Irish poet, but once, and got it wrong', *Fall of Feudalism in Ireland* (London, 1904), p. 652.

12   Ibid.

13   Morley, *Gladstone*, III, pp. 376–7.

14   Ibid., pp. 313, 448, 450–1.

15   Barry O'Brien, *Life of Charles Stewart Parnell*, I, p. 74.

16   J. G. Swift MacNeill, *What I Have Seen and Heard* (London 1925), pp. 145–6.

17   Barry O'Brien, *Life of Charles Stewart Parnell*, I, pp. 74–5.

18   Michael MacDonagh, *The Life of William O'Brien* (London, 1928), p. 50.

19   O'Day, 'Parnell: orator and speaker', p. 205.

20   Barry O'Brien, *Life of Charles Stewart Parnell*, I, p. 85.

21   7 Oct. 1875. Barry O'Brien, *Life of Charles Stewart Parnell*, I, p. 86.

22   Ibid., pp. 86–7.

23   Ibid., p. 99.

24   T. P. O'Connor, *The Parnellite Movement* (London, 1886), pp. 237–8.

25   Swift MacNeill, *What I Have Seen*, pp. 145–6; HC Debs, CCLXXVI, 482.

26   Walter Bagehot, *The English Constitution* (London, 1866).

27 D. George Boyce, 'Parnell and Bagehot', in D. George Boyce and Alan O'Day (eds), *Parnell in Perspective* (London, 1991), pp. 107–28.

28 One of the most enduring myths about Parnell is that he was ignorant of Irish history. However, both William O'Brien and Michael Davitt explicitly rejected this. Davitt stated that Parnell had read and understood well the history of Ireland from the Norman invasion; O'Brien attested his detailed knowledge of 1798. William O'Brien, *Recollections* (London, 1905), pp. 396–7; Davitt, *Fall of Feudalism*, pp. 114–15; P. S. O'Hegarty, *A History of Ireland Under the Union* (London, 1952), p. 589.

29 For the Cincinnati speech, see above, chapter 3, p. 51, and F. S. L. Lyons, *Charles Stewart Parnell* (London, 1978), pp. 110–11.

30 M. V. Hazel, 'First link: Parnell's American tour, 1880', *Eire Ireland* xv, no. 1 (1980), p. 9.

31 MacDonagh, *Life of William O'Brien*, pp. 59–61.

32 *Nation*, 6 Jan. 1885; *Freeman's Journal*, 6 Oct. 1885; James Loughlin, *Gladstone, Home Rule and the Ulster Question* (Dublin, 1986), p. 54.

33 Loughlin, *Gladstone*, p. 29; James Loughlin, 'Constructing the political spectacle: Parnell, the press and national leadership, 1879–1886', in D. George Boyce and Alan O'Day (eds), *Parnell in Perspective* (London, 1991), p. 225.

34 Davitt, *Fall of Feudalism*, p. 205. For Parnell's American speeches, see above pp. 48–53.

35 Admirable pieces of detective work by historians including Emmet Larkin and Michael Hazel have helped clarify the situation about the Cincinnati affair considerably. Hazel, 'First link', pp. 6–24; Lyons, *Parnell*, p. 111.

36 Hazel, 'First link', pp. 17–18. See also *Special Commission Act, 1888. Proceedings and Evidence* (London 1889) pp. 7, 22–3, 110–17, 282.

37 Hazel, 'First link', pp. 7 and 24.

38 Lyons, *Parnell*, pp. 110–14; Barry O'Brien, *Life of Charles Stewart Parnell*, I, p. 206.

39 *Freeman's Journal*, 18 May and 9 June 1886.

40 Morley, *Gladstone*, III, p. 313.

41 Ibid., p. 337. Davitt rated this as probably Parnell's final parliamentary speech; it was, he said, Parnell 'at his best . . . dignified in tone and excellently delivered', *Fall of Feudalism*, p. 494.

42 Brian MacArthur, *The Penguin Book of Historic Speeches* (London 1996), pp. 71–3.

43 Lionel A. Tollemache, *Talks with Mr Gladstone* (London, 1898), pp. 127–8.

44 4 Mar. 1881. HC Debs, CCLIX, 335–57.

45 11 Mar. 1881. HC Debs, CCLIX, 829–33.

46 O'Hegarty, *History of Ireland*, pp. 597–8.

CHAPTER 5   PARNELL'S WOMEN

Delivered at the Parnell Society's Spring Day, 15 April 2000.

1   *Wicklow Newsletter*, 3 Dec. 1887, quoted in R. F. Foster, *Charles Stewart Parnell: The Man and His Family* (Sussex, 1976), p. 238

2   Parnell to Katharine O'Shea, 4 Jan. 1888, in Katharine O'Shea, *Charles Stewart Parnell*, 2 vols (London, 1914), II, p. 134.

3   *Irish Weekly Independent*, 6 Oct. 1894, quoted in Foster, *Parnell*, p. 329.

4   Jane McL Côté, *Fanny and Anna Parnell* (Dublin, 1991), p. 23.

5   Foster, *Parnell*, p. 46.

6   Delia Parnell to T. D. Sullivan, 21 Jan. 1880, quoted in Foster, *Parnell*, p. 225

7   R. Barry O'Brien, *The Life of Charles Stewart Parnell* (London, 1910 [1898], 1 vol. edn), pp. 29–30.

8   Ibid.

9   F. S. L. Lyons, *Ireland Since the Famine* (London, 1971), p. 148.

10   Foster, *Parnell*, pp. 92–4; R. F. Foster, *Modern Ireland 1690–1972* (London, 1988), p. 401.

11   O'Shea, *Charles Stewart Parnell*, I, p. 127.

12   Tim Healy to Maurice Healy, 20 Mar. 1880, in T. M. Healy, *Letters and Leaders of My Day*, 2 vols (London: 1928), I, p. 87.

13   T. W. Moody, *Davitt and the Irish Revolution 1846–1882* (Oxford, 1981), p. 8.

14   Côté, *Fanny and Anna Parnell*, p. xiii.

15   Foster, *Parnell*, pp. 55, 60–4, 237

16   John Howard Parnell, *Charles Stewart Parnell: A Memoir* (London, 1916), p. 10.

17   Foster, *Parnell*, p. 238; Barry O'Brien, *Life of Charles Stewart Parnell*, p. 162.

18   O'Shea, *Charles Stewart Parnell*, II, p. 176.

19   John D. Fair, 'Letters of mourning from Katharine O'Shea Parnell to Delia Tudor Stewart Parnell', *Irish Historical Studies* XXI, no. 122 (Nov. 1998), pp. 241–6.

20   For Fanny and Anna Parnell, see Côté, *Fanny and Anna Parnell*; also Foster, *Parnell*.

21   J. H. Parnell, *Parnell: A Memoir*, p. 70.

22   *Gaelic American*, 16 Jan. 1907.

23   R. F. Foster, *Paddy and Mr Punch* (Harmondsworth, 1993), p. 44.

24   Foster, *Parnell*, p. 246.

25   Côté, *Fanny and Anna Parnell*, p. 59.

26   Charles Stewart Parnell, 'The Irish land question', *North American Review* CXXX, no. 281 (Apr. 1880), 388–406. In her bibliography, Côté (*Fanny and Anna Parnell*, p. 316) attributes an article, 'The Irish Land Situation' [*sic*], *North American Review*, Mar. 1881, to Fanny Parnell. No such article appears.

27   Michael Davitt, *The Fall of Feudalism in Ireland* (London, 1904), pp. 292–3.

28   Ibid., pp. 291–2 for the rest of this ballad.

29   Quoted in Côté, *Fanny and Anna Parnell*, pp. 133–4.

30   F. H. O'Donnell, *The History of the Irish Parliamentary Party*, 2 vols (London, 1910), II, p. 51. For the Ladies' Land League, see Côté, *Fanny and Anna Parnell*; Margaret Ward, *Unmanageable Revolutionaries: Women and Irish Nationalism* (Dingle, 1983); Marie O' Neill, 'The Ladies' Land League', *Dublin Historical Record*, Sept. 1982.

31   Anna Parnell, *The Tale of a Great Sham* was eventually published by Arlen House, Dublin in 1986, edited with an introduction by Dana Hearne.

32   Anna Parnell, *Tale of a Great Sham*, p. 69; Côté, *Fanny and Anna Parnell*, p. 247.

33 A. Parnell, *Tale of a Great Sham*, p. 164.

34 J. H. Parnell, *Parnell: A Memoir*, pp. 80–1.

35 Healy, *Letters and Leaders*, I, pp. 107–10. Patrick Egan (1841–1919) was a former member of the supreme council of the IRB and treasurer of the Land League.

36 F. S. L. Lyons, *Charles Stewart Parnell* (London, 1978), p. 149.

37 Noel Browne's story about J. C. McQuaid's antics in the upstairs of a pub in Drumcondra on a GAA Sunday afternoon has as much or as little credibility. John Cooney, *John Charles McQuaid: Ruler of Catholic Ireland* (Dublin 1999), pp. 285–7.

38 O'Shea, *Charles Stewart Parnell*, I, p. 4.

39 See Frank Callanan, *T. M. Healy* (Cork, 1996), pp. 47, 52–5, 639 n. 69.

40 O'Shea, *Charles Stewart Parnell*, I, p. 4.

41 Healy, *Letters and Leaders*, I, p. 327.

42 O'Shea, *Charles Stewart Parnell*, I, p. 135.

43 See W. E. H. Lecky, *Democracy and Liberty* (London, 1896), II, pp. 166–70 for a discussion of the divorce legislation as it then stood; also Sybil Wolfram, 'Divorce in England, 1700-1857', *Oxford Journal of Legal Studies* 2–5 (1985), pp. 155–86.

44 See above, pp. 36–7.

45 O'Shea, *Charles Stewart Parnell*, I, p. 261; see below, pp. 130–2.

46 Ibid., I, p. 275.

47 Healy, *Letters and Leaders*, I, p. 242.

48 W. H. O'Shea to Katharine O'Shea, 2 Nov. 1885 (O'Shea, *Charles Stewart Parnell*, II, p. 90).

49 Joyce Marlow, *The Uncrowned Queen of Ireland: The Life of Kitty O'Shea* (London, 1975), p. 259.

50 Ibid.

51 Healy to his wife, 28 Nov. 1890 (Healy, *Letters and Leaders*, I, pp. 326–7).

52 Marlow, *Uncrowned Queen*, p. 263.

53 Ibid., p. 277.

54 Ibid., p. 288.

55 Ibid., p. 278.

56 For a more detailed and perceptive analysis of Healy's animosity towards Parnell and Katharine O'Shea, see Frank Callanan, *The Parnell Split 1890–91* (Cork, 1992) and his *Healy*.

CHAPTER 6 'UNDER THE GREAT COMEDIAN'S TOMB'

1 Oliver MacDonagh, *States of Mind: A Study of Anglo-Irish Conflict, 1780–1980* (London, 1983), p. 101. MacDonagh cited the example of Eamon de Valera's meeting with Lloyd George where Lloyd George was struck by the Irish leader's tendency to speak of Oliver Cromwell and the seventeenth century as if they lived on and 'generated still unexpiated and irredeemed injustices'. Ibid., p. 1. Of course, the great example of the invocation of the dead generations is the 1916 Proclamation.

2   This paper was first delivered to a Parnell Spring Day at Avondale in 1992. Revision of the paper has been facilitated by access to 'The funeral of Charles Stewart Parnell' a transcription of the coverage of the funeral in the *Freeman's Journal* undertaken by Pat Power as part of a Parnell commemoration of the funeral in October 2004.

3   *Irish Times*, 12 Oct. 1891.

4   *United Ireland*, 10 Oct. 1891.

5   See W. B. Yeats, *Autobiographies* (London, 1955), p. 199; John Kelly, 'Parnell in Irish Literature', in D. George Boyce and Alan O'Day (eds), *Parnell in Perspective* (London, 1991), p. 244.

6   For a more detailed discussion of these funerals, see Pauric Travers, 'Our Fenian dead: Glasnevin cemetery and the genesis of the republican funeral', in James Kelly and Uaitear MacGearailt (eds), *Dublin and Dubliners* (Dublin, 1990), pp. 52–72; on Glasnevin cemetery in its social context, see Carmel Connell, *Glasnevin Cemetery, Dublin, 1832–1900* (Dublin, 2004).

7   P. H. Pearse, *Political Writings and Speeches* (Dublin, 1922), pp. 133–7.

8   The most complete account of the split is Frank Callanan's complex but masterful *The Parnellite Split 1890–1* (Cork, 1992).

9   The Catholic bishops did not publicly pronounce against Parnell until 3 December 1890; indeed they were berated by *The Times* for their tardiness.

10 Jennie Wyse Power, *Words of the Dead Chief: Extracts from the Public Speeches and Other Pronouncements of Charles Stewart Parnell* (Dublin, 1892), pp. 170–1.

11 *Freeman's Journal*, 12 Oct. 1891.

12 *Irish Times*, 8 Oct. 1891.

13 *Irish Times*, 8, 9 Oct. 1891; F. S. L. Lyons, *Charles Stewart Parnell* (London, 1978), pp. 602–3. For a detailed discussion of the cause of Parnell's death, see J. B. Lyons, 'Charles Stewart Parnell and his doctors', in Donal McCartney (ed.), *Parnell, The Politics of Power* (Dublin, 1991), pp. 176–81. He concludes that the most likely cause of death was coronary thrombosis.

14 *Cork Examiner*, 8 Oct. 1891.

15 *Sheffield Independent*, 8 Oct. 1891.

16 *Irish Catholic* 8 Oct. 1891. A rumour that Archbishop Walsh had written the *Irish Catholic* editorial gained currency particularly in the United States and added to the animosity towards the clerical authorities. Thomas J. Morrissey, *William J. Walsh Archbishop of Dublin, 1841–1921: No Uncertain Voice* (Dublin, 2000), pp. 137–9.

17 *United Ireland*, 9 Oct. 1891.

18 *Freeman's Journal* 10 Oct. 1891; *Irish Times* 12 Oct. 1891.

19 *Irish Times*, 10, 12 Oct. 1891; *Freeman's Journal*, 12 Oct. 1891.

20 *Irish Times*, 10, 12 Oct. 1891; Katharine O'Shea, *Charles Stewart Parnell: His Love Story and Political Life* ([1914] Dublin, 2005 edn), p. 287. A proposal to have a death mask cast by Miss Grant, a sculptor who travelled from London for that purpose, had to be abandoned because of the state of the remains. *Freeman's Journal*, 10 Oct. 1891.

21 Henry Harrison to H. T. Parnell, 9 Oct. 1891; published in *Irish Times*, 13 Oct. 1891. Coincidentally, Parnell had attended the funeral of O'Gorman Mahon in Glasnevin in June 1891 and had become unnerved by the crush of the crowd around the grave. Frank Callanan, *The Parnellite Split* (Cork, 1992), p. 166.

22 Emily Dickinson, *A Patriot's Mistake: Reminiscences of the Parnell Family by a Daughter of the House* (London, 1905), pp. 186–7.

23 R. F. Foster, *Charles Stewart Parnell: The Man and His Family* (Sussex, 1976), p. 283.

24 Henry Harrison to H. T. Parnell, 9 Oct. 1891, published in *Irish Times*, 13 Oct. 1891.

25 *Freeman's Journal*, 10 Oct. 1891. There were touching tributes at a number of stations along the line from Willesden to Holyhead, including Chester where a wreath was handed in with the inscription 'In fond memory of one of Erin's greatest chieftains, who was murdered in his struggle for independence, from a few of her loving children, Chester.' At Holyhead, the train was met by senior Parnellites who had crossed from Dublin by the steamer *Ireland*.

26 *Irish Times*, 10, 12 Oct. 1891.

27 For Dr Kenny, see above, p. 32.

28 *Freeman's Journal*, 10 Oct. 1891. At 171 feet high, George Petrie's round tower which was completed in 1861 at a cost of £18,000, far exceeded any of the structures on which it was modelled.

29 Ibid.; *Irish Times*, 10 Oct. 1891; W. F. Mandle, *The GAA and Irish Nationalist Politics 1884–1924* (London, 1987), pp. 85–6.

30 Maud Gonne travelled with the remains from London and Yeats was there to meet her.

31 Onlookers seeking souvenirs quickly cut the deal case into pieces using penknives. *Freeman's Journal*, 12 Oct. 1891.

32 While marching in procession to the Rotunda for one of his last public speeches in Dublin, Parnell had paused symbolically at the site of the old parliament building.

33 The French radical republican Leon Gambetta died in 1882; his funeral was a public occasion of considerable ceremony and spectacle.

34 *Irish Times*, 12 Oct. 1891; *Freeman's Journal*, 12 Oct. 1891.

35 Ibid.; Jules Abels, *The Parnell Tragedy* (London, 1966), p. 379.

36 *Irish Times*, 12 Oct. 1891.

37 *Irish Times*, 12 Oct. 1891; *Freeman's Journal*, 12 Oct. 1891; Abels, *Parnell Tragedy*, p. 379.

38 *Irish Ecclesiastical Gazette*, 16 Oct. 1891. Alderman Meade's chaplain, Rev Malley, travelled in the Lord Mayor's carriage.

39 On 15 August 1882, Parnell had attended the unveiling of the O'Connell monument along with the Archbishop of Dublin.

40 *Irish Times*, 12 Oct. 1891; *Freeman's Journal*, 12 Oct. 1891.

41 Ibid. Vincent was later called on to explain why he had dared to preside at such a funeral.

42 'Parnell's Funeral' from 'A full moon in March', *Yeats's Poems*, ed. A. Norman Jeffares (Dublin, 1992), pp. 395–6.

43 R. Barry O'Brien, *The Life of Charles Stewart Parnell*, 2 vols (London, 1898), II, p. 352.

44 The next great political funeral to Glasnevin was that of Jeremiah O'Donovan Rossa in 1915. It was more in the tradition of the MacManus funeral and served a similar purpose; it was used by the IRB as a rallying cry for rebellion. Travers, 'Our Fenian dead', pp. 65–7.

CHAPTER 7   AT THE GRAVESIDE

This chapter brings together orations delivered at four gravesides: Charles Stewart Parnell's in Glasnevin; Katharine Parnell's in Littlehampton, Sussex; Fanny Parnell's in Mount Auburn cemetery, Boston; and Anna Parnell's in Ilfracombe, Devon.

1   An address at the graveside of Charles Stewart Parnell in Glasnevin Cemetery, 3 October 1982

2   He also intended that Ulster unionists would be accommodated within a Home Rule Ireland. He was referring specifically to the Protestants of Ulster when speaking on the first Home Rule Bill (1886) he said: 'No, Sir; we cannot afford to give up a single Irishman. We want the energy, the patriotism, the talent and works of every Irishman to ensure that this great experiment shall be a successful one.' [*Hansard*, 3rd ser., CCCVI, 1168–74 (7 June 1886)]. A slightly different wording is given in *Freeman's Journal*, 9 June 1886]. In Belfast in 1891, he said: 'until the religious prejudices of the minority, whether reasonable or unreasonable, are conciliated . . . Ireland can never enjoy perfect freedom, Ireland can never be united' (Quoted in Paul Bew, *C. S. Parnell* (Dublin, 1980), p. 129). For a discussion of Parnell's attitude to Ulster see: Pauric Travers 'Parnell and the Ulster question' in Donal McCartney (ed.), *Parnell: The Politics of Power* (Dublin 1991), pp. 57–71.

3   The Manifesto is published in Tom Corfe, *The Phoenix Park Murders* (Dublin, 1968), pp. 206–7. It was drafted by Davitt and edited by the Party leaders meeting in Davitt's hotel room. According to Davitt (*The Fall of Feudalism in Ireland* (London, 1904), p. 359), a significant contribution to the final version of the Manifesto was made by A. M. Sullivan.

4   *Hansard*, 3rd ser., CCLXIX (8 May 1882), 323.

5   R. Barry O'Brien, *The Life of Charles Stewart Parnell*, 1 vol. edn (London, 1910 [1898]), p. 556.

6   Littlehampton Cemetery, Sussex, 23 April 2003.

7   For Katharine Wood's family background see Joyce Marlow, *The Uncrowned Queen of Ireland: The Life of Kitty O'Shea*, (London, 1975); Jane Jordan, *Kitty O'Shea: An Irish Affair* (London, 2005).

8   Emma, whose married name was Emma Barrett Lennard. Among the poems she set to music was 'Up the airy mountain / Down the rushy glen' (The Fairies) by the Ballyshannon poet, William Allingham.

9   Anna, whose married name was Anna Steele.

10   Joseph Gillis Biggar. See above, p. 82.

11   For Healy's sexual invective against Katharine O'Shea see Frank Callanan, *T. M. Healy* (Cork, 1996); and the same author's *The Parnell Split, 1890–91* (Cork, 1992).

12 *National Press*, 2 Nov. 1891 quoted in Callanan, *Parnell Split*, p. 187.

13 James Joyce, *Ulysses* (Minerva edn, 1992), p. 632; (Bodley Head edn, 1986), p. 581.

14 Nor did Parnellites rush to defend her honour. Out of loyalty to Parnell, however, they thought it best to remain discreetly silent on the subject of Parnell's love.

15 Katharine O'Shea, *Charles Stewart Parnell: His Love Story and Political Life*, 2 vols (London, 1914), I, p. 189.

16 E. A. D'Alton, *History of Ireland*, (Dublin, 1912), VI, p. 382.

17 Quoted in Callanan, *Parnell Split*, p. 127.

18 For details of this notorious case see Angela Bourke, *The Burning of Bridget Cleary* (Dublin, 1999); Thomas McGrath, 'Fairy faith and changelings: the burning of Bridget Cleary, 1895', *Studies* (Summer 1982), pp. 178–84.

19 The following address was delivered on 11 April 2001 to mark the placing of a commemorative stone of Wicklow granite from Avondale on the grave of Fanny Parnell (1848–82) at Mount Auburn cemetery, Boston.

20 O'Shea, *Charles Stewart Parnell*, II, pp. 44–5.

21 Jane McL. Côté, *Fanny and Anna Parnell: Ireland's Patriot Sisters* (Dublin 1991), pp. 223–4 and pp. 304–5, nn. 13, 14.

22 Ibid.

23 Mr Leslie Armstrong, Rathdrum.

24 John O'Leary, *Recollections of Fenians and Fenianism* (Dublin, 1896), II, pp. 30–1.

25 John Howard Parnell, *Charles Stewart Parnell: A Memoir* (London, 1916), pp. 70–1.

26 T. M. Healy, *Letters and Leaders of My Day*, 2 vols (London, 1928), I, p. 81.

27 Charles Stewart Parnell, 'The Irish land question', *North American Review*, CXXX (Apr. 1880), pp. 388–406. Healy, *Letters and Leaders*, I, p. 87, claimed that every word of this article was written by Fanny. Of course, it incorporated her brother's own views. The speech to the House of Representatives is given in Davitt, *Fall of Feudalism*, pp. 198–203.

28 Quoted in Côté, *Fanny and Anna Parnell*, p. 144.

29 Davitt, *Fall of Feudalism*, pp. 291–3. For another verse of this ballad, see above, p. 73.

30 Quoted in Côté, *Fanny and Anna Parnell*, p. 168.

31 J. H. Newman, *Sermons on Various Occasions* (London, 1891), p. 219.

32 *Pilot* (Boston), 2 Nov. 1878, quoted in Thomas N. Brown, *Irish-American Nationalism* (Philadelphia and New York, 1966), p. 42.

33 F. Sheehy Skeffington, *Michael Davitt* ([1906] London, 1967 edn), p. 98.

34 See her poem 'After Death'.

35 O'Shea, *Charles Stewart Parnell*, II, p. 44.

36 Holy Trinity cemetery at Ilfracombe, Devon, 5 April 2002. A marble stone was placed on the grave bearing an inscription with Anna's own words: 'The best part of independence . . . the independence of mind.' A message from Mary McAleese, President of Ireland was read at the graveside where an address was given by His Excellency, the Irish Ambassador to the United Kingdom, Mr Daithí Ó'Ceallaigh. A sapling beech from Avondale was planted in memory of Anna.

37 She reported her parliamentary observations in the *Celtic Monthly* (New York), for May, June and July 1880 in a three-part article entitled 'How they do in the House of Commons: Notes from the Ladies' Cage'.

38 Anna Parnell, *The Tale of a Great Sham*, with an introduction by Dana Hearne (Dublin 1986), p. 178.

39 Quoted in Côté, *Fanny and Anna Parnell*, p. 53.

40 Anna Parnell, *The Tale*, p. 49.

41 Quoted in Foster, *Parnell*, p. 254.

42 *Freeman's Journal*, 12 Mar. 1881, cited in Emmet Larkin, *The Roman Catholic Church and the Creation of the Modern Irish State 1878–1886* (Dublin, 1975), pp. 96–7.

43 Anna Parnell, *The Tale*, pp 171–2.

44 Davitt, *Fall of Feudalism*, p. 300.

45 Katharine Tynan, *Twenty-five Years: Reminiscences* (London, 1913), p. 99, quoted in Foster, *Parnell*, p. 266.

46 *Nation*, 2 Apr. 1881, cited in Foster, *Parnell*, p. 271.

47 Foster, *Parnell*, p. 275; Côté, *Fanny and Anna Parnell*, p. 204.

48 *Irish Weekly Independent*, 8 Oct. 1898, quoted in Edward Byrne, *Parnell: A Memoir*. ed. Frank Callanan (Dublin, 1991), pp. 30–1.

CHAPTER 8   IN THE FOOTSTEPS OF JOHN HOWARD PARNELL

Delivered at the Parnell Summer School, 15 August 2001.

1 Jane McL. Côté, *Fanny and Anna Parnell: Ireland's Patriot Sisters* (Dublin, 1991), p. 20.

2 Emily Dickinson, *A Patriot's Mistake: Reminiscences of the Parnell Family by a Daughter of the House* (London, 1905), pp. 37–8.

3 *Bordentown Register*, 28 July 1882.

4 Ibid.

5 Côté, *Fanny and Anna Parnell*, p. 89.

6 Michael Davitt, *The Fall of Feudalism in Ireland* (London, 1904), p. 208.

7 From a ballad written in honour of the occasion by Fionnuala Waldron, Mary Moore and Pauric Travers.

8 James Joyce, *Ulysses* (Minerva edn, 1992), p. 173.

9 F. S. L. Lyons, *Charles Stewart Parnell* (London, 1978), p. 604.

10 R. F. Foster, *Charles Stewart Parnell: The Man and His Family* (Sussex, 1976), pp. 296, 297.

11 Robert Kee, *The Laurel and the Ivy: the Story of Charles Stewart Parnell and Irish Nationalism* (London, 1993), p. 22.

12 Côté, *Fanny and Anna Parnell*, p. 47.

13 John Howard Parnell to George Gardiner, 1 June 1866 (quoted in John D. Fair and Cordelia C. Humphrey, 'The Alabama dimension to the political thought of Charles Stewart Parnell', *Alabama Review* 52, no. 1 (Jan. 1999), p. 30).

14 Ibid., p. 33.

15 *Bordentown Register*, 28 July 1882. For a deconstruction of the myth that John Howard Parnell was the 'father of commercial peach-growing in the South', see John D. Fair, 'Parnell and peaches: a study in the construction of historical myth', *Alabama Review*, Apr. 2005.

16 Fair and Humphrey, 'Alabama dimension', p. 37.

17 Côté, *Fanny and Anna Parnell*, p. 275 n. 29. See also St John Ervine, *Parnell* (London, 1925), p. 67.

18 Henry Harrison, *Parnell Vindicated: The Lifting of the Veil* (London, 1931), p. 109.

19 Dickinson, *A Patriot's Mistake*, p. 34.

20 John Howard Parnell, *Charles Stewart Parnell: A Memoir* (London, 1916), p. 45.

21 Foster, *Parnell*, p. 289.

22 *Hansard Parliamentary Debates*, 16, 28 July 1896; 15 July 1897.

23 Ibid., 5 Mar. 1896.

24 Ibid.

25 Ibid.

26 Foster, *Parnell*, p. 69.

27 *Hansard*, 5 Mar. 1896.

28 Ibid., 5, 9, 10 May 1896.

29 R. F. Foster, *Paddy and Mr Punch: Connections in Irish and English History* (London, 1993), pp. 56–61.

CHAPTER 9   'NO TURNING BACK'

First delivered to Ilfracombe historical society, March 2002.

1 See bibliographical note below.

2 Other important contributions were various works by Margaret Ward notably *Unmanageable Revolutionaries* (Dingle, 1983) and Jane McL. Côté and Dana Hearne, 'Anna Parnell', in Mary Cullen and Maria Luddy (eds), *Women, Power and Consciousness in Nineteenth Century Ireland* (Dublin, 1995), pp. 263–94. See also Judith Thompson, 'Fanny and Anna Parnell, the uncrowned queens of Ireland', MA thesis, Sussex University, 1996.

3 Michael Davitt, *The Fall of Feudalism in Ireland* (London, 1904), p. 110.

4 L. C. B. Seaman, Victorian *England: Aspects of English and Imperial History, 1837–1901* (London, 1973), p. 5.

5 Avondale House was built in 1779 by Samuel Hayes MP. On his death in 1795, it passed to his cousin and political ally, Sir John Parnell – he was great grandson of the original Thomas. Avondale became synonymous with the Parnells, especially Charles Stewart and his patriot sisters Fanny and Anna.

6 Their social standing in Wicklow has been well explored by Foster in *Parnell*; see also Foster, 'Parnell, Wicklow and nationalism', in Donal McCartney (ed.), *Parnell: The Politics of Power* (Dublin, 1991), pp. 19–34.

7   *Life of Frances Power Cobbe by Herself* (London, 1894) I, p. 186; St John Ervine, *Parnell* (London, 1925), p. 42. On Cobbe see Lori Williamson, *Power and Protest: Frances Power Cobbe and Victorian Society* (Chicago, 2005) and Deirdre Raftery, 'Francis Power Cobbe', in Mary Cullen and Maria Luddy (eds), *Women, Power and Consciousness in Nineteenth Century Ireland* (Dublin, 1995), pp. 89–124. She founded the Society for the Protection of Animals Liable to Vivisection in 1875 and the British Union for the Abolition of Vivisection in 1898, was a leading member of National Society for Women's Suffrage and wrote extensively on suffrage issues and property rights for women – a subject also raised by Anna Parnell.

8   Jane McL. Côté, *Fanny and Anna Parnell: Ireland's Patriot Sisters* (Dublin, 1991).

9   Alexis de Tocqueville, *Democracy in America* (London, 1968), II, pp. 762–3. On the 'tyranny of the majority', see II, pp. 304–20.

10 Jennie Wyse-Power, *Words of the Dead Chief: being extracts from the public speeches and other pronouncements of Charles Stewart Parnell from the beginning to the close of his memorable life* (Dublin, 1892), with an introduction by Anna Parnell, p. xvi.

11 Emily Dickinson, *A Patriot's Mistake: Reminiscences of the Parnell Family by a Daughter of the House* (London, 1905), p. 12; R. Barry O'Brien, *The Life of Charles Stewart Parnell*, 2 vols (London, 1898), I, p. 37. O'Brien recounts a humorous incident when the young Charles intervened to protect Anna whom he considered was being too harshly treated by their governess; he placed her on a table and stood guard with a stick to repulse the governess. Ibid. John Howard says Anna was Fanny's 'special chum'. John Howard Parnell, *Charles Stewart Parnell: A Memoir* (London, 1916), p. 13.

12 Jules Abels, *The Parnell Tragedy* (London, 1966), p. 20.

13 Ibid., p. 161.

14 T. M. Healy, *Letters and Leaders of My Day* (London, 1928), I, p. 157; *The Times*, 9 May 1882.

15 Healy, *Letters and Leaders*, I, pp. 81 and 157.

16 Emily Dickinson, *A Patriot's Mistake: Reminiscences of the Parnell Family by a Daughter of the House* ((London, 1905), p. 206.

17 Anna Parnell, *The Tale of a Great Sham*, with an introduction by Dana Hearne (Dublin, 1986), pp. 85–6.

18 Healy, *Letters and Leaders*, I, pp. 80–1. This was organised by John Dillon, of whom she was fiercely critical from time to time. Côté, *Fanny and Anna Parnell*, pp. 239–40.

19 *Celtic Monthly*, May, June, July 1880.

20 William O'Brien, *Recollections* (London, 1905), p. 376. O'Brien describes Anna as 'the soul of the League', p. 463.

21 The Fenian movement had a Prisoners' Aid Association from 1865 which was concerned exclusively with welfare; Isabella Todd established her Woman's Suffrage Association in 1872 while Anna Haslam's Irish Women's Suffrage Association was established in 1876.

22 Katharine Tynan suggested that it be called the Women's Land League but some women felt than this was 'too democratic'. Marie O'Neill, *From Parnell to De Valera: A Biography of Jennie Wyse Power* (Dublin, 1991), pp. 16–17. Davitt and Anna Parnell later

disagreed publicly about the precise origins of the Ladies' League. Côté, *Fanny and Anna Parnell*, pp. 241–9.

23 T. J. O'Dempsey diary, NLI, MS351, p. 6.

24 L. J. Kettle (ed.), *Material for Victory: The Memoirs of Andrew J. Kettle* (Dublin, 1958), p. 48.

25 Anna Parnell, *The Tale*, p. 120.

26 William O'Brien, *Recollections*, p. 463.

27 Archbishop McCabe (Dublin), pastoral letter 12 Mar. 1881. See above, chapter 7. p. 107; A. M. Sullivan challenged McCabe saying that he was proud his wife was a member. Healy, *Letters and Leaders*, I, p. 157.

28 Davitt, *Fall of Feudalism*, p. 356; Healy, *Letters and Leaders*, I, p. 157.

29 Katharine Tynan, *Twenty-five Years: Reminiscences* (London, 1913), p. 89. Although critical of Parnell's actions, William O'Brien attributed them to 'his financial soul alone' and suggests that nobody appreciated more than he their 'daring and unselfishness'. *Recollections*, p. 463.

30 See pp. 36–7 above.

31 Katharine O'Shea, *Charles Stewart Parnell: His Love Story and Political Life*, 2 vols (London, 1914), I, p. 261.

32 William O'Brien, *Evening Memories*, p. 188; William O'Brien, *Recollections*, p. 463.

33 Anna Parnell to *National Press*, 27 Mar. 1891; Frank Callanan, *T. M. Healy* (Cork, 1996), p. 310. The suggestion also appeared in *Pall Mall Gazette*, 13 Jan. 1891.

34 John Howard Parnell, *Charles Stewart Parnell: A Memoir* (London, 1916), p. 211.

35 Côté, *Fanny and Anna Parnell*, p. 228.

36 Jennie Wyse Power published an account of the Ladies' Land League in *Sinn Féin*, 16 Oct. 1909.

37 Wyse Power, *Words of the Dead Chief*, pp. xi–xvi.

38 *Gaelic American*, 19 Feb. 1908. Quoted in Richard Davis, *Arthur Griffith and Non-Violent Sinn Féin* (Dublin, 1974), p. 46.

39 *Gaelic American*, 7 Mar. 1908, quoted in Davis, *Arthur Griffith*, pp. 47–8.

40 R. M. Fox, *Rebel Irishwomen* (Dublin, 1935), p. 123. Molony was one of the first women jailed for a political offence since the days of the Ladies' Land League.

41 See above p. 75; for a short account of the circumstances of her drowning, see Ervine, *Parnell*, pp. 323–4.

42 It was published in instalments in William O'Brien's *Irish Peasant* between March and August 1907. For some of the provenance of the manuscript, see Dana Hearne's introduction, Anna Parnell, *The Tale*, pp. 9–10. Máire Comerford unsuccessfully attempted to interest Eamon de Valera in sponsoring its publication.

43 For good discussions of her differences with Davitt and the writing of the *Tale*, see Côté, *Fanny and Anna Parnell*, pp. 237–49 and Hearne, introduction to Anna Parnell, *The Tale*.

44 Anna Parnell, *The Tale*, pp. 177–81.

45 See above, p. 75.

46 Ervine, *Parnell*, pp. 199-200. Ervine described Anna Parnell as 'mad'. He cited P. S. O'Hegarty's *The Victory of Sinn Féin* (Dublin, 1924) which expresses similar sentiments in relation to women's involvement in the independence movement.

47 Anna Parnell, *Old Tales and New* (Dublin and London, 1905). All the poems quoted here are drawn from this collection.

48 Ibid., p. 240.

49 O'Shea, *Charles Stewart Parnell*, I, p. 156.

50 Bishop Heber (1783-1826) was lord bishop of Calcutta. He was famous for his evangelical activities and for his travelogues, particularly in India.

51 The Treaty of Paris 1898 which ended the Spanish American war seemed likely to herald Cuban independence but it was the American rather than the Cuban flag which was raised in Havana giving rise to a period of conflict between the USA and Cuban nationalists.

52 *Nation*, 26 Mar. 1881.

CHAPTER 10 'THE THURIBLE AS A WEAPON OF WAR'

1 James Joyce, 'Ivy Day at the committee room', *Dubliners* (Penguin Modern Classics, 1956), pp. 131–2.

2 I should stress that I do not use myth here in a pejorative sense – but merely to denote the evolving public view or views of Parnell in the years after his death. For a useful extended discussion of Parnell, myth and history, see William Michael Murphy, *The Parnell Myth and Irish Politics 1891–1956* (New York, 1986).

3 The Parnell GAA club was founded in 1893 in Donnycarney. Originally the club had been known as the Parnell Volunteers. In the late 1880s, tournaments were held in various parts of the country to raise funds for the National Monument Fund, to erect monuments on Fenian graves in Glasnevin. Clubs were required to register their names and colours. When it transpired that the Parnell Volunteers had the same colours as a club in Dundalk, also called Parnell's, a match was held between the two teams at Avondale in 1888 to decide who should retain the right to the name and the colours. St James Brass and Reed band from the Liberties played both teams on to the lawn and the ball was thrown in by Parnell. The match was won by the Dublin team. 'The Life and Times of Parnell's GAA Club', www.cumannparnell.com.

4 Irish cities and towns which named or re-named major streets in memory of Parnell include Bandon, Clonmel, Dublin, Ennis, Kilkenny, Limerick, Mountmellick, Navan, Thurles, Waterford. In Britain, the USA and Australia, the Irish diaspora followed suit with Parnell Streets in Airdrie, Hammersmith, Strathfield NSW, Waroona WA. The Parnell district in Auckland boasts a Gladstone Rose Gardens Shopping Centre where 'passion and style collide'. While it may seem an appropriate motto for his career, the place name predates the career of Charles Stewart Parnell. Parnell Street in Fairfield NSW is named after Samuel Parnell, champion of the 8-hour day who lived there from 1843 to 1875 while Parnell Avenue, Chicago is named after Thomas Parnell 1679-1718.

5   In 1895, it was announced that a monument was to be erected on the great Sugar Loaf Mountain in County Wicklow to the memory of Parnell. A prize of £5 was offered for the best design. John O'Leary, Thomas Drew RHA and Thomas Farrell PRHA were to act as assessors. *Irish Builder*, 15 Dec. 1895.

6   See above, pp. 86–9.

7   Pauric Travers, 'Our Fenian dead: Glasnevin cemetery and the genesis of the republican funeral', in U. MacGearailt and J. Kelly (eds), *Dublin and Dubliners* (Dublin 1989), pp. 60–5.

8   On the Manchester Martyr demonstrations, see Owen McGee's article 'God save Ireland: Manchester-martyr demonstrations in Dublin, 1867–1916', *Eire-Ireland*, Fall–Winter (2001), pp. 39–66; on the martyrs in nationalist iconography, see Gary Owens, 'Constructing the martyrs: the Manchester executions and the nationalist imagination', in Lawrence McBride (ed.), *Images, Icons and the Irish Nationalist Imagination* (Dublin, 1999), pp. 18–36.

9   R. Barry O'Brien, *The Life of Charles Stewart Parnell*, 2 vols (London, 1898), I, pp. 97–8.

10   *Irish Times*, 12 Oct. 1891.

11   *Irish Daily Independent*, 4 and 5 Oct. 1892.

12   Murphy, *Parnell Myth*, p. 18; *Irish Times*, 6 Oct. 1892.

13   *Irish Daily Independent*, 1 Oct. 1982.

14   *Irish Times*, 10 Oct. 1892; *Daily Telegraph*, 10 Oct. 1892; *Freeman's Journal*, 9 Oct. 1893.

15   *Irish Times*, 8 Oct. 1894 & 12 Oct. 1896.

16   *Freeman's Journal*, 10 Oct. 1892; Frank Callanan, *T. M. Healy* (Cork, 1996), pp. 416–17.

17   *Freeman's Journal*, 10 Oct. 1892.

18   *Hazell's Annual Cyclopedia*, 1887 (London, 1887); *Hayden's Dictionary of Dates* (London, 1892).

19   *Morning Post*, 10 Oct. 1892 (quoted in *Irish Times*, 11 Oct.); *Daily Telegraph*, 10 Oct. 1892 (quoted in *Irish Times*, 11 Oct.); *Dublin Evening Mail*, 10 Oct. 1892; *Irish Times*, 10 Oct. 1892.

20   *Daily Chronicle*, quoted in *Irish Daily Independent*, 9 Oct. 1893. In Dublin, the *Irish Times* reported that everyone at the procession 'wore either the badge of the dead Nationalist leader or the ivy leaf which has now become the recognised emblem of the Parnellite party – an outward and visible sign, it may be supposed, that though deserted by some of his colleagues, they continued to cling to him in life, and to his principles now that he is gone.' Even the *Freeman's Journal* conceded that 'a great many people displayed ivy leaves and other green favours' but added that the absence of such tokens being worn by spectators indicated that they were unsympathetic to the Parnellite cause and were attracted only by curiosity. *Irish Times*, 9 Oct. 1893; *Freeman's Journal*, 9 Oct. 1893.

21   *Irish Times*, 8 Oct. 1894; *Freeman's Journal*, 8 Oct. 1894.

22   *Irish Times*, 7 Oct. 1895 and 12 Oct. 1896; *Freeman's Journal*, 7 Oct. 1895 and 12 Oct. 1896; *Irish Daily Independent*, 5 and 7 Oct. 1895. The *Freeman* lamented the attempt to use the ivy leaf to perpetuate disunion.

23   The newspaper reports of the processions from 1897 to 1901 make few specific references to ivy. In 1902, the *Freeman's Journal*, now a supporter of a reunited nationalist party, commented that the ivy was generally worn in the procession. *Freeman's Journal*,

13 Oct. 1902. Conversely the *Irish Times* which had enthusiastically reported the proceedings as long as they highlighted nationalist division, lost interest. There was no *Irish Times* report in 1900 or 1902.

24 *Pace* Gary Owens, the fact that the starting point of the procession was near the foundation stone of the Tone memorial was coincidental. Gary Owens, 'National Monuments in Ireland *c.* 1870–1914: symbolism and ritual', in B. Kennedy and R. Gillespie (eds), *Ireland: Art into History*, (Dublin 1994), pp. 103–17.

25 The original funeral had not passed through Grafton Street.

26 *Irish Times*, 12 Oct. 1896 and 13 Oct. 1941; *Irish Independent*, 13 Oct. 1941.

27 See above, chapter 6. On Dublin bands, see Timothy Dawson, 'The city music and city bands', *Dublin Historical Record* 25 (1971–2), pp. 102–16, and 51 (Spring 1998), pp. 82–3.

28 *Freeman's Journal,* 8 Oct. 1894.

29 *Freeman's Journal,* 12 Oct. 1896.

30 *Irish Times* 12 Oct. 1896; *Freeman's Journal,* 12 Oct. 1896.

31 *Irish Times,* 12 Oct. 1896.

32 *Freeman's Journal,* 11 Oct. 1897 and 10 Oct. 1898; Plunkett Kenny, letter to *Irish Times,* 8 Oct. 1894.

33 *The Times* and *Daily Telegraph,* 10 Oct. 1892, quoted in *Irish Times* 11 Oct.; *Irish Times,* 11 Oct. 1892; *Wicklow Newsletter,* 15 Oct. 1892.

34 *Irish Times,* 9 Oct. 1892.

35 There was 'absolute unanimity' that the procession took one hour and twenty minutes to pass the GPO. This was the same time as the first anniversary procession. *Irish Times,* 8 Oct. 1894; *Freeman's Journal,* 8 Oct. 1894.

36 *Irish Times,* 7 Oct. 1895 & 12 Oct. 1896; *Freeman's Journal,* 7 Oct. 1895 and 12 Oct. 1896.

37 *Irish Times,* 11 Oct. 1897, 10 Oct. 1898, 9 Oct. 1899; *Freeman's Journal,* 11 Oct. 1897, 10 Oct. 1898, 9 Oct. 1899. In 1898, the parade took only 35 minutes to pass a given point and, in 1899, 30 minutes but it was contended that the marching pace was much brisker than before. *Irish Times,* 10 Oct. 1898 and 9 Oct. 1899.

38 DMP report, 9 Oct. 1905, CO 904/10.

39 DMP reports, 6 Oct. 1907, 10 Oct. 1909 & 9 Oct. 1910. CO 904/11,12.

40 *Freeman's Journal,* 10 Oct. 1892.

41 Frank Callanan, *T. M. Healy* (Cork, 1996), p. 417.

42 *Freeman's Journal,* 6 Oct. 1892.

43 Callanan, *Healy,* pp. 416–17

44 *Pall Mall Gazette,* quoted in *Freeman's Journal,* 11 Oct. 1892.

45 *Irish Times,* 10 Oct. 1892. The choice of speaker became a matter of great contention and significance at the funerals of both Bellew MacManus and O'Donovan Rossa; and the oration at the Manchester Martyrs' Commemoration was often the occasion for an IRB rallying cry. See Travers, 'Our Fenian dead'.

46 See, for example, 'important' speech by Redmond to meeting at Rotunda. *Irish Times,* 10 Oct. 1893.

47 See for example DMP police reports, 9 and 11 Oct. 1911. CO 904/13.

48 Parnell had organised Stephens's return from exile in Paris and supported a public subscription to buy a home for Stephens; Stephens visited his grave in the days after the funeral. Travers, 'Our Fenian dead', p. 71.

49 McGee, 'God save Ireland'; *Irish Independent*, 21 Nov. 1893; NLI, CSO News Cuttings, vol. 43.

50 Owen McGee, *The IRB* (Dublin, 2005), p. 229.

51 Ibid., p. 264; *Freeman's Journal*, 16 Aug. 1898.

52 *Irish Times*, 9 Oct. 1899; *Freeman's Journal*, 9 Oct. 1899. The Lord Mayor was Daniel Tallon.

53 *Irish Times*, 9 Oct. 1899.

54 There were faint echoes of the 1899 disturbances a decade later when the Parnell statue was finally unveiled. The ceremony was one of the largest in Dublin since the unveiling of the O'Connell monument – however the Lord Mayor, John J. Farrell's carriage was hissed and booed and he was forced to retreat even before reaching Sackville Street. Mindful of the earlier debacle, the organisers allowed only one speech at the unveiling – that by Redmond, symbolising his dominant position politically at the moment. *Freeman's Journal*, 2 Oct. 1911.

55 *Freeman's Journal*, 25 Nov. 1911.

56 For the Parnell monument, see Timothy J. O'Keefe, 'The art and politics of the Parnell monument', *Eire-Ireland* XIX, no. 1 (Spring 1984), pp. 6–25; Sean Rothery, 'Parnell monument: Ireland and American beaux arts', *Irish Arts Review*, IV, no. 1 (Spring, 1987), pp. 55–7; *Souvenir Brochure of the Unveiling of the Parnell National Monument* (Dublin, 1911).

57 *Irish Times*, 2 Oct. 1911.

58 DMP report, 2 Oct. 1911, CO 904/13.

59 *Independent*, 9 Oct. 1911.

60 *Irish Times*, 2 Oct. 1911; *Freeman's Journal*, 2 Oct. 1911; *Sinn Féin*, Oct. 1911. The *Irish Times* commented that 'it may be presumed that if Mr T.P. O'Connor, Mr Dillon and certain others among Mr Parnell's lieutenants and followers were present they were discretely silent'. Dillon was indeed present – hence Griffith's retort. Some of those on the platform narrowly escaped serious injury when the railing on one side gave way precipitating those in the vicinity into the crowd.

61 *Irish Times*, 6 Oct. 1916. Public gatherings in Dublin were banned.

62 *Freeman's Journal*, 7 Oct. 1921

63 The story of this commemorative endeavour was eloquently recounted in an unpublished talk to the Parnell Society by Nuala Jordan, daughter of Niall Harrington and granddaughter of Tim Harrington.

64 *Irish Weekly Independent*, 6 Oct. 1894; *Irish Builder*, 15 April 1893. In the immediate aftermath of the funeral, a Sunday Guard of Honour was maintained at the grave by Dublin branches of the National League.

65 McGee, 'God save Ireland'.

66 Boland to O'Broin, 20 Aug. 1937, NLI, MS 40,469.

67 The account which follows is taken from the papers of Niall Harrington, recently deposited in the NLI (Collections list 100). I am grateful to Nuala Jordan for copies of the papers related to Parnell's grave.

68 *Irish Times*, 2 May 1938.

69 Harrington to Boland, 1 Oct. 7 9 Oct. 1937. NLI, MS 40,649.

70 Boland to Harrington, 31 Mar. 1938. NLI, MS 40,649.

71 Ibid., 3 May 1938.

72 Ibid., 31 May 1938.

73 Ibid., 15 July 1938.

74 Ibid.; Report by Harrington and Boland to General Committee, September 1938. NLI, MS 40,648.

75 Purcell was Professor of Civil Engineering at UCD from 1909 to 1953.

76 *Irish Press*, 9 Oct. 1939; Boland to Harrington, 31 May 1938, 23 Feb., 14 Mar. 1939; Parnell's Grave; Proposed Name-stone, Report to Executive Committee. n.d. NLI, MSS 40,648, 9.

77 *Irish Times*, 11 Oct. 1937; Boland to Harrington, 6 Oct. 1937, NLI, MS 40,469. McDonnell was a teacher in Donore Avenue School.

78 *Irish Independent*, 11 Oct. 1938, 9 Oct.1939, and 7 Oct. 1940; *Irish Times*, 10 Oct. 1938, 9 Oct. 1939 and 7 Oct. 1940. Mathews was from Skerries.

79 *Irish Times*, 7, 9, 13 Oct. *Irish Independent*, 7, & 13 Oct. 1941; *Irish Press*, 7 and 13 Oct. 1941. This account of the 1941 commemoration draws on 'Ivy Day at Glasnevin, 6 Oct. 1941', an unpublished paper by Cassie Travers.

80 Memorandum by Harrington on Parnell Commemoration Association. 1971. NLI, Ms 40,646.

81 Dáil Éireann Debates, Vol. 399, 23 May 1990, question 2; Vol. 404, 18 Dec. 1990, questions 8 & 9;

82 In 1982, the oration was given by Professor Donal McCartney and, in 1990, it was delivered by Dr Pauric Travers.

83 *Irish Times*, 9 Oct. 1939.

84 *The Bell*, Oct. 1945. The centenary of Parnell's birth was marked in 1946 by the unveiling of a plaque at Avondale by a Wicklow Commemoration Committee.

CHAPTER 11   FROM POLITICS TO HISTORY

Delivered at Parnell Summer School, 16 August 2004.

1   Davitt to Croke, 20 Nov. 1890; (Mark Tierney, 'Dr Croke, the Irish Bishops and the Parnell Crisis, 18 Nov. 1890 –21 Apr. 1891', *Collectanea Hibernica*, no. 11 (1968), p. 114.

2   *Labour World*, 20 Nov. 1890. Quoted in P. J. Walsh, *William Walsh: Archbishop of Dublin* (Dublin and Cork, 1928), p. 407.

3   Croke to Walsh, 22 November 1890 (Walsh, *William Walsh*, pp. 409–10).

4   Walsh, *William Walsh*, p. 419.

5   *The Tablet*, 27 Dec. 1890.

6   Brownrigg to Croke, 11 Dec. 1890 (Tierney, 'Dr Croke', p. 122).

7   F. H. O'Donnell, *The Lost Hat: The Clergy, the Collection, the Hidden Life* (London, n.d. [?1914]), p. 9

8   Brownrigg to Croke, 19 December 1890 (Tierney, 'Dr Croke', p. 123).

9   Croke to Kirby, 29 January 1891 (Tierney, 'Dr Croke', p. 139).

10   'Confidential circular to the clergy of Cashel and Emly and to them alone, 2 March 1891'. Tierney, 'Dr Croke', pp. 142–3.

11   F. S. L. Lyons, *Charles Stewart Parnell* (London, 1978), p. 582.

12   Tierney, 'Dr Croke', p. 244.

13   Logue to Kirby, 21 February 1891 (Tierney, 'Dr Croke', p. 141).

14   *National Press*, 27 May 1891.

15   Logue to Croke, 14 Mar. 1891 (Tierney, 'Dr Croke', p. 147).

16   *Irish Catholic*, 8, 15, 22 August 1891 (Quoted in Frank Callanan, *T. M. Healy* (Cork, 1996), pp. 366–9).

17   Ibid., 10 Oct. 1891.

18   Ibid., 9 July 1892. The pastoral is also given in full in *The Irish Priest in Politics: the South Meath Election Petition*, published by the Irish Unionist Alliance, pp. 7–23.

19   *Freeman's Journal*, 14, 10 Oct. 1892 (Callanan, *T. M. Healy*, p. 417).

20   Timothy O'Keefe, 'The art and politics of the Parnell Monument', *Eire-Ireland* (Spring 1984), pp. 6–23.

21   Ibid. See above, pp. 151–2.

22   O'Donnell, *The Lost Hat*, p. 15.

23   John Redmond, 'Preface' to R. Barry O'Brien, *The Life of Charles Stewart Parnell* (London, 1910 [1898]).

24   Barry O'Brien, *Charles Stewart Parnell*, pp. 553–63.

25   P. H. Pearse, *Collected Works of Padraic H. Pearse: Political Writings and Speeches*, (Dublin and London, 1922), III, p. 241.

26   James Joyce, 'Ivy Day in the Committee Room', in *Dubliners*, (Penguin Modern Classics, 1956), p. 132.

27   W. B. Yeats, 'Come Gather Round Me, Parnellites', in various selections of his poetry.

28   Barry O'Brien, *Charles Stewart Parnell*, p. 517.

29   For a more detailed listing of the work of the historians, see bibliography below.

Bibliographical Note

I EARLY BIOGRAPHICAL WORKS

The earliest books on Charles Stewart Parnell were published in his own lifetime and before the split in the Irish party. As well as catering for the public interest in Parnell's ancestry and his meteoric rise to power, these works reflected the remarkable impact which he had already made even before Gladstone, faced with the strength of the Parnell movement, had committed himself to Home Rule. In chronological order these included:

T. Sherlock, *Charles Stewart Parnell* (New York, 1882; London edn, 1945).

J. S. Mahoney, *The Life of Charles Stewart Parnell* (New York, 1885).

T. P. O'Connor, *The Parnell Movement* (London, 1886).

R. Johnston, *Parnell and the Parnells: A Historical Sketch* (London and Dublin, 1888).

The divorce scandal, followed by the split in the party and the death of Parnell in 1891, resulted in a noticeable shift of emphasis. The personality whose characteristics had brought him to such dazzling heights and yet also had dragged him down to utter ruin required explanation. Fascination with this question of Parnell's personality began with two books that appeared immediately after Parnell's death. One was written by a former admiring colleague turned anti-Parnellite; the other, published in America, was a compilation including information (not always reliable) from Parnell's mother, Delia. These were:

T. P. O'Connor, *Charles Stewart Parnell: A Memory* (London, 1891).

R. M. McWade, *The Uncrowned King: the Life and Public Services of the Hon. Charles Stewart Parnell* (Philadelphia, 1891).

In 1898 was published what for long afterwards was considered by far the best biography of Parnell, and was widely relied upon by successive biographers and historians:

R. Barry O'Brien, *The Life of Charles Stewart Parnell*, 2 vols (London, 1898). One vol. edn (London 1910).

O'Brien's biography was based upon his personal acquaintance with the Irish leader and on interviews with several of Parnell's colleagues and contemporaries. Loyal to Parnell throughout the split, R. Barry O'Brien has been described as Parnell's Boswell.

2 MEMOIRS AND CONTEMPORARY NARRATIVES

Davitt, Michael, *The Fall of Feudalism in Ireland* (London and New York, 1904): Michael Davitt acknowledged Parnell's 'claim to greatness', but faulted him on the divorce scandal and held him solely responsible for the tragedy of the split.

Devoy, John, *Recollections of an Irish Rebel* (London, 1929).

———, *Devoy's Post Bag*, 1871–1928, ed. William O'Brien and Desmond Ryan, 2 vols (Dublin, 1948, 1953): A valuable collection of letters with many references to the Irish-American dimension of Parnell's career.

Healy, T. M., *Letters and Leaders of My Day*, 2 vols (London, 1928.: useful contemporary comments in letters to members of his family by Parnell's arch-enemy.

McCarthy, Justin, and R. M. Campbell Praed, *Our Book of Memories* (London, 1912): has comments on the split.

MacNeill, J. G. Swift, *What I have Seen and Heard* (London, 1925).

O'Brien, William, *Recollections* (London, 1905): deals with the period up to 1883.

———, *An Olive Branch in Ireland and its History* (London, 1910): deals with the split.

———, *Evening Memories* (London and Dublin, 1920): covers the years 1883–1890.

O'Connor, T. P., *Memoirs of an Old Parliamentarian*, 2 vols (London, 1929).

O'Donnell, F. H., *History of the Irish Parliamentary Party*, 2 vols (London, 1910): bitterly anti-Parnell.

O'Leary, John, *Recollections of Fenians and Fenianism*, 2 vols (London, 1896).

Sullivan, A. M., *New Ireland* (London, 1894).

Sullivan, T. D., *Troubled Times in Irish Politics* (Dublin, 1905).

Wyse-Power, Jennie, *Words of the Dead Chief: being extracts from the public speeches and other pronouncements of Charles Stewart Parnell from the beginning to the close of his memorable life*, compiled by Jennie Wyse-Power, with an introduction by Anna Parnell (Dublin, 1892).

3 FAMILY MEMOIRS

Chronologically, the first of the memoirs by members of Parnell's immediate family was written by his sister, Emily; the second was by his wife, Katharine; the third was by his brother, John Howard; and the fourth,

which is different in nature was by his sister Anna and relates to the Ladies'
Land League.

Emily Monroe Dickinson, *A Patriot's Mistake: Reminiscences of the Parnell Family
by a Daughter of the House* (London, 1905).

Katharine O'Shea (Mrs Charles Stewart Parnell), *Charles Stewart Parnell: His
Love Story and Political Life*, 2 vols (London, 1914). One vol. edn, with an
introduction by Martin Mansergh (Dublin, 2005).

John Howard Parnell, *Charles Stewart Parnell: A Memoir* (London, 1916).

Anna Parnell, *The Tale of a Great Sham*: with an introduction by Dana Hearne
(Dublin, 1986).

Emily's book reveals far more about herself and her tastes than about
Charles. It is also factually unreliable. But for all its lack of modesty and its
exaggerations, it does provide glimpses of the family life at Avondale. By
comparison, John's book is notably self-effacing; and although not always
accurate on the larger political issues, insofar as it concentrates its attention
on his famous brother, it has been indispensable for all Parnell's biographers.
Because Katharine O'Shea was Parnell's lover and confidante from 1880 until
his death in 1891, her personal account of their love story and of his political
life remains particularly valuable. And since Parnell committed comparatively
little to writing, the inclusion of his many letters to her from Kilmainham is
exceptionally useful. Anna's impassioned memoir of the Ladies' Land
League was completed in 1907 but was not published until 1986.

4 EARLY BIOGRAPHICAL

Between R. Barry O'Brien's seminal biography in 1898 and F. S. L. Lyons's
scholarly full-length biography in 1977, a number of biographical studies of
Parnell appeared. Although not altogether replaced by Lyons, they have
been relegated to a role of lesser significance. These include:

Abels, Jules, *The Parnell Tragedy* (London, 1966).

Ervine, St John, *Parnell* (London, 1925).

Haslip, Joan, *Parnell: A Biography* (London, 1936).

O'Brien, William, *The Parnell of Real Life* (London, 1926): a defence of his former
leader against St John Ervine's biography.

Ó Broin, Leon, *Parnell: Beathaisnéis* (Áth Cliath, 1937).

O'Hara, M.M., *Chief and Tribune: Parnell and Davitt* (Dublin, 1919).

Robbins, Alfred, *Parnell, the Last Five Years: Told from Within* (London, 1926).

5 SPECIAL STUDIES

Parnell and Mrs O'Shea had chosen not to offer a defence in the divorce court. Henry Harrison's book was a closely reasoned vindication of Parnell's role in the fatal triangle. It may also be seen as the final shot in the 40-year war of words between Parnell's former colleagues:

Harrison, Henry, *Parnell Vindicated: The Lifting of the Veil* (London, 1931).

Following what has been called the Irish historiographical revolution, which has been associated chiefly with the names of Professor T. W. Moody of Trinity College, Dublin, and Professor R. Dudley Edwards of University College Dublin, academics began to give their attention to Parnell studies. In the early 1940s, Conor Cruise O'Brien began work on Parnell's party as a thesis for his PhD. When the thesis was eventually published as a book, he acknowledged the guidance and 'lucid judgements' of T. W. Moody, the supervisor of his thesis, as well as the 'stimulating criticisms' of R. Dudley Edwards. O'Brien's pioneering study represented a move away from the political controversy and partisanship of Parnell's contemporaries to the more objective scholarship of the professionally trained historians.

O'Brien, Conor Cruise, *Parnell and his Party* (Oxford, 1957).

Another of Moody's pupils, F. S. L. Lyons, became a leading specialist in the Parnell period with a succession of original studies:

Lyons, F. S. L., *The Irish Parliamentary Party 1890–1910* (London, 1951).
_____, *The Fall of Parnell* (London, 1960).
_____, *Parnell* (Dundalk, 1963).
_____, *John Dillon: A Biography* (London, 1968).
_____, *Charles Stewart Parnell* (London, 1978).

The last work was the first full-length modern biography surpassing in depth and research all preceding ones.

While Lyons's standard biography was still in the press, a work appeared which had also begun as a thesis under Professor Moody's supervision and which proved invaluable for placing Parnell in the context of his family's political background, the Anglo-Irish Ascendancy and his County Wicklow environment:

Foster, R. F., *Charles Stewart Parnell: The Man and his Family* (Sussex, 1976).

Meanwhile, an American historian was working on a multi-volume history of the Roman Catholic Church in Ireland (1780–1918). Three of his volumes related to the Parnell period. They are based on the private correspondence of the bishops and give a clear indication of the role of the clergy during the Parnell era.

Larkin, Emmet, *The Roman Catholic Church and the Creation of the Modern Irish State 1878–1886* (Dublin, 1975).

———, *The Roman Catholic Church and the Plan of Campaign in Ireland 1886–1888* (Cork, 1978).

———, *The Roman Catholic Church in Ireland and the Fall of Parnell 1888–1891* (Liverpool, 1979).

Alongside the seminal works of Cruise O'Brien, Lyons, Foster and Larkin listed above, other scholars have made important contributions to several aspects of Parnell studies. These include:

Bew, Paul, *C. S. Parnell* (Dublin, 1980): an excellent short assessment which emphasises the social and political context more than the individual life.

———, *John Redmond* (Dublin, 1996): a useful short study of Parnell's successor as leader of the Parnellite faction.

———, *Land and the National Question in Ireland, 1858–1882* (Dublin, 1978).

———, *Conflict and Conciliation in Ireland, 1890–1910: Parnellites and Radical Agrarians* (Oxford, 1987). This and the previous title are valuable accounts of agrarian politics.

Brown, Thomas N., *Irish-American Nationalism 1870–1890* (Philadelphia and New York, 1966).

Boyce, George, and O'Day, Alan (eds), *Parnell in Perspective* (London, 1991): essays written for the centenary of Parnell's death.

Callaghan, Mary Rose, *Kitty O'Shea: A Life of Katharine Parnell* (London, 1989).

Callanan, Frank, *The Parnell Split, 1890–91* (Cork, 1992).

———, *T. M. Healy* (Cork, 1996). This and the previous title are important in-depth examinations of their topics.

Samuel Clarke, *Social Origins of the Irish Land War* (Princeton, 1979).

Côté, Jane McL., *Fanny and Anna Parnell: Ireland's Patriot Sisters* (Dublin, 1991): provides a welcome account of the Parnell sisters whose contribution has tended to be underestimated by some historians.

Curtis, L. P., Jr, *Coercion and Conciliation in Ireland 1880–1892: A Study in Conservative Unionism* (Princeton, 1963).

Eugene Doyle, *Justin McCarthy* (Dundalk, 1996).

Foster, R. F., *Paddy and Mr Punch: Connections in Irish and English History* (London, 1993). A collection of essays three of which relate directly to Parnell.

Hurst, Michael, *Parnell and Irish Nationalism* (London, 1968).

Jordan, Jane, *Kitty O'Shea: An Irish Affair* (Sutton Publishing, 2005).

Kee, Robert, *The Laurel and the Ivy: The Story of Charles Stewart Parnell and Irish Nationalism* (London, 1993). The most recent full-length biography.

King, Carla, *Michael Davitt* (Dundalk, 1999).

McCartney, Donal (ed.), *Parnell: The Politics of Power* (Dublin, 1991). A selection of papers read to the Parnell Society.

Marlow, Joyce, *The Uncrowned Queen of Ireland: The Life of Kitty O'Shea* (London, 1975).

Moody, T. W., *Davitt and Irish Revolution 1846–82* (Oxford, 1981).

Murphy, William Michael, *The Parnell Myth and Irish Politics 1891–56* (New York, 1986): an interesting exploration of the nature and dimensions of the Parnell 'myth'.

O'Day, Alan, *Parnell and the First Home Rule Episode 1884–7* (Dublin, 1986).

Ward, Margaret, *Unmanageable Revolutionaries: Women and Irish Nationalism* (Dingle, 1983).

Sally Warwick-Haller, *William O'Brien and the Irish Land War* (Dublin, 1990).

Several significant works have allowed Parnell's career to be placed in the context of British politics. These include Gladstone's diaries which have been published and a number of excellent biographies of Gladstone.

A. B. Cooke and J. R. Vincent, *The Governing Passion: Cabinet Government and Party Politics in Britain, 1885–1886* (Brighton, 1974).

J. L. Hammond, *Gladstone and the Irish Nation* (London, 1964).

Roy Jenkins, *Gladstone: A Biography* (London, 2002).

H. C. G. Matthew (ed.), *The Gladstone Diaries with Cabinet Minutes and Prime Ministerial Correspondence*, vols 10–12 (1990, 1994).

H. C. Matthew, *Gladstone 1875–1898* (Oxford, 1995).

John Morley, *The Life of William Ewart Gladstone*, 3 vols (London, 1903): particularly interesting because of Morley's own political career and for his portrait of Parnell.

Alan O'Day, *The English Face of Irish Nationalism: Parnellite Involvement in British Politics, 1880–1886* (Dublin, 1977).

6 DOCUMENTS

Two useful collections of Parnell related documents:

Paul Leahy and Paul Nolan, *Kilmainham Gaol Document Pack: Parnell* (Dublin, 1994).

Kissane, Noel, *Parnell: A Documentary History* (Dublin, 1991).

.

Index